Liberal Democracy, Citizenship & Education

Liberal Democracy, Citizenship & Education

Edited by
Oto Luthar
Keith A. McLeod
and Mitja Žagar

mosaic press

in cooperation with the
Scientific Research Institute, Ljubljana, Slovenia

National Library of Canada Cataloguing in Publication Data

Main entry under title:
    Liberal democracy, citizenship and education

Includes bibliographical references.
ISBN 0-88962-781-9

    1. Civics—Study and teaching. 2. Democracy—Study and teaching.
I. Luthar, Oto II. McLeod, Keith A., 1935- III. Zagar, Mitja

JC423.L52 2001   370.11'5   C2001-903615-9

Published by Mosaic Press, offices and warehouse at 1252 Speers Road, Units 1 and 2, Oakville, Ontario, L6L 5N9, Canada and Mosaic Press, PMB 145, 4500 Witmer Industrial Estates, Niagara Falls, NY, 14305-1386, U.S.A.

Mosaic Press acknowledges the assistance of the Canada Council and the Department of Canadian Heritage, Government of Canada, for their support of our publishing programme.

Mosaic Press, in Canada:
1252 Speers Road, Units 1 & 2,
Oakville, Ontario
L6L 5N9
Phone/Fax: 905-825-2130
mosaicpress@on.aibn.com

Mosaic Press, in U.S.A.:
4500 Witmer Industrial Estates
PMB 145, Niagara Falls, NY
14305-1386
Phone/Fax: 1-800-387-8992
mosaicpress@on.aibn.com

Le Conseil des Arts   The Canada Council
    du Canada   for the Arts

Table of Contents

Part II
Governance: Citizens, Citizenship, And Education

Contributors

Andrew Calabrese is a Professor at Boulder University, Colorado, U.S.A.

Douglas F. Challenger is an Associate Professor of Sociology and Director of the New Hampshire Center for Civic Life at Franklin Pierce College, Rindge, New Hampshire, U.S.A.

Karmen Erjavec is a Professor's assistant at the Faculty of Social Sciences, University of Ljubljana, Slovenia.

Slavko Gaber is the former Minister of Education and Sports of the Republic of Slovenia and an Associate Professor at the Faculty of Education, University of Ljubljana, Slovenia.

Ralph Ketcham is a Professor at the Maxwell School of Citizenship and Public Affairs, Syracuse University, New York, U.S.A.

Janez Krek is an Assistant Professor of Philosophy at the Faculty of Education, Centre for Educational Policy Studies, University of Ljubljana, Slovenia.

Mojca Šebart Kovač is an Assistant Professor of Sociology of Education and Theory, Pre-school Education at the Department of Pedagogy, Faculty of Arts, University of Ljubljana, Slovenia.

Oto Luthar is a Director of the Scientific Research Centre of the Slovene Academy of Science and Arts.

Keith A. McLeod is a Professor Emeritus at the Ontario Institute for Studies in Education, (Adult Education and Teacher Education), University of Toronto, Canada.

Jamie Myerfeld is Associate Professor of Political Science at the University of Washington. He is the author of *Suffering and Moral Responsibility* (Oxford University Press, 1999).

Henri Peña-Ruiz.'s most recent publication is *Dieu et Marianne, philosophie de la laïcité.* (Presses Universitaires de France, collection "Fondements de la politique". Paris: 1999).

Mojca Peček is an Assistant Professor at the Faculty of Education, University of Ljubljana, Slovenia.

Sabrina P. Ramet is a Professor at the Henry M. Jackson School of International Studies, University of Washington, Seattle, Washington, U.S.A.

Rudolf M. Rizman is a Professor at the Faculty of Arts, University of Ljubljana, Slovenia.

Geri Smyth is a multicultural educator from the University of Glasgow, U.K.

Mirko Vaupotič is a deputy director of the Office of the Republic of Slovenia for Youth, Ministry of Education and Sport.

Zala Volčič is a Doctoral student at the University of Colorado, Boulder, U.S.A.

Mitja Žagar is the Director of the Institute for Ethnic Studies in Ljubljana, Slovenia.

Acknowledgments

Firstly, we would like to thank those who assisted with the planning, operation, and success of the conferences which led to this publication. Secondly, we also like to thank those who contributed their articles for this volume. Thirdly, we would like to express our appreciation for the support provided by the following: The Scientific Research Center; The Institute for Ethnic Studies (INV/IES); The Trade Union of Education and Scientific Workers of Slovenia (SVIZ); The Council of Europe; Slovene National Commision for UNESCO; the Public Affairs Section of the American Embassy, Ljubljana; and the Government of the Republic of Slovenia: Ministry of Education and Sport; and the Ministry of Science and Technology. Lastly, we would like to thank all those who helped with this publication. Most especially, we would like to thank Alenka Koren for her continuous support and attention to the adminstrative details.

The Editors

-Introduction-

Oto Luthar, Keith A. McLeod, and Mitja Žagar

The development of liberal democracy brought a new role to the people in their states; they became citizens. Being the 'subject' of a monarch, an oligarchy, or a dictator was replaced by participation in the power and authority of the state and by the acceptance, equally, of the responsibilities of citizenship. Liberal democracies featuring liberty, tolerance, human rights, equality and freedom did not come about suddenly or easily. Furthermore, when liberal democracy was instituted in many countries, there were limits on the participation, rights, freedom, and responsibilities of some members of society which rendered their citizenship not equal. From the blacks in the United States, and the lower classes in Britain and Canada as well as in many other countries, to women and to ethnic or cultural minorities in many countries, many groups were more subjects than citizens even into the twentieth century. Moreover, in countries which professed democracy, there were people who did not have access to full citizenship. Similarly, in countries where control in the state was accorded to only members of a particular party, religion, class, or gender, liberal democracy was limited or absent. In states where Marxist philosophy prevailed, there was often little pretence about the liberal portion of the concept; these states referred to themselves as socialist democracies.

The conferences in Ljubljana, Slovenia in 1998 and 1999 on citizenship and civic education enabled the speakers or presenters to unburden themselves of a number of questions, views, analytical perspectives, and historical assertions regarding citizenship and civic education. There were several papers that analyzed citizenship, the nature of the state, the role of nationalism, and the nature of liberal democratic government. Many of the speakers made particular reference to "societies or states in transition" by which they meant the changed socio-political culture where liberal democracy had replaced the Marxist-socialist political paradigm.

There was a keen awareness among the participants, many of whom were teachers, that questions related to learning how to function as citizens in the new liberal democratic political framework was very crucial to the work of teachers and to the expectations of Slovenian society. What, they inquired, should teachers be doing to enable students to learn to be citizens?

The foregoing question was a focus of the conferences. Speakers addressed their views in their own ways depending upon their background, areas of study and their experience. There were papers that explored liberty and freedom, democratic representative government, securalism, and human rights as the bases of citizenship. There were questions regarding the separation of church and state as a fundamental basis of citizenship and liberal democracy. There were presentations on nationalism, media literacy, liberal arts in education, adult education, post-modernism, multicultural or plural societies, and on citizen participation through dialogue and community participation. The presenters, in addition to focussing upon Slovenia, also made reference to many other countries including Poland, France, Canada, the United Kingdom, the United States and others. There were discussion related to the new democracies in Eastern and Central Europe. In addition, participants were provided with information regarding the work of the Council of Europe in the field of citizenship education.

There were also presentations that explored the value of the state, and whether the state was primarily a territorial entity or an association of people with socio-cultural affinities. There were discussions about whether differentiated citizenship is valid in liberal democracies and whether it had been more characteristic of early liberal democracies, where entrenched groups insisted on their rights or on their values or even privileges. Some participants provided evidence to support their view that countries with multicultural policies were actually diminishing diversity by their work on equality, access, and inclusion. There were also discussions about whether the nation state was being superseded by a new political order with the advent of globalization or whether the nation state would remain the basic political unit. There was also a sense at the conferences that while the practice of liberal democracy in particular states might be fragile, the concept of liberal democracy was forceful, persistent and enduring. An interesting footnote is that there was comparatively little discussion about the concept of the welfare state or the value of social rights. However, there seemed to be a major assumption of the importance of social rights or of a positive role for the collective action of citizens.

Beyond the intellectual thoughts regarding human or political questions relating to states and citizenship, there were opportunities at the conferences to address major questions that teachers face: How does one teach civic education and citizenship? Again, the answers varied depending upon the particular perspective of the presenter or participant. How does a teacher choose what to teach? Stated in more liberal democratic or even post-modern educational terms, how would a teacher help students to learn what is needed to be a citizen? Thus, there were discussions about content that included such topics as human rights, tolerance, democratic procedures, and ethnic and racial diversity.

There were also ideas expressed regarding what teaching techniques teachers might employ. Experiential learning, where the students participate in simulations or "real-life situations", such as dealing with racism, voting in elections, practicing tolerant behaviour, or establishing the rules of their conduct in school or in class, was discussed. Inevitably, many kind of materials which school students and teachers and adult learners could use were discussed. We might add here that teaching materials in educational settings today might be simply a question, an exercise, an experience, or a community event rather than a book or a glossy booklet. In the post-modern world, the learning 'material' needed may only be as far away as the community, a keyboard, or a screen.

Finally, the participants became engaged in the discussion about who can help teachers to prepare their classes on civic education and how this could be done. Teachers in Slovenia, like all citizens facing 'the advantages of free choice', have become after ten years of democracy much more sceptical about the instructions (and instructors) which they have been receiving from the West. After the initial period of enthusiasm for everything connected with the Western world, they have become more critical about the educational goods they have been offered from Western Europe and the U.S.A. Along the way, they have discovered some of their own resources and traditions. In the Czech Republic, Poland, Hungary, and especially in Slovenia, the *resources* were discovered in the philosophy of the civic movements of the 1980s. The *traditions*, on the other hand, were found in emancipatory minority legislation and even in the primary school curriculum.

Unfortunately the 'civil society movements' with their notions of a new style of governing which was supposed to oppose old-style politics, with its sterile battles between left and right, lacked new ideas. Instead of proposing new ideas, the movements were rather offering local versions of arrangements to be found already somewhere else in the world. Do the 'new democracies' have conventional Western-style party politics, accompanied by typical side effects such as corruption and clientelism?

Self-confidence has been shown by some of the new democracies when they have addressed the question of minorities. In the Slovenian case, this confidence has been shown by embracing emancipatory minority legislation inherited from the former Yugoslavia. By incorporating this legislation in the new constitutional democratic system, the Slovenian parliament created a liberal atmosphere based on equal opportunities and responsibilities for all citizens. Another example of how democracy has been combined with Slovene tradition has been the reconstruction of that part of the primary school curriculum which is concerned with civic education known under the term 'Ethics and Society'. In the preamble to this curriculum, it is stated that besides economic ideas pupils should also understand concepts such as democracy, pluralism, cooperation, cultural unity, diversity, conflict and change, migration, environmental protection, preservation of cultural heritage, and the good and bad aspects of European integration. With such improvements and the discussion of such isues as "the problems of democracy" and "marginal communities", democratic citizenship education can resist different kinds of cultural, religious and ethnic determinism and reductionism.

In the following chapters, you will find some of the life of the conferences. The papers in this volume will provide you with the opportunity to share some of what happened at the conferences. The papers will also provide you with the opportunity to think over many of the issues that were discussed, shared, and debated by the participants. What do you think should be the role of civic education? What do you think citizens should learn? What are the fundamentals of a liberal democracy and of participating as a citizen in one?

Part 1 Governing:

Liberal Democracy, the State, and Education

- Chapter 1 -

Laicity: Questions of Principle

Henri Peña-Ruiz

Translated by Lise Fournier

The Principle of Laicity

"Laicity" is first and foremost a *principle*: it makes the people as a whole, without discrimination and without privilege, the focus not only of the political community, but of the spiritual sphere as well. This was the too-easily forgotten wish of Auguste Comte, who understood the end of the collusion between temporal and spiritual power as a universalization of the spiritual life based on culture and the autonomy of judgment. The human community that has been liberated by this process can from now on be called a republic - an entity that is shared by all people. The ancient Greek word for people was *laos*, and this etymology sheds light on the concern to prioritize that which unites all people, but without the tutelage of a single group charged with a mission to establish social norms. There should be no clerical privilege, and no official creed. Neither is there any need for a moral or spiritual magisterium. Religious groups may be led by members of the clergy as long as the latter are content to perform religious duties on behalf of those who freely recognize their role. But if religious leaders decide to exercise power over all people, they are doing a grave injustice to those who have opted for other forms of spirituality. History has shown us the kinds of crimes that have been committed against freedom in the name of such appropriations of power.

This principle is concerned with uniting people on a level that transcends their differences, or perhaps it would be more accurate to say that this union take places at a more fundamental level. Laicity, while not essentially anti-religious, becomes anti-clerical out of necessity, if we understand clericalism to mean the desire to control the political sphere. What is true for some, cannot be imposed on all, unless, of course, it is imposed through violence. A believer and a free-thinker are able to enter into dialogue by virtue of the fact that they share a common language - a common ground that enables them to transcend the particularity of their spiritual options. Laicity leads to the sanctioning of this common ground. The neutrality demanded by laicity is a positive stance because it privileges those things that unite people without specifically denying those things that differentiate them, and it assigns all spiritual options - whether they are religious in nature or not - to the *private sphere*. Thus the way is cleared for a united civil and spiritual base that is free from all tutelage, and does not lead to the balkanization of different communities.

The private sphere can have a collective, or social, dimension – as in the example of a mass or a gathering of free-thinking humanists - but this dimension, which pertains to the freedom to gather together around a common set of beliefs, cannot lay claim to the public and civil spheres. And if this public sphere were defined only in relation to one or several groups, it would no longer have the characteristics that make it a legitimate reference for all people. This is why the shift in meaning from "collective" to "public" is illegitimate in this context. Critics routinely accuse supporters of laicity of wanting to reduce religion to an individual phenomenon because it understands religion to be a private matter. It is uncertain whether the apparent confusion around the terms of the debate is legitimate, or a matter of bad faith. "Individual" is the opposite of "collective", and "private" is the opposite of "public". Religion can have a collective dimension without extending it to include all members of society. The collective dimension of Catholicism in France is unmistakable, yet Protestants, Jews, Muslims, agnostics, and free-thinkers are not included in that particular collectivity. It is obvious that they do belong to the larger political community known as a "republic". It would be stating the obvious to say that a republic as such can be nothing other than secular in nature. And so it is equally obvious that this *res publica*, which by definition belongs to all people, cannot continue to exist if it becomes lost in a mosaic of publicly sanctioned communities.

It follows that all confusion or collusion between the state and any religious group - no matter which one it is – undermines the universal character of public power and makes a mockery of the principle of the civil and ethical equality of citizens. It even undermines the principle of freedom of conscience. When the president of the United States of America swears an oath on the Bible, only those Americans who identify with this text feel that they are being represented. When religious education is made mandatory for all Polish schools, free-thinking Poles become victims of discrimination, and questions of equality and freedom of conscience are brought to the fore.

Laicity therefore entails a separation of Church and State in order to restore each of these to its proper sphere. The laws of the political sphere, common to all people because they transcend differences, win their independence by refusing to privilege a particular religious option. In other words, this separation promotes the fundamental equality of all religious groups, as well as the greatest freedom possible with regard to other spiritual postures, whether or not they are religious in nature. As long as religious or other groups do not confuse collective expression with the right to seize public power, a secular state allows religious and philosophical beliefs the greatest freedom of expression. This is not the paradox it might appear to be. The facts are clear: believers aren't oppressed in secular countries, but free-thinkers are, to varying degrees, wherever a single religious confession is imposed by the state. Pagans, Christians, Jews, and Muslims have all at one time or another been excluded from some aspect of society as a result of the clerical interpretation of social cohesion and spirituality. The particular religious group being persecuted at any given time varied, depending on the historical period in question, but atheists, agnostics, and free-thinkers suffered almost constant persecution.

Such an historical perspective highlights the liberation issues involved in the radical secularization of public power and civil society. Religious belief itself can only be fully liberated within the context of a religious pluralism that upholds freedom of conscience and the legal equality of religious convictions. This equality extends to atheism and free-thought, which are viewed as equally legitimate spiritual options. The public sphere's openness to spiritual options is rooted in the double principle of equality and freedom, values which show their mutual dependence in the secular recasting of social cohesion and the conditions of spiritual life. An obstacle to democratic debate has been removed, and, even more significantly, society is now free to come together to articulate the principles specific to the construction of a unified society. Laicity can replace a regime based on fear and discrimination with an ideal of peace and harmony, because the search for a common good isn't distorted from the outset by official religious privilege. But this is not simply a matter of constructing a spiritual pluralism that makes peace with the 'differences' that are juxtaposed. It means constructing a common society based on judgment and reason, where people can live together peacefully because they have learned to relativize and transcend their particular spiritual options. This is what Spinoza meant when he said that reason could unite all people.

But it would be naïve to think that all we need to achieve freedom are the right legal conditions. And it would be wrong to assume that people are able to distance themselves spontaneously from their own beliefs and live them serenely and tolerantly.

Pressure groups prevalent in civil society want not only to control public opinion, but also to be sanctioned by public institutions. They are as much of an obstacle to the construction of a harmonious secular society as clerical control. We see it in the United States, where certain Protestant groups have successfully banned the teaching of Darwinian biology in schools on the grounds that it contradicts biblical accounts of creation. Using the legal system, they have even invaded the private lives of politicians, all the while holding the public sphere ransom in the name of their particular world-view.

It is therefore necessary to uphold the freedom of each person by ensuring that it is grounded in the principle of the autonomy of judgment - a principle essential to the secular and public education provided by the *École de la République* in France. Laicity, then, is more than a legal principle and a political articulation of a common public space, it is also a philosophical ideal that is concerned with the true autonomy of the individual in thought and action. Laicity cannot be articulated without a solid construction of this autonomy. The time and place of this construction, like the culture it involves, must be protected as much as possible from religious or other pressure groups. The separation of religion from public power - from the power that we all share - is what unites the principles of freedom of conscience and the equality of citizens, regardless of their individual spiritual convictions. Such a separation ensures a public school system that is dedicated to teaching the values of freedom of judgment to each and every student, as well as to exposing them to a wide variety of spiritual options, without exclusion or preference. Inversely, as soon as schools are influenced by religious groups, discriminatory practices - even purely symbolic ones - follow close behind, such as when a supposedly 'public' power sanctions a state religion or a particular world view that many individuals do not share.

We see all too clearly that this kind of submission to religion poses a danger to educational institutions. Culture would be revised and corrected as it was for many years by the Church, when works were blacklisted because they did not conform to Church teachings: Hugo, Molière, Freud, Descartes, Rousseau, and many others, were all placed on the *Index librorum prohibitorium* - the Index of Forbidden Books - a project that was only abandoned in 1965.

The role of the secular school is to inspire a high level of thinking in all students, by exposing them to a universal culture that draws from humanity's finest achievements. All schools should be free to fulfill this role without interference. When it is not distorted or censured, cultural knowledge enables future citizens to distance themselves from the illusions of the moment as well as to free their judgment from tutelage. A universal and authentic spiritual life begins to take shape when students of culture come to know its great traditions: myth, religion, science, philosophy, art, and every other accomplishment whose study may contribute to humanity's self-fulfillment. But it accomplishes this by forbidding all proselytism. This means, among other things, that it does not confuse the study of religion and the works it has inspired with a "religious culture", a slightly ambiguous expression that might lead some to think that the religious point-of-view may be legitimately introduced in contexts where there should only be objective instruction and dispassionate reflection.

The Status of the Secular Ideal

Wagering on freedom, a demanding notion relating to the autonomy of judgment, and concerned to create a world of common understanding where differences do not mean isolation, laicity is more than the empty shell of cultural or spiritual pluralism than some would like to reduce it to. Without privileging any particular spiritual option, laicity recasts the conditions of the spiritual life by separating it from all worldly tutelage. It upholds the equality of believers of all persuasions, including religious believers, agnostics, and free-thinkers. But, as we have seen, it does not stop at legal reform. The argument that would link laicity with religious disenchantment and despiritualization is as dubious as it is widespread. It seems to be a variant of the biased theory that would reduce the spiritual to the religious, but most importantly, it seriously misunderstands the reasons for the current disenchantment with the spiritual, attributing it to secularization rather than to the effects of social or economic changes. Moreover, the idea that a profane humanism - one that deals with the meaning of human behaviour as well as more existential questions - could coexist with religious approaches to spiritual questions, is stubbornly rejected by adversaries, both open and disguised, of secularization. It is as though by liberating the spiritual sphere from the old clerical constraints, and by protecting it from the will of the moral magisterium from whom religious groups demand official recognition, laicity's advocates are creating a spiritual void.

As a result of this kind of exasperating criticism, laicity is often misunderstood, and finds itself in an awkward position. Indeed, it seems that laicity has been put in an impossible situation. If it incorporates a rationalist and critical humanism, and a certain notion of the fullness of human accomplishment, critics are quick to accuse it of having adopted a particular philosophy and abandoned the neutral position which befits it. It doesn't seem to matter that they are knowingly confusing religious neutrality, which is fundamental to the conception of a genuinely 'public' power, with legal and ethical neutrality, which cannot be applied to the secular ideal, because it strongly supports clearly recognized principles and values (freedom of conscience, the equality of believers and non-believers, the universalization of the autonomy of judgment and of the culture that supports it, and a concern for public space and a common good that does not resort to apartheid-style divisions). If, however, in the name of neutrality, laicity refrains from all references to norms or ideals, then critics will be quick to imply that its spiritual silence and ethical vacuity make it an empty shell that must be filled as quickly as possible by religious groups. Within the framework of this significantly diminished notion of laicity, these groups would monopolize the search for meaning. Those who argue that the political empowerment of religion is inevitable, are often quick to criticize laicity's efforts to bring about the ideal of a life of harmony and human accomplishment. These attempts are immediately labeled as examples of "republican mysticism" and "sacralization" of the state. Here the sacred is invoked in a pejorative sense, which may seem paradoxical coming from those who normally protect religious thought from the kind of sociological relativizations they blithely use to characterize the secular ideal and Enlightenment rationalism.

It is therefore necessary to explain in some detail the relationship that exists between the critical humanism of laicity, and spirituality, including the eternal question of meaning. There is really nothing new about this discussion, when we consider that the whole reflexive tradition of philosophy has always been concerned with truth and rationality, which did not always depend exclusively on faith in a transcendent god, except according to those who chose to think in those terms. As we move into this new area, we must keep in mind that the spirituality debate takes on renewed form as soon as the process of secularization liberates human conscience from all tutelage and official belief systems, and establishes its autonomy through rigorous education.

The secular state cannot privilege particular spiritual options any more than it can hand over the field of public and spiritual life to the myriad of religious groups and exclusive world-views. This is a reiteration of the above question of "neutrality". To solve the problem, we must consider how laicity situates itself on a plane which is completely distinct from that upon which various spiritual options confront one another. In fact, laicity ensures their freedom of expression with a strict respect for their basic equality, and for the integrity of the public good, so that groups are not isolated by difference. In this regard, Montesquieu appealed to a love of laws and of the equality they make possible, which is the foundation of republican virtue. Such a virtue is added to a profound understanding of the significance and the challenge of secular emancipation for all spiritual options. The co-existence of the republican virtue and different spiritual options only requires that people do not live their religion in a fanatical manner – that is, that they do not impose it on others by taking control of the public sphere. Like adherence to the principles and values of laicity, this virtue transcends the particularity of each spiritual option by creating a universal space where they are free from persecution and where they may enter into dialogue with other spiritualities.

Because they both respect the public sphere that emphasizes what brings people together rather than what keeps them apart, an atheist and a believer can learn to respect one another. This does not mean that they must refrain from critiquing each other's options, because that would mean giving in to *religious correctness* (or *ideological correctness*). This kind of respect is the result of republican laicity - of the protection of shared values and mutual understanding, all of which make it possible for those who adhere to different belief systems to come together and to dialogue with one another. This is *secular transcendence*, an authentic source of harmony and fraternity, where no one feels that they have been injured because of a privilege given to another, or that they have been stigmatized because of their spiritual beliefs. The philosophy that informs this secular transcendence is *generosity*, which holds that all people have the desire for freedom within them, and that they are capable of going beyond themselves. Everyone should be able to live a spiritual life in such a way that allows them to distance themselves far enough from the public sphere that they can respect its neutrality, without having to sacrifice individual or collective expression, and all of this within the purview of recognized secularized law. When all is said and done, this transcendence of transcendences actually enhances spiritual life by giving it an awareness of its singularity, and by purging it of the temptation to dominate. Transcendence plays an essential role in neutralizing new forms of clericalism, whether they are fundamentalist in character or whether they consist of plans to restore the concordat between Church and State. Many people are coming to understand that this peaceful way of living one's faith or one's secular commitments – a way that does not intrude in the temporal sphere – promotes a more authentic, impartial and unfettered form of spiritual expression. This is a sharp contrast to the political ambitions of religious authorities who still want their social role officially recognized. A religion with political aspirations may attempt to adorn itself in the discourse of cultural identity and spiritual expression, but it is still a political entity and it should therefore be treated as such.

The originality of the register in which the secular ideal defines itself enables it to steer clear of the most common misunderstandings concerning its status and scope, and particularly those misunderstandings that have already been touched on in this discussion.

Reconsideration of the Founding Ideals

But this originality is obstructed by two serious misunderstandings currently overshadowing the laicity debate. First, there is the lumping together of laicity and atheism, and then there is the charge that Enlightenment ideals are responsible for the aberrations of our era. Some critics reduce laicity to one of many spiritual options in order to diminish its universal scope; others reject the entire intellectual and moral process that leads to secular emancipation, saying that its founding ideals are the direct cause of suffering in our time. And yet all of these critics are strangely silent on the subject of atrocities that were committed during the period when religion was in a position of temporal power and could have done something to prevent them. This amounts to a new 'formatting' of collective memory that discriminates against certain ideals, depending on whether they are religious ideals or secular ones, such as the philosophy of human rights that emerges from Enlightenment rationalism.

The origin of the first misunderstanding is partly due to the confusion of two points-of-view - one legal, and one historical - that should in fact be totally distinct. From a legal persepective, as we have seen, laicity does not actively support any particular spiritual option. But in reality, the historical struggle for the emancipation of rights could make it seem as though laicity had allied itself with those spiritual options that were oppressed during certain historical periods: atheistic humanism during a time when it wasn't deemed an acceptable spiritual posture; Protestantism when it was subject to persecution; Judaism when its adherents have been persecuted; and even Catholicism where it has been stigmatized, such as in countries where reformed Christianity was made the official religion. The mere enumeration of these *solidarities of resistance* discredits the persistent idea that atheism has been granted some special status. It is true, of course, that philosophical humanisms based on atheistic spiritualities have played a role in secular emancipation throughout history, partly because they have revealed the unacceptably partisan character of official religion and its monopoly on thought, but also because they have contributed to the emancipation of political thought from theological-political doctrines that subject political power to religious power. But the idea that the political organization of human societies can manage without a religious foundation does not in any way mean the destruction of religions: it only returns them to their status as spiritual options that may be freely chosen by those who are interested. An optional God is not a forbidden or imprisoned God. It is time to absolve the secular ideal of the transgressions that have been attributed to it because of a confusion between the process that led to its recognition and the principles that define it and upon which it is founded. We can no longer say that secular emancipation of rights and laws - which hasn't even yet been achieved, as the opposition to "Pacs"[1] clearly shows - is hostile to religion.

Let us move now to the contemporary trial of Enlightenment ideas. Those who see a direct link between these ideas and the deplorable historical events of our era, will sing the virtues of Christian values in the same breath, distancing these values from the real oppression they have sanctioned throughout history. There is something overtly discriminatory, even aberrant, about the unilateral trial of ideas; this is exemplified by Monsignor Lustiger's suggestion that Auschwitz was a result of Enlightenment rationalism - a statement which seems to purposefully confuse the applied rationality of the techniques of extermination put to use in the service of a mystical ideology of race and power, with philosophical reason, which is understood as the ability to question, and to make ethical and political choices. Such an interpretation of the link between ideals and historical developments is patently unfair. On the one hand, there seems to be a remarkable amnesia when it comes to atrocities committed in the recent past in the name of religion, coupled with unadulterated praise for the 'Christian sources' of human rights and humanism. On the other hand, there is a systematic stigmatization of Enlightenment rationalism and the ideals of social and intellectual emancipation that have continued its work, particularly in the struggle to liberate society from unchecked capitalism and its brute instincts, which reappear whenever the balance of power permits it. Included in all of this is a dishonest rewriting of history that attributes the origin of human rights solely to Christianity and entirely forgets the rationalist humanism that goes back to ancient Greek philosophy and the Cartesian emancipation of judgment. Less than a century ago, Monsignor

Freppel said that these human rights went hand in hand with the "denial of original sin".

That the 'Black Book of Christianity' has never been written is therefore symptomatic. The difficult issue of the link between ideals and historical events obviously deserves rigorous study - a study that would be attentive to the status of texts and their relationship with historical realities, as well as with the relative autonomy of their meaning. Spinoza was exemplary in his application of this rational hermeneutic to biblical texts in his *Theological-Political Treatise,* in which he critiques the notion of a chosen people - a notion he considers to be dangerously ambiguous. In much the same way, other thinkers have critiqued the rationalist ideals of the Enlightenment and its revolutionary doctrines, bearing in mind that the relation between texts and historical developments is far from easy to understand, and that modern anti-rationalism is itself irrational. In fact, depending on whether we are discussing religion or varieties of secular humanism, the issue seems to have been settled, without further deliberation, in two contradictory ways. Certain religious ideals seem to be cleansed of all responsibility for known crimes (the innumerable victims of the Inquisition and the Crusades), retaining only their purely spiritual expression. Curiously enough, the official programs of history suggest that we come to understand this spiritual expression independent of historical manifestations of religious political power. But in the case of rationalist ideals and secular humanisms, the same generosity is hardly ever shown. They say it is obvious that the emancipatory message of Enlightenment philosophers or the social thought of the nineteenth century had a direct relation to the tragic disappointments of the twentieth, including the monstrosities of Stalinism. But the 'Black Book of Stalinism' is no more of a direct expression of these ideals than the 'Black Book of Clericalism' is a direct result of the Christian message. And this is precisely why these titles have been deliberately altered here - to inspire a more impartial principle of reading. The fact that a single verse of the Bible could have been an inspiration to Itzak Rabin's assassin, or to the holy fool who murdered Palestinians chased from their land, should give pause. That a certain reading of the gospels could lead someone to carry out a bomb attack on a cinema that was playing *"The Last Temptation of Christ"* is cause for concern. That one verse of the Qu'ran could be read in such a way by a terrorist that it revives the infamous "holy war " – a notion common to all three "religions of the Book", as attested by their historical writings – clearly demonstrates that memory, if it is to steer clear of deception, cannot be selective. There cannot be double standards in the interpretation of texts and their relation to concrete reality.

Which secular humanism?

The extensive list of charges relating to the predispositions already mentioned above inspires us to imagine a critical humanism of a different kind. The general construction of this humanism opens up the philosophical grounds of secular emancipation where a genuine reformulation of spiritual life can begin to be articulated. It brings five main strategies into play. The first strategy involves a critical definition of the ideal of human accomplishment, one that clarifies its points of reference as well as its expectations of liberation. The second strategy is a political philosophy of law and its legitimate scope of application, understood within a dialectic of emancipation that enables us to grasp the scope of each of the registers of emancipation, thereby contextualizing and evaluating secular emancipation. The third strategy is a theory of education entirely oriented toward the construction of intellectual autonomy, and an accompanying universalization of the spiritual life. The fourth strategy, a critical concept of rationalism, eliminates all confusion concerning the registers of rationality, and all scientistic reductions of existential lucidity concerning the meaning of practices, knowledge, and belief. The last strategy is a reflexive distancing, and a restrained and rational attitude towards different varieties of metaphysical questioning. This attitude is essential to the philosophy of laicity: by ensuring its independence from various metaphysical and religious options, it can have a relationship with each one of them and at the same time enjoy universal recognition. For the first time, the thirst for a spiritual life is compatible with liberty. Secularization does not mean the end of metaphysical questioning; it is not the dark and empty shell of total relativism; it is instead an encouragement of the spiritual power in each of us and of our ability to exercise that power free from tutelage. It should be noted here that the spiritual dimension is best expressed when it isn't tinged with any worldly control or compromise. Religious groups and sects that want – or even demand - worldly power and institutional recognition, may be suspected of distorting the spiritual, and, in fact, of having very little respect for it. It is time to put an end to the old prejudice handed down to us by Tocqueville: that a people without religion as a point of reference are plunged into metaphysical chaos and ethical alienation.

In light of these issues, the *status of the ideal* and its role must be clarified. The secular ideal renews classical humanism by updating it with a critical version free from the ideological illusions and naïve metaphysical notions that have long given it a certain ambiguity. It envisions humanity as an ensemble of possibilities to be fulfilled. It is an ideal that uncovers the extent of actual injustices and fills the gap so that each person can achieve his or her full potential. Understood in this way, the ideal is not a pious wish or an ideological fiction: it has a real effect on those who aspire to a better life because it gives them a way of measuring the transformations that are necessary. The idea that humanity can achieve self-fulfillment is itself likely to evolve as time passes; ideas of transcendence will be conceived in terms of what now is and what will reveal itself to be possible in the light of critical discernment. Distinguished from all arbitrary trends, the historicity of the ideal goes hand in hand with its critical function: to free human aspirations from conformist ideas that ensnare them in the ideologies of the moment. On the other hand, abstract references to humanity can weave fictions of freedom, no matter what the actual conditions of existence are, as we see all too often in certain kinds of legal abstractions, where the register of the ideal is the product of a kind of mystification. Lucidity means understanding that the language of rights may ring false if temporal power denies the human subject the freedom of self-expression that it is supposed to have according to abstract legal language. From this point of view, laicity cannot work without a critical theory of the subject and the many relations that will delineate the subject's scope of action.

Second, it is therefore timely to imagine a *dialectic of emancipation* in order to evaluate laicity's contribution. The legal emancipation promised by the secular ideal strictly delimits the scope of the law to include the double principle of the freedom of conscience and the equality of all people, so that spiritual options become a strictly private matter. However, there can be no autonomy of the subject without the other registers of emancipation. The secular emancipation of the state and of rights requires an intellectual and cultural emancipation that clears the way for the universal democratization of an authentic spiritual life. But economic and social emancipation are also required, which will make public realities just as credible as the promises of critical rationalism. It is therefore necessary that we avoid abstract exaltations of the registers of emancipation, that we give meaning to ideals by including them within the dialectic of registers of liberation, and that we refuse the kind of hypocrisy that would support or promote the belief that legal equality is the only kind of equality that we need.

Areas of legitimate state intervention are to be understood in terms of what differentiates and legitimizes them. Vague liberal ideas must now clarify their shape and sphere of influence, and ideas of political volunteerism must do the same. In fact, secular emancipation radically liberalizes the state's relationship to spiritual options, because it does not permit the imposition of mandatory beliefs or ethical or ideological persecution, and because it promotes freedom of conscience and equality of spiritual options. But this kind of restraint on the part of the state does not at all mean that it withdraws from legitimate areas of intervention. It means that in a republican democracy, the state is not a transcending, controlling force: it implements the public will and does whatever is in the public interest. Public schools, social rights, and public services, among other things, fall under its jurisdiction, as does the concern for a republican and social readjustment that ensures that these services stay independent from market forces. The political philosophy of laicity is not a kind of unrestrained liberalism, but rather a balanced theory that articulates the basis upon which the state either intervenes in or abstains from public affairs. We know that unchecked economic liberalism can lead to humanitarianism, as well as to the anointing of a 'social role for religions' and the accompanying demands for the restoration of clerical power.

Secular humanism is therefore not of the same order as the republican dictate, which resembles an idealistic and unrealistic *petito principii*, such as that which posits that as the master of his own thought and actions, the human subject can fully exist apart from the conditions and relations that make his ascent possible. Because of the way in which it understands the dialectic of the registers of emancipation and their interrelationships, this humanism assumes a materialist understanding of the conditions that ensure that the ideal is not pure fiction. We should add that secular advances into spiritual sphere do not prevent people from isolating themselves in various communities as long as there is social injustice. This does not mean that laicity must give up its specificity in the general struggle for social justice, because laicity has a great deal to contribute to its unfolding. But it must restore the conditions necessary to authentic emancipation, so that there are no more misunderstandings and errors in the analysis of deviations too often attributed to the secularization process.

Third, the secular ideal strives to realize the Enlightenment ideal for "the people" - that is, for all people. Laicity's wager on freedom is made more explicit and becomes a wager on the real intellectual and cultural autonomy of every person: it will not abandon future generations to ideological power struggles without giving them the means to think for themselves. Public and secular education does not promote any one spiritual option, but it does promote both sound judgment and the culture in which that judgment is grounded. Secular education falls under the jurisdiction of the state, and it is therefore the duty of the state. Its mission involves more than professional instruction; its *raison d'être* is the promotion of personal accomplishment through cultural education.

Public and secular education understood in these terms aims to make reason accessible to everyone. Reason is understood as the faculty that allows us to investigate matters freely and critically, but also as the ability to think about the meaning of knowledge, to judge right from wrong, and to do all of this within a clear existential framework. In short, this kind of education has as much to do with what is reasonable as with what is rational. It means that the rationalism to which it refers cannot be reduced to the kind of soulless, practical rationality that it is accused of by those who still support a clerical program and want to more effectively chip away at notions of secular emancipation. In reality, laicity extends to all people the privilege previously accorded to religious leaders as learned guardians of a conformist spirituality. It does abolish to some extent the élitist expression of the spiritual life, at the same time as it frees it from clerical control and religious monopolies. This kind of rationalism has nothing in common with the caricatures still being drawn by anti-Enlightenment critics.

The final - but not the least important - aspect of the secular conception of spirituality is the liberation of the spiritual sphere through a refusal to impose metaphysical dogmatism, to hand down political rulings concerning beliefs, or to have some of them officially sanctioned. A republican state must not delve into the metaphysical, nor must it make a distinction between 'good religions' and 'bad sects' by evaluating their doctrines. On the other hand, it must ensure that the exercise of free will is respected, which means condemning and checking all efforts to manipulate or subject others, especially the kind of deceitful manipulation that goes on today within certain religious groups. While actions are to be condemned, belief systems are not, otherwise we are submitting to religious correctness. If it is true that certain ideas are dangerous or deadly, they are only so in a virtual sense in the beginning. But their *expression*, because it is an action, can be criminal, as in the case of racist statements which in themselves already constitute a concrete injury, even a provocation to violence. In cases such as these, secular law in France has sufficient means to take action. But the law may not try citizens on the basis of what they intend to do. The best way to stop sectarian brainwashing is, as Condorcet envisioned, by public debates informed by intellectual autonomy and reason, rather than by a new wave of spiritual discrimination.

In order to ensure that society is not once again taken prisoner by such personalities, all people must be able to think clearly and critically, and to express their spiritual life through unfettered access to the resources of universal culture. The human capacity for reflection, when it is nourished by these resources, can clearly differentiate knowing and believing, which are two different registers of conscience whose confusion leads to obscurantism. Freedom of conscience does not mean that Darwinian science and Christian beliefs about creation can be placed on the same level. The secular state's retreat from these issues is a sharp contrast to the violent clerical attitudes of recent history, but it is not true that this retreat leads to indifference and unbridled relativism. A thousand years of collusion between theology and politics has clearly shown us all we need to know about what happens when we mix these two together; we need no further examples to prove the point. The secular state's refusal to pass judgment on the relative value of various belief systems is an intangible principle upheld by the 1905 French law governing the separation of Church and State. It does not permit confusion, but it recognizes the fact that the life of the spirit cannot be nor should be desecrated, which is exactly what happened over a long period of history when society was ruled by a "religion of love". It cannot be dissociated from the active promotion of theoretical reason and its practice, just as it cannot be separated from the principles and values that enable human beings to live together. Therefore there is nothing about this civil and moral disarmament that is the result of a general relativism: rather, it calls for an intellectual vigilance that does not compromise the requirements of truth, and does not renounce any critical resources.

Critical rationalism as set out by laicity brings into play an essential distinction between beliefs, including general metaphysical and religious options, and the principles of rights or truths that cannot be challenged. Its function is partly to draw out the consequences of the status of beliefs and world views that support one another. While they are free, they are also private, and therefore they must not impose themselves in any way on the public sphere, since nothing about them is universal. This corresponds to a certain attitude in each person living in a secular state. The believer must know that he or she only believes, and that the structure of the interior life cannot be confused with the structure of knowing, or with the general will, the faculty present in each one of us to want that which has value for all. This self-distancing of the living and thinking subject is obviously a condition of tolerance, which is understood as the respect not of the beliefs of the other, but of the other's freedom to believe. It also signals a clarity of reflection that prevents people from slipping into fanaticism. Finally, it retains a subjective openness to the universal by assigning particular spiritual options to their appropriate status. The spiritual option one chooses is a personal matter that must not be imposed on others, or on the public sphere where dialogue takes place. These things hold true for all spiritual options, regardless of the importance of the people who share that option. It is also necessary to define the legitimate scope of intervention for society's laws, by ensuring that all people are recognized by the principles and values that form the basis not only of communal existence, but also of authentic harmony, without at the same time having to give up the power to judge and criticize, or the capacity to share and admire.

Spinoza made it clear that there is no need for the state to exercise religious or metaphysical tutelage by legislating dogmas or by empowering religious authorities to oversee communal norms. After Spinoza, Kant also discussed the necessity of state abstention. In his view, this meant reassigning metaphysical beliefs to the spiritual status that befits them so that they don't lead to dogmatism. This is the status of the probable and of the hypothetical, where human beings can only hope to know things subjectively, alongside an awareness of this subjective character, and all of this arising from the self-distancing required to achieve clarity. This does not imply that metaphysical thinking is useless or harmful. Kant thought that the opposite was true. But all of this emphasizes the need to distinguish clearly the registers of the spiritual life and the function that each one could fulfill in the context of personal conduct and in state life. The political retreat from metaphysical and theological matters does not open up a void. Instead, it brings people back to their essential responsibility: the mastery of critical thought, a qualification that cannot be delegated to others. But it does more. It liberates that which is common to particular axiologies and the elective spiritual options in which they originate. By doing this, it does not open the door to any particular immorality or spiritual void.

At a time when the Christian creed was mandatory, Bayle stated that "it is not more peculiar that an atheist lives virtuously than it is that a Christian engages in all kinds of crime. If we see the latter monster every day, why do we think that the other cannot possibly exist?" Since Epicurus, we should know that neither public-spiritedness nor ethical righteousness imply a religious spirituality, nor more than they require a particular variant of metaphysical questioning. Hume, imagining a dialogue between Epicurus and the Athenians who were scolding him for his lack of piety, brings up this point forcefully. Truth itself cannot be imposed on others except through the free consent of an enlightened mind that accepts it as its own: in matters of the mind, there can be absolutely no violence, no matter what form it may take.

"Man is the measure of all things". A critical humanism accepts this well-known formula, but examines it further. The "things" in question are those that need to be decided on in order to organize public life. But there are other "things", things that go beyond what is necessary, and these can only come from human freedom. This is the realm of spiritual beliefs and options that the law can neither order nor officially recognize. If humanism involves a certain confidence in the autonomy of each person, laicity does not, for all that, dismiss reflection on the finite, and on the tragic knowledge that may go along with it. But metaphysical unrest must not find its way into the political sphere, and no one has a legal right to it. Some religious authorities like to insist on the role of religions in the spiritual dimension of human beings, but besides the fact that these groups do not have a monopoly on this dimension, there can be no public recognition of this function without illegitimately encroaching on the political sphere. Should believers be offended by the fact that the secular can be structured around a political references to humanity, without imposing an official creed? No, unless their spirituality still includes a program of temporal domination and universal influence. Again, a vision of a secular state that does explicitly refer to God is not the same as a denial of God. It is, as we have come to see, an affirmation of shared humanity.

---

[1] *Translator's note*: "Pacs", or "le Pacte" civil de solidarité", refers to 1999 French law that recognizes the right of couples who "do not want to or cannot marry" to sign a contract of mutual support and to receive social benefits.

- Chapter 2 -

Human Rights and Civic Education[1]

Jamie Myerfeld

In this essay I will explore the meaning of human rights and their connection to democracy. If civic education means education for democracy, and if, as I shall argue, the proper understanding of democracy is rooted in human rights, then human rights should be the starting point for reflection on civic education.

The Idea of Human Rights

Today the concept of human rights commands universal allegiance. The Universal Declaration of Human Rights, now in its 52nd year, is accepted by virtually all nations. Many governments violate human rights systematically, but none admit to doing so. A few governments try to water down the concept of human rights in the name of local cultural values. But the appeal to a distinct cultural perspective rings hollow, since these same governments silence and intimidate those among their citizens who would express a robust commitment to human rights; they also show a predilection for the violent repression and sometimes the attempted extermination of cultural minorities residing in their territory.

In Europe, almost all countries are bound by the European Convention on Human Rights. Governments can be sued before the European Court of Human Rights, and must adjust their policies in light of its findings. Most national constitutions entrench human rights, and many countries, such as Slovenia, include a Constitutional Court empowered to overturn legislation that violates human rights.

Thus the idea of human rights is affirmed throughout Europe and the world. It enjoys pride of place in the political rhetoric of our time. But as we all know, reality lags far behind rhetoric. In many countries rights are threatened, or slighted, or routinely trampled. Nor is it inevitable that human rights will retain their current prestige. Inattention to their value, or attraction to incompatible doctrines, could dislodge them from the favored position they now enjoy in our scheme of values. If we want to preserve the idea of human rights, and if we hope to convert the idea into reality, we must make an effort to understand their meaning and rationale.

The recognition that humans possess rights is only a few centuries old. Though the enterprise of political theory spans over 2500 years, during most of that time no such idea is articulated. Ancient religious and philosophical traditions from around the world include teachings on the dignity of the human person; these, however, do not amount to a theory of human rights, even if they help us to construct such a theory. The medieval period, in which barons and townsmen successfully checked the pretensions of aggrandizing monarchs, developed a set of concepts useful for resisting arbitrary power. But medieval liberties, privileges, and immunities were invoked to defend a hierarchical order grounded in custom and tradition, rather than a democratic vision of equal freedom. We might say that the medieval period created the vocabulary of rights without the content (or with only half the content).

The full articulation of the idea of human rights awaits the 17th century, when it appears in the political program of the Levellers, the radical party during the English Civil War. In a revolutionary departure, whose origins are difficult to trace, the Levellers demanded universal male suffrage and government by consent, freedom of conscience, and the abolition of conscription. They gave democratic meaning to an older vocabulary of personal entitlements. Their vision is captured in the famous assertion of Colonel Rainsborough during the Putney Debates that "the poorest he that is in England has a life to live as the greatest he."[2] Needless to say, the Levellers were too radical for their time. They were defeated militarily, and their program shelved indefinitely.

The theory of human rights begins to send down roots in the Age of Enlightenment. To the Enlightenment we owe the notion that people can rely for their beliefs on reason rather than authority or custom. To it, we also owe the idea of autonomy--roughly, the notion that it is the individual who is ultimately responsible for charting the direction of his or her life. Certain thinkers are particularly important: John Locke, who articulated the notion of self-ownership (the idea that one is owned by oneself and not another) and who asserted that human beings enjoy natural rights prior to government and establish government only to protect those rights;[3] Immanuel Kant, who asserted that human beings must always be treated as ends in themselves, never as means only, and who insisted that no one is authorized to impose his or her conception of happiness on another;[4] and John Stuart Mill, who argued that we must protect idiosyncratic beliefs and practices from repressive legislation as well as social intolerance.[5] In our own day, John Rawls has done more than anyone to help us conceive a just political order which grants all citizens an equal opportunity to pursue their own conception of the good life.[6]

The primacy of rights was asserted in the great revolutionary manifestoes of the 18th century--the American Declaration of Independence and the French Declaration of the Rights of Man and of the Citizen--but for generations only a tiny proportion of the world's inhabitants possessed the entitlements proclaimed by these documents as a common human birthright. The horrors of World War II led to the inclusion, in the Charter of the United Nations, of a general commitment to the promotion of "human rights and fundamental freedoms," and spurred the creation, three years later, of the Universal Declaration of Human Rights.[7] Eleanor Roosevelt hoped that the Declaration would become "an international Magna Carta of all mankind." More than fifty years after its adoption, it continues to challenge and inspire, and still repays careful study.

The Declaration announces several kinds of rights. The variety is instructive, since it reminds us of the diverse ways in which people can be degraded, demeaned, and abused. The rights asserted by the Declaration can be divided into five broad categories:

1. Security rights: a right not to be killed, a right not to be tortured, a right not to be arbitrarily detained, a right to a fair trial;
2. Liberty rights: a right to freedom of speech, freedom of conscience, freedom of assembly, freedom of movement;
3. Political participation rights: a right to vote, a right to run for office;
4. Right to non-discrimination: that is, a right against discrimination based on arbitrary or irrelevant group classifications;
5. Economic and social rights: These include a right to subsistence, defined by the Declaration as "the right to a standard of living adequate for ... health and well-being ... including food, clothing, housing, and medical care." Economic and social rights also include the right to education, the right to work, and the right to leisure.

Like other commentators, I believe that all these rights are united by a fundamental connection to human dignity. The connection is recognized in the Declaration, whose Preamble begins: "Recognition of the inherent dignity and of the equal and inalienable rights of all members of the human family is the foundation of freedom, justice and peace in the world." It is hard to discuss dignity in simple and precise terms. Let us just say that the dignity of each person consists in a status shared equally with all other human beings, a status that requires respect for essential human capacities and protection against common human vulnerabilities. When one's rights are violated, one is treated as less than human.

The assault on human dignity is most blatant in the deprivation of physical security and economic subsistence. However, human dignity is assaulted through the violation of other rights as well. The violation of liberty rights denies the capacity of each person to think his or her own thoughts and to lead a life of his or her own choosing. Discrimination relegates one set of people to a subordinate status. The deprivation of political rights attacks human dignity by subjecting people to rules not under their control.

Essential to the concept of human rights is the recognition that we all share a double interest in security and autonomy. Our vulnerability entitles us to certain protections; our independence entitles us to certain freedoms. To put it another way, the success of each person's life depends partly on the avoidance of certain fates we all recognize as evil, and partly on the individual's independent judgment of what defines success. The point is well captured by Ronald Dworkin: "Government must treat those whom it governs with concern, that is, as human beings who are capable of suffering and frustration, and with respect, that is, as human beings who are capable of forming and acting on intelligent conceptions of how their lives should be lived."[8] George Kateb echoes this insight, though he notes as a third feature of the human condition our capacity to recognize the equal moral status of others: "Public and formal respect for rights registers and strengthens awareness of three constitutive facts of being human: every person is a creature capable of feeling pain, and is a free agent capable of having a free being, of living a life that is one's own and not somebody else's idea of how a life should be lived, and is a moral agent capable of acknowledging that what one claims for oneself as a right one can claim only as an equal to everyone else."[9] Theorists of human rights have long recognized that our interests in security and autonomy are closely intertwined.[10] A standard means of depriving persons of autonomy is to threaten them with assault or severe deprivation if they try to act freely (for example: throwing them in prison if they criticize the government). A well-designed human rights regime must take into account the specific structure, or architecture, of the conditions which make possible a dignified human existence.

The preceding paragraphs sketch a principled argument for human rights, but there is an instrumental justification that deserves equal emphasis. The fact is that regimes which disregard human rights display a general pattern of "botching things up." You don't have to believe in the intrinsic importance of human rights to be troubled by the legacy of illiberal regimes, particularly in the twentieth century: genocide, famine, terror, civil war, economic instability and collapse, ecological catastrophe, the breakdown of public health, official sponsorship of lunatic science, spectacular corruption. As William Talbott has argued, this is exactly what we should expect. [11]A strong human rights regime establishes a set of mutually overlapping and reinforcing protections against governmental incompetence and criminality. Moreover, it is a well-established fact that liberal democracies rarely if ever go to war with each other. Scholars debate the implications of this finding, but it seems to suggest that in a regime which respects human rights certain hurdles are raised to the pursuit of war.

Those of us concerned about rights need a clear conception of the agencies and entities that threaten rights most seriously. The state is the first object of suspicion. It wields the greatest power, and can do the worst harm. States violate rights with chilling ease and horrifying casualness. Rights require unceasing vigilance. But the state is not the only threat. Any institution with the power to interfere with people's lives and confine their freedom must be an object of distrust. Mill took pains to emphasize this point in *On Liberty*, where he wrote that society may exert a tyranny more powerful than government itself. Feminists have shown that an excessive focus on the state too often has blinded us to the abuses visited on women by society. Human rights must be asserted not only against the state, but also against economic corporations, schools, religions, families, and a host of other social institutions, as well as dominant cultural practices. Consciousness of our rights obliges us to challenge these forces, even if some disruption of social harmony is the inevitable result.

Democracy

There is an essential connection between human rights and democracy. I base this assertion, not on the etymology of the word "democracy," but on what the democratic ideal has come to stand for after centuries of political experience and reflection. "Democracy" originally meant rule by the *demos*--the common people, or those who form a majority of the population. Aristotle, who employed this definition, classified democracy as an unjust constitution. He feared that the common people would use the power of the majority to expropriate and oppress the wealthier class; an empowered *demos* would rule in its collective interest rather than the common good. When democracy simply means rule by the *demos* or rule by a majority, there is no necessary connection between democracy and justice.

If we were tied to Aristotle's definition of the term, there would be little reason to take interest in democracy. But the meaning of the concept has evolved with time. Today the best and most interesting conception of democracy--the one which gives us an ideal worthy of aspiration--is that which is based on the principle of political equality.[12] Democracy is a form of government which seeks to honor equally the independence and sovereignty of all citizens.

Notice that if we start from the premise of equal human dignity, the very idea of government is placed under moral suspicion. Any system of compulsory laws, backed by the coercive power of the state, seems antithetical to individual freedom. The democratic response to this difficulty is to seek the informed consent of all citizens to any laws that are enacted. Democracy makes laws the outcome of a sustained and continuous effort of public justification. It institutionalizes debate. Those who seek legislative office must first defend their proposals before the electorate. A system of checks and balances offers repeated opportunities to reconsider legislation, and gives diverse groups a chance to exercise their veto. Policies are contested in parliament, in a free press, in the universities, and a host of other spaces. Minorities are constitutionally protected against the danger of an overweening majority, and human rights are constitutionally guaranteed. Under the rubric of "civil disobedience," room is made for citizens to refuse compliance to laws they regard as unjust. Democracy is rooted in the idea of individual autonomy, and must remain faithful to that idea in all its operations.

Democracy refers not only to a set of rules, but also to a kind of culture.[13] Democratic institutions depend on, but also inspire and reinforce, a particular collection of attitudes. These include a belief in the equal dignity of all individuals; a resistance to hierarchy; a reluctance to identify with the exercise of power; a willingness to have one's beliefs questioned and challenged; a tolerance for a certain measure of conflict, tension, and disorder in political life. The culture of democracy is the culture of human rights. At the same time, the idea of human rights is democratic at its core. When one believes in human rights, one looks for groups whose rights have been denied. Over time, the concept of human rights has inspired struggles on behalf of religious minorities, including atheists; national and ethnic minorities; women; blacks and other people of color; homosexuals, bisexuals, transsexuals, and other sexual minorities; workers; poor people; the homeless; immigrants; refugees; prisoners; criminal suspects; the mentally ill; the disabled; and children. The idea of human rights even pushes beyond the human. The animal rights movement owes much to the idea of human rights. One need not believe that the interests of animals are identical to those of humans to believe that animals have a moral status of their own, and that certain ways of treating them are morally unacceptable.[14]

Community, Culture, and Nationality

I do not claim that human rights occupy the entire moral universe. There are other values that exist in combination and in tension with human rights. Part of the challenge of political theory is to formulate an understanding of supplementary and competing values that does not displace the centrality of human rights.

I want to look very briefly at three concepts that have attracted a great deal of theoretical attention in recent years: community, culture, and the nation. Liberal democrats (my shorthand for those who give priority to human rights) must approach these concepts with great care.

Community. Human beings need community. We are bound to each other by numerous ties of dependency. Community enables and enhances our existence. Life without it is unimaginable.

The question is: what sort of community do we need? Liberal democracy prefers a conception of community that is oriented to the needs and aspirations of its members, and is preserved only by their consent. Community is not an end in itself. It takes its life from the goals and commitments of the individuals who constitute it and who may withdraw their membership if they wish. We should expect that old communities will dissolve and new ones will form, and that the character of ongoing communities will change over time, sometimes beyond recognition.

Frequently, however, community is invoked to limit individual freedom. People are told that their self-realization is achieved through the fulfillment of pre-assigned social roles and the subordination of individual purposes to those of the group.[15] This conception of community has been dominant throughout history, and has been the reigning ideology of several twentieth-century regimes. It is obviously incompatible with a robust commitment to human rights.

Such a conception of community is encouraged (wittingly or not) by those political theorists who like to claim that people depend on their community for their values and beliefs. [16] Since the community is the source of our values and beliefs - of our very identity - the picture of individual agency presupposed by the doctrine of human rights is an illusion. This line of thinking has proven widely seductive, but I think it is plainly contradicted by experience. Individuals are not bound by a script. They are capable of thinking and feeling and observing on their own. They are not passive receptacles of inherited wisdom, but exercise their own understanding. Even when people draw on ideas present in their community, by far the most interesting part of this story is the creativity they employ in combining, interpreting, evaluating, and re-articulating those ideas.

To repeat: I do not question the value of community; rather, I mean to indicate the danger of certain conceptions of community. Many of those who worry about the weakening of community raise legitimate concerns: the general indifference to the poor and unfortunate in our midst, the fraying of social trust, the inability to sustain intricate forms of human cooperation required for the solution of complex social problems. These problems can be addressed, I believe, without displacing the centrality of human rights.

Culture. Culture is as great a human need as community; life without it is no less unimaginable. The standard human rights catalogues - by recognizing such rights as freedom of expression and freedom of religion - protect our ability to take advantage of cultural offerings around us and to transmit cultural forms to anyone willing to adopt them.

The multiculturalist movement has rightly insisted on the need for tolerance toward and understanding of people of diverse backgrounds and experiences.[17] What ought to be avoided, though not all adherents of multiculturalism succeed in avoiding it, is the suggestion that one's identity is defined by the culture to which one is said to belong, and that what is most worth preserving is the diversity of cultures *per se*, rather than the freedom of individuals to choose their preferred mode of cultural expression. There is an unfortunate tendency to imagine that the world is divided into discrete and largely self-contained cultures, corresponding to ethnic, religious, and linguistic categories. In a world of accelerating communication and travel, this picture is rapidly losing any plausibility it may once have had, and it ought particularly to be disavowed by those who prize the freedom of the individual to chart the direction of his or her own life. In any case, the most significant cultural divides are often those of occupation and class, rather than ethnic, religious, or linguistic group.[18]

Issues that ought to be addressed separately too often are lumped jointly under the heading of "culture." Take the question of language as an example. In multilingual societies there are often good reasons for recognizing more than one official language: languages possess intrinsic aesthetic value; each one is tied to a rich literary heritage; people are naturally attached to the languages in which they are raised, and insofar as possible should not have to abandon them in order to enjoy opportunities available to other citizens. However, linguistic differences lack the cultural implications which are frequently attributed to them. A difference of mother tongue does not by and large entail a difference of worldview or ethical belief. The assimilation of language to culture simultaneously exaggerates the differences between people and diminishes the richness of language. Language is both less and more than what we generally imply by the term "culture." There is much to be gained by recollecting the distinction.[19]

The relation of democracy to religion is a large question, which I cannot address here. To Locke goes the credit for insisting that religion must be conceived as a form of voluntary association. Individuals should be free to espouse a religion of their choice, to change religion, or to profess none at all. Parents are entitled to raise children in their own religion, but not to deprive children of the capacity, as they grow into adults, to evaluate their own religion rationally and to consider the religious alternatives available to them.[20]

The Nation. We are all familiar with the ravages unleashed by nationalism. Yet the primary form of political organization in our day remains the nation-state. Certain democratic theorists have argued that citizens must form some kind of bond with the nation if they are to carry out the hard work involved in the maintenance of democracy. Hence the call for civic nationalism as an alternative to ethnic nationalism.

If civic nationalism is to be adopted, it must be firmly subordinated to, and seen to be derived from, democratic values of freedom and equality. The democratic ideal, rightly understood, tempers the attachment to the nation and reminds us of obligations that transcend national divisions. Liberal democrats must be permanently wary of nationalism.[21]

Conclusion

My objective in this essay has been to show that the democratic values to be transmitted through civic education are ultimately the values of human rights. In any program of civic education, democracy should be understood as existing primarily for the sake of human rights. Partly for this reason, human rights should be an important part of the curriculum.[22] Students should be exposed to the major legal and philosophical texts on human rights. They should be made aware of the human rights protections afforded by their own governments, by the European Convention on Human Rights, and by various international treaties. They should learn about the struggles that have been waged on behalf of human rights in their own country and elsewhere - struggles that transcend differences of culture, community, and nationality. The message is that human rights can be claimed by anyone on behalf of anyone. The universal meaning and import of human rights is unfortunately obscured by the nationalist narratives that are dominant in many school systems around the world.

As I remarked earlier, human rights depend not only on a set of rules, but also on a certain kind of culture. Schools should take a self-conscious role in transmitting, through instruction and example, the norms which underlie and sustain democracy. These include norms of tolerance, mutual respect, and free rational inquiry. When it comes to education, democracies should not hesitate to promote these particular values and to oppose contradictory ones. [23] I do not deny, on the contrary I insist, that in a free society individuals should be allowed to express the widest spectrum of views, including those antithetical to the values of a free society. But we cannot be quite so permissive in the realm of primary and secondary education. Children must be prepared for freedom, as for much else. We must equip them with the ability to take full advantage of the opportunities available to them in a free society, and we must inculcate in them the values on which the preservation of a free society depends.[24]

Democracy is more than popular elections or parliamentary votes. It is an effort to give political form to the vision of equal human dignity. It is the political corollary to the idea of human rights. That is only the beginning of the story, of course. There is much work that remains to be done - work that perhaps can never be completed - in understanding the meaning of human rights. The greatest task is to make the promise of human rights a reality for all people, now and in the future. It is a task which necessarily involves the instruction of succeeding generations, and which must inform our approach to civic education.

Endnotes

1 This essay draws freely from the work of my teacher, George Kateb. See Kateb, *The Inner Ocean* (Ithaca: Cornell University Press, 1992). I have also relied on Jack Donnelly, *Universal Human Rights in Theory and Practice* (Ithaca: Cornell University Press, 1989); Donnelly, *International Human Rights* (Boulder: Westview Press, 1998); Henry Shue, *Basic Rights* (Princeton: Princeton University Press, 1980); and Jeremy Waldron, *Liberal Rights* (Cambridge: Cambridge University Press, 1991).

2 Agreement of the People; *Putney Debates.*

3 *Second Treatise of Government*; A Letter Concerning Toleration.

4 Groundwork of the Metaphysics of Morals; The Metaphysics of Morals; On the Proverb: That May Be True in Theory, but Is of No Practical Use.

5 *On Liberty*; The Subjection of Women.

6 A Theory of Justice; Political Liberalism.

7 On the story of the drafting of the Declaration, see Mary Ann Glendon, "Knowing the Universal Declaration," *Notre Dame Law Review* 73 (1998): 1153-80.

8 *Taking Rights Seriously* (Cambridge, Massachusetts: Harvard University Press, 1977), p. 272.

9 *The Inner Ocean*, p. 5.

10 See especially Shue, *Basic Rights.*

11 William J. Talbott, Why Human Rights Should Be Universal (typescript).

12 See Charles R. Beitz, *Political Equality: An Essay in Democratic Theory* (Princeton: Princeton University Press, 1989).

13 This is a main theme in Kateb, *The Inner Ocean.*

14 See Peter Singer, *Animal Liberation*, 2nd ed. (New York: New York Review of Books, 1990); Tom Regan, *The Case for Animal Rights* (Berkeley: University of California Press, 1983); David DeGrazia, *Taking Animals Seriously* (Cambridge: Cambridge University Press, 1996).

15 Donnelly, *Universal Human Rights in Theory and Practice*, p. 83.

16 Alasdair MacIntyre, *After Virtue* (Notre Dame: University of Notre Dame Press, 1984); Michael Sandel, *Liberalism and the Limits of Justice* (Cambridge: Cambridge University Press 1982); and Sandel, *Democracy's Discontent* (Cambridge, Massachusetts: Harvard University Press, 1996). Both MacIntyre and Sandel are explicit in their opposition to rights.

17 For an excellent statement, see Martha Nussbaum, *Cultivating Humanity: A Classical Defense of Reform in Education* (Cambridge, Massachusetts: Harvard University Press, 1997).

18 For a lucid exposition of several fallacies common to the 'culturalist' argument, see Brian Walker, "Plural Cultures, Contested Territories: A Critique of Kymlicka," *Canadian Journal of Political Science* 30 (June 1997): 211-34.

19 For an illuminating examination of these and other issues, see Jacob Levy, *The Multiculturalism of Fear* (New York: Oxford University Press, forthcoming).

20 For an excellent discussion, see Stephen Macedo, *Diversity and Distrust: Civic Education in a Multicultural Democracy* (Cambridge, Massachusetts: Harvard University Press, 1999).

21 See Attracta Ingram, "Constitutional Patriotism," *Philosophy and Social Criticism* 22 (1996): 1-18; and Jamie Mayerfeld, "The Myth of Benign Group Identity: A Critique of Liberal Nationalism," *Polity 30* (Summer 1998): 555-78.

22 On the subject of human rights education, see Tania Bernath, Tracey Holland, and Paul Martin, "How Can Human Rights Education Contribute to International Peace-Building?,"*Current Issues in Comparative Education* 2 (November 15, 1999) [http://www.tc.columbia.edu/cice/vol02nr1/bhmart1.htm]. See also George Andreopoulos and Richard Pierre Claude, eds., *Human Rights Education for the Twenty-First Century* (Philadelphia: University of Pennsylvania Press, 1997).

23 See Macedo, *Diversity and Distrust.*

24 On the challenge of civic education in liberal democracies, see Amy Gutmann, *Democratic Education* (Princeton: Princeton University Press, 1987); Macedo, *Diversity and Distrust*; Nussbaum, *Cultivating Humanity*; and Alan Ryan, *Liberal Anxieties and Liberal Education* (New York: Hill and Wang, 1998**).**

- Chapter 3 -

The Classical Liberal Tradition: Versions, Subversions, Aversions, Traversions, Reversions

Sabrina P. Ramet

More than sixty years ago, the Gershwin brothers, George and Ira, gave us the memorable song, "I Got Rhythm". The song seems to celebrate simplicity itself, with its refrain,

I got rhythm
I got music
I got my man
Who could ask for anything more?

The song was, of course, about appreciating the simple things in life, the basics one might say. But one could also treat it as if it were a code, substituting *rithen* for the original *rhythm*. The song could then serve as a summons to the liberal-democratic project. RITHEN could stand for

Rule of law

Individual rights & duties derived from Natural Law

Tolerance of differences in religion, life styles, and culture

Harm principle: do not harm others (except in defense of life or limb or kin) or tolerate the infliction of harm

Equality

Neutrality of the state in matters of religion.

RITHEN, in short, serves as an acronym for the classical liberal project itself, the project for a secular liberal state which protects individual rights to "life, liberty, and the pursuit of happiness" -- except when one person's happiness seems to entail depriving others of *their* happiness. It is fashionable in 21st-century America to imagine that the formula for liberalism provided above is some sort of 'Eurocentric prejudice' and to pretend that non-European societies have other, equally legitimate 'traditions'. In fact, it is this objection which is 'Eurocentric', by imagining that non-Europeans prefer to live under lawless tyranny, without respect for human rights and without any binding moral code, and in conditions of bigotry, wanton infliction of harm on others, class or caste inequality, and theocracy. Such an inverted system could look fine, at best, to the tyrant or to his hangers on.

But to return to the song, one might treat MUSIC as an encrypted code for the recipe for democracy:

Multiparty elections
Uncensored press
Separation of powers
Informed public
Campaign funding from government, rather than from corporate, sources.

Multiparty elections would presume independent parties not beholden to economic interests. *Uncensored press* is vital to public airing of views concerning the public interest, and hence need not include freedom for outright pornography in order to assure the possibility for the frank discussion of public issues. *Separation of powers* would include the functioning of an independent judiciary, among other things. Many people will no doubt question my inclusion of an *informed public* as an essential component of democracy, on the argument that there is no need for people to understand the issues on which they vote, let alone the consequences of their voting choices. After all, people of that orientation might argue, the point is not whether people know what they are doing, but that they are free to do it. On this argument, it makes no difference if government "of the people, by the people, for the people" may operate, in practice, *against* the people. The argument for public information, to the contrary, holds that the integrity of the voting process requires that people are able to judge the issues honestly – which they cannot do if officeholders withhold essential information.

As for excluding corporate funders from making contributions to the coffers of candidates for public office, the argument is a simple one, viz., that unless such an exclusion is effected, there is nothing to keep a democracy from degenerating into plutocracy, with "rule by the people" ending as rule by the wealthy.

Returning to the Gershwin song, the third line, "I got my man", could be treated as a reference to the responsibility of elected officials to the electorate (hence, more properly, "I got my representative").

Thus translated, the Gershwin text reads,

I got the liberal project
I got democracy
I got elected officials responsible to the electorate
Who could ask for anything more?
Who indeed?

Versions

The classical liberal tradition, as adumbarted by Hooker, and expostulated by Hobbes,[1] Locke, and Kant,[2] presumes the existence of a higher moral law discernible by unaided human reason; in other words, it presumes that there are some principles on which rational persons may agree. Richard Hooker (1554—1600) put it this way:

"The main principles of reason are in themselves apparent. For to make nothing evident of itself unto man's understanding were to take away all possibility of knowing anything....From which relation of equality between ourselves and them that are as ourselves, what several rules and canons natural reason hath drawn for direction of life, no man is ignorant, as namely, That because we would take no harm, we must therefore do none; That since we would not be in any thing extremely dealt with, we must ourselves avoid all extremity in our dealings [with others]; That from all violence and wrong we are utterly to abstain...Wherefore the natural measure whereby to judge our doings, is the sentence of reason."[3]

John Locke (1632—1704), an admirer of Hooker's writings, put it more simply:

"The State of Nature has a Law of Nature to govern it, which obliges every one: And Reason, which is that Law, teaches all Mankind, who will but consult it, that being all equal and independent, no one ought to harm another in his Life, Health, or Possessions."[4]

So central is the moral law to classical liberal theory that one may, without distortion, describe classical liberalism as the project to make politics conform to the moral law.[5]

If, further, the challenge is to make state and politics conform to moral precepts, then it is fatuous to imagine that the state may stand above Right, above morality, above duty. Even Hobbes, who is sometimes mistaken for an advocate of state absolutism, took the moral law (whether one calls it Natural Law or Universal Reason) as his starting point.[6] Locke is, perhaps, the most articulate in taking the moral context in which states exist to its logical consequence. In Locke's words:

"...if a long train of Abuses, Prevarications, and Artifices, all tending the same way, make the design visible to the People, and they cannot but feel, what they lie under, and...'tis not to be wonder'd, that they should then rouze themselves, and endeavour to put the rule into such hands, which may secure to them the ends for which Government was at first erected."[7]

This justification of a right of rebellion against tyranny found its way, in Jefferson's paraphrase, into the American Declaration of Independence. But if the people serve as the ultimate check on the government, the government, in turn, serves as a check on the people. "If men were angels, no government would be necessary," James Madison tells us.[8]

Yet, out of this common fount, three distinct 'versions' of liberalism have developed: the *universalist-idealist* tradition which may trace its heritage to Locke, Kant, and Madison; the *conventionalist-realist* tradition with which Hobbes ought not to be too firmly identified (inasmuch as he remained within the Natural Law tradition) but which may, all the same, trace its heritage to Hobbes' influence and to the writings of the "Hobbists"[9]; and the *consequentialist-relativist* tradition, which I view as a corruption of the ideas of John Stuart Mill.

For the *universalist-idealists*, as Madison put it, "justice is the end of government. It is the end of civil society."[10] And further,

> "...the aim of every political constitution is, or ought to be, first to obtain for rulers men who possess most wisdom to discern, and most virtue to pursue, the common good of society; and in the next place, to take the most effectual precautions for keeping them virtuous whilst they continue to hold their public trust."[11]

In other words, good laws and good institutions are not enough; the character of the officeholders is also of crucial importance.

As universalists, adherents of this first branch of the liberal tradition place their emphasis squarely on the moral framework of rights and duties, and see human reason as the gateway to a moral understanding, even to a (perhaps limited) moral consensus.

For *conventionalist-realists*, the emphasis is shifted from human potential to grow in moral excellence, to human depravity; in accordance with this view, the purpose of government cannot be Justice in any grand sense, but is reduced to the more modest task of maintaining civil order. For conventionalist-realists, the police figure as the living symbol of the state. Nor is Reason of much avail. In Hobbes' words, "Reason...is nothing but reckoning, that is adding and subtracting, of the consequences of general names agreed upon for the marking and signifying of our thoughts," and hence, "no man's reason, nor the reason of any one number of men, makes the certainty; no more than an account is therefore cast up, because a great many men have unanimously approved it."[12] But if Reason is so uncertain a tool, then it would be vain to presume that anyone's understanding of *justice* ought to be treated as having intrinsic or essential worth, or to be capable of serving as a measure against which to measure the compliance of the state with presumed rational standards. For conventionalists, one need not dispense with the word "justice", of course, only 'recognize' that it can have no greater meaning than the sum of the laws of the land. Frank Coleman argues the point, giving Hobbes' philosophy a somewhat different interpretation from that advanced here. In Coleman's words, "according to Hobbes, the authority exercised by public officials is absolute...Public authority must be absolute because there must be in society a determinate person, or body of persons, responsible for saying what the law is."[13] The aim of government, then, cannot be justice in any transcendent sense, for 'justice' is seen by conventionalists as merely the tool whereby the government is to realize its 'true' aim, which, as already noted, is seen as the preservation of civil order. This is why Samuel P. Huntington, a latter-day 'conventionalist-realist', holds that the most important distinction in politics is between those governments capable of maintaining civil order and those not capable of such, even positing a functional equivalence between communist governments and democratic governments.[14] Or, in Hobbes' words, "...men have no pleasure, but on the contrary a great deal of grief, in keeping company, where there is no power able to overawe them all."[15]

Consequentialist-relativism is the third heir to the liberal tradition, and though it may trace a noble genealogy to Jeremy Bentham (1748—1832)[16] and John Stuart Mill (1806—1873),[17] and count among its proponents such brilliant minds as L. W. Sumner[18] and Russell Hardin,[19] it is ultimately a bastard son of the liberal commitment to individual rights and the capitalist urge to accumulate wealth, and in this illicit union, Natural Law is pushed to the side and moral determination is hitched to the dual standard of "the end justifies the means" (a slogan to which consequentialism owes its name) and "the greatest good for the greatest number". It is not that Kant or Locke, or even Hobbes for that matter, would have contemned "the good", much less "the greatest good". The rub is that, by specifying "for the greatest number" and by associating the moral calculus with consequences (hence, consequences for the majority), consequentialism admits its willingness to sacrifice the interests of minorities to those of 'the majority' as well as its denial of an external rational standard for judging human behavior (a denial also implicit in conventionalism, as we have seen), thereby reducing the moral calculus to the democratic outcome of majorities and minorities. In this way, consequentialism beguilingly offers itself as the 'most democratic' of the three heirs to the liberal tradition, even as it gives rise to what I have elsewhere called *moral hedonism*[20] and allows its subscribers to suspect that there are no objective facts about right or wrong, no objective basis, for example, for judging whether cruelty to children or rape or mass murder should be condemned, no basis for assessing whether kindness, honesty, and charity, on the other side, ought to be admired. But the problem lies in the writings of the consequentialists, rather than in the nature of the moral law as such. Along such lines, Robert Adams has argued that "if we are tempted to say...that there are no objective facts of right or wrong at all, it is chiefly because we have found so much obscurity in theories about objective, non-natural ethical facts."[21]

As is often the case, the ideas of this current's (co-)founder are more subtle than those of many of his inheritors. Thus, in exalting utility as "the ultimate appeal on all ethical questions" -- a phrasing which, taken alone, could give encouragement to those given to the abuses and deformations which have become ever more commonplace in our so-called "post-modern" age -- Mill immediately adds the specification that "it must be utility in the largest sense, grounded on the permanent interests of man as a progressive being."[22] As for the government, consequentialists tend to view government as a facilitator of the pursuit of *individual interests*, rather than as either an absolute enforcer of Order or the vehicle for maximizing either the common good or justice.

Subversions

Subversions may be distinguished from frontal attacks insofar as they begin from within, taking their start with one or another of the rival legacies of the liberal tradition, and modulating or transforming the emphases, purposes, and even values to be defended.

On the understanding of the liberal tradition as outlined in the preceding section, I count at least four spurious claimants to the liberal tradition, each of which undermines and subverts one or more of the central values of the liberal project. These spurious claimants are libertarianism, the absolutization of the state, the denial of reason, and moral consequentialism-relativism. Separately and collectively, these claims are able to pose a serious threat to the liberal heritage, precisely because their advocates (in many cases) believe that they remain within the liberal tradition (with others simply reviling liberalism as a 'Eurocentric' prejudice, to cite a criticism favored by fin-de-siecle American bigots).

Libertarianism, the advocacy of a minimal state, is linked with ultra-individualism and the cult of uniqueness through conformity. Libertarians may, to be sure, cite suitable passages from John Stuart Mill, among others, but the minimal state reduces equality to equality of 'right' while stripping away social services. Is special documentation required to prove that the right to self-expression and to personal security enjoyed 'equally' by a billionaire media-mogul and by an indigent homeless shift worker will not be enjoyed equally by *both,* or that the whittling away of the state requires that one peg one's hopes for other planks of the liberal project (specifically the assurance of individual rights, tolerance, and respect for the harm principle) on the good intentions of all citizens and the voluntary self-restraint of those who might be tempted to violate these values? In other words, libertarianism reveals an unmistakable naïvete. It draws its energy from a one-sided emphasis on individual rights at the expense of other elements in the liberal project.

The absolutization of the state takes the form of assertions that state sovereignty is the supreme principle, that 'sovereign' states may treat their subjects as they will, and that there is no higher court of justice to which an appeal may be brought – not to Universal Reason (which state absolutizers deny), not to the moral law (which state absolutizers either deny or qualify), not to international covenants, nor even to international bodies established for the purpose of defending certain supposed norms of international behavior. For state absolutizers, the sanctity of human rights is not so much denied, as ignored or set aside. This line of argument became fashionable in certain circles in the U.S., Britain, France, and Germany[23] during the Bosnian war of 1991—95 and the Kosovo crisis of 1998—99. Affirming the unbreachable and inviolable state sovereignty of Serbia, state absolutizers sought to deny Bosnian Muslims and Kosovo Albanians alike any *right* either to rebel or to appeal to the international community for assistance (much less to secede), and to deny the international community any right but to acquiesce in the continued oppression of Muslims (even in towns controlled by the Serbs from the early stages of the war, such as Banja Luka) and of Kosovo's Albanians. Hence, for example, in the words of two well-known state absolutizers, "...fundamental principles...most notably the right of states to defend their sovereignty and territorial integrity and to conduct their internal affairs free from external intervention," regardless of the levels of oppression in which the given government might be implicated, militated, in their view, "against intervention on any basis other than that recognized in the United Nations Charter: to preserve international peace."[24] In other words, in their view, only a threat to international peace and international security could ever justify intervention in a state's internal affairs, and, further, the sovereign rights of both legitimate and illegitimate states should be seen as equivalent and interchangeable. That such counsel could offer solace and satisfaction not to Balkan dictators but also to the Pinochets, Somozas, Khomeinis, and Pol Pots of this world should be clear, since for state absolutizers, it is the office-holders who enjoy 'sovereignty', not the subjects of their rule.

Along similar lines, Susan Woodward, a literal-minded conventionalist, treated the 1974 Yugoslav constitution as the ultimate arbiter of justice in writing that

> "The rights to territorial self-governance on the basis of national self-determination or to national sovereignty were not at all clear in the case of the ethnic Albanians. Their constitutional classification as a nationality rather than [as] a constituent nation made them ineligible for such rights...."[25]

Leaving aside the question of whether national difference should be taken as justifying secession in any and all cases – without which claim there can be no "right of national self-determination" as such[26] -- this position entails the notion that there is no higher court of appeal than the constitution and laws of the land, whatever they might be. Yet, while this is conventionalism in its purest form, it proves to be *inconsistent* conventionalism, because Woodward elsewhere endorses the Serbian position that self-determination took precedence over *Croatian* sovereignty, writing, "To grant Croatian sovereignty in 1991—92 over the territories it claims historically, therefore, as Vladimir Gligorov puts it, is to 'open the Serbian question'."[27]

For consistent state absolutizers, the existence of such organizations as Amnesty International and Human Rights Watch could even appear to be a bit of foolishness, insofar as they have been erected precisely to protect and enforce universal standards which state absolutizers treat as pure illusion. In this way, their cynicism about the reliability of human reason ends with the apotheosis of the written law, the letter of the law, and with the exaltation of state sovereignty.

Inspired by the Hobbist (but not Hobb'sian)[28] reading of the moral law ("the question of the supposed moral law" consistent state absolutizers might say), conventionalists of this strain place undue stress on the rule of law, distorting its meaning in the process. That this position is irreconcilable with the Lockean-Jeffersonian defense of a right of rebellion against illegitimate government should be self-evident (and is implicit, for that matter, in the denial of a right to request international intervention). That this position, when advanced in the supposed defense of local 'traditions' of non-Western nations is potentially racist, reflecting a deep contempt for non-Western peoples, should also be more than evident. The classical liberal tradition, at least as espoused by Hooker, Locke, Kant, and Jefferson, draws a clear distinction between legitimate and illegitimate states, on the basis of which one might presume to set forth the proposition that only legitimate states may be said to be sovereign.[29]

The denial of reason. There are two arguments which profess to deny reason its place in the moral calculus, either qualifying as a manifestation of philosophical skepticism. The first is that since 'people' have had different values and different moral presuppositions and conclusions in the course of history, there is no such thing as Universal Reason, no such thing as "a system of *a priori* knowledge from concepts alone,"[30] such as Kant outlined, and no such thing as a categorical imperative. Instead of thinking in terms of postulates such as Kant's "Act upon a maxim that can also hold as a universal law,"[31] the skeptic would have us judge each situation "on its own merits," on the basis of empirical grounds alone, disregarding Kant's warning about the inadequacy of empirical grounds as a guide to moral action and blithely assuming that one can judge the merits of a case without some *a priori* non-empirical assumptions or standards.

The second argument for skepticism is that since reasonable people may disagree about many things, one is not entitled to assume or postulate that any argument or principle may have any greater claim to rationality than any other, not even the argument, for example, that genocide, mass rape, and the torture of infants are morally wrong.[32]

There are at least three replies to this skepticism – one formal, and two substantive. The formal reply is that the skeptic is using *a priori* argumentation for the purpose of debunking a priori argumentation, in effect declaring that the only legitimate a priori argument about morality is that a priori arguments about morality are, *a priori,* invalid. This smacks of casuistry and is redolent with anti-intellectualism.[33] The first substantive reply is that moral discourse is not purely self-referential, but, on the contrary, is used to refer to relations in the world; the proof of this is that moral discourse exists not merely in the academe, but is, on the contrary, the lifeblood of politics. The second substantive reply is that the concept of Universal Reason does not presume either static understandings of the moral law over the course of history or universal assent in all details, any more than the concept of good etiquette requires that everyone in the world, and across time, agree as to whether, for example, one should send a thank-you note to one's host after enjoying a fine meal at the host's expense or say "excuse me" when attempting to exit a crowded bus; in Japan, in fact, either of these behaviors would be considered at best 'curious' or 'American', at, at worst, 'suspicious' or 'foolish'. And yet, Japan is clearly a society with a marked emphasis on etiquette, and, I would go so far as to suggest, one could reasonably even speak of some "universals" in etiquette, such as not to insult one's host, not to express contempt for gifts, and so forth. By extension, the moral law may be seen as grounded in rational standards, even if articulate persons may differ both about those standards and about their applications, just as, for that matter, mathematicians may differ about some of the principles and applications of higher mathematics, without being required to deny that mathematics as a field has any universally rational basis. For Kant, indeed, the metaphysics of morals is seen as comparable, in this sense, with mathematics and, further, with the natural sciences.[34] As Allen Wood explains:

"Kant thinks rational principles (including but not limited to moral principles) are "universally valid" in the sense that they are normative for all beings capable of rational conduct. This does not imply that all rational beings, irrespective of their nature or situation, must find exactly the same actions rational or irrational, or even that they must recognize the same rules about this. (Still less does it imply that any individual's or culture's view about the norms of rationality are ever infallible or incontrovertible.) It means only that insofar as what we take to be rational really is such (i.e., really is rationally binding), it must be understood in terms of the same fundamental principles (whatever the degree of understanding of those we may have acquired)."[35]

Moral consequentialism. I have already discussed consequentialism-relativism in the previous section, but may add here that, in contemporary America, this orientation tends to take either of two forms. The first is a hybrid with the aforementioned 'skepticism', and the arguments brought to bear against that skepticism apply with equal force to the hybrid. The second is the epiphenomenon in the moral field of the lust for commodities and commodity-induced 'pleasure' fostered and encouraged by the materialist culture of monopoly capitalism. Insofar as I construe capitalism as an economic system having little or nothing to do with liberal morality, its discussion belongs more properly to the next section.

Aversions

Under this rubric, I propose to discuss (briefly) four threats to or dangers for liberalism. I shall pass over such obvious dangers as Taliban-style theocracy, neo-fascism, and neo-Naziism, and reserve my space for less obvious dangers.

The first on my list, to continue the thread from the previous section, is the *capitalist economic system*. Capitalism lures the consumer with consequentialist snares such as "what's good for no. 1" or invitations to attain individual 'uniqueness' through the acquisition of brandname merchandise and conformity to prefabricated models of acceptable fashion and taste. This at least hints at the reasons why I believe that capitalism, while masquerading as the economic avatar of liberalism, is, in fact, virulently corrosive of the liberal project. Among other things, we find that capitalism substitutes the rule of the market for the rule of law, the right to consume for other more important rights, or apathy for true tolerance,[36] wholesale destruction of the ecosphere (with all of its consequences) and the continued impoverishment of both foreign and domestic working classes for respect for the harm principle in all its manifestations, and the equality of equal money for the liberal understanding of equality. Of the six components of the liberal project, only the neutrality of the state in matters of religion remains untouched by monopoly capitalism.

Clericalism likewise poses a danger to liberal society. By "clericalism" I mean the *organized* effort on the part of certain religious bodies or their front organizations to impose their denominational moral agendas on the public at large; this effort has been assayed in the United States through the initiative process (as manifested, for example, in the Christian Right's efforts in several states in the course of the 1990s to reduce gays and lesbians from second-class citizens to third-class citizens), through violence and intimidation (as manifested in the murders of a series of physicians by anti-abortion fanatics and the recurrent blockades of clinics and other medical facilities by anti-abortion activists over the last two decades of the twentieth century, and especially during the Reagan and Bush administrations), and through not-so-subtle propaganda targeted, in the first place, at members of intolerant religious associations themselves.

The third danger to the liberal project comes from *nationalism*, which affirms the rights of the designated group over the rights of the majority (as shown, for example, in Serb nationalists' and Serb apologists' denunciations of the winter 1992 referendum on independence in Bosnia-Herzegovina), over the rights of individuals (as illustrated in the process of "ethnic cleansing"), and over the rights of the society as a whole (among which rights, as both Hobbes and Locke would agree, is the right to peace and security).

And finally, as mentioned earlier in this chapter, an *uninformed public* may itself pose a threat to liberal democracy. Liberalism may find itself, as Shklar puts it, in a "marriage of convenience" with democracy,[37] but the freedoms assured by democracy are open to all sorts of uses, including media campaigns to mislead the public. Hence, for example, when the voters of the State of California approved Proposition 13 in the early 1980s, thereby slashing property taxes, and when the voters of the State of Washington approved Initiative 695 in autumn 1999, reducing vehicle registration fees to a flat $30 and legislating that there be no further increases in taxes or new taxes without voter approval, the result should be seen – according to apologists for these initiatives – as "triumphs" of the General Will (to use Rousseau's terminology), in spite of the fact that the California vote resulted in a curtailment of police and fire protection, while the Washington vote resulted in the curtailment of bus service (on which the less well-to-do depend), the firing of public health nurses, and discussions of dramatic increases in ferry fares, which many of the ferry's users could ill afford. In essence, in both cases, the upper classes were able to reduce their contribution to public expenditures by a disproportionate amount, hurting the working classes disproportionately.

It might be thought that the chief threat of poor information would be to democracy, rather than to the liberal project, and, insofar as I have listed "an informed public" as one of the components of *democracy*, this would be technically correct. But votes on the basis of poor information may *also* threaten individual rights and, depending on the specific content of the initiative, any of the other components of the liberal project.

Traversions

The collapse of the communist organizational power monopoly across Eurasia between 1989 and 1991 signalled the inception of a new phase in the political history of the region. Prominent figures in the post-communist societies, including the leading personalities in relatively young non-communist parties, confronted the challenge of attempting to move their societies in the direction of liberal democracy. Spain, Portugal, and various countries in Latin America and Africa had traversed the road from authoritarianism to liberal democracy (defying the anti-Western skepticism of would-be 'champions' of moral 'diversity') beginning in the 1960s, in some cases. Could the post-communist societies do likewise?

Fareed Zakaria and Marc Plattner recently debated the nature of liberal democracy in the pages of *Foreign Affairs.* Where Zakaria construed liberal democracy as a hybrid consisting of separable parts, worrying about the proliferation of a new hybrid which he called "illiberal demcracy",[38] Plattner took a more sanguine view, declaring liberalism and democracy indissolubly linked, so that one need not worry, in his view, about illiberal fruit in democratic systems.[39] My own understanding is closer to Zakaria's here than to either Plattner's or Shklar's (Plattner wrote that one could not have either liberalism or democracy without the other,

- 60 -

while Shklar wrote merely that one could not have liberalism without democracy).

Following Zakaria's line of thought, one may distinguish among four hybrid systems: liberal democracy, illiberal authoritarianism, liberal authoritarianism (including liberal monarchy), and illiberal democracy. Of these four, we may count liberal democracy and liberal monarchy as fully legitimate,[40] and the two illiberal permutations as illegitimate systems. But in the present historical context, liberal monarchy may figure, at best, as a transitional order (except insofar as one might speak of constitutional monarchy on the British or Spanish model), while illiberal democracy, as a strategy for transition to liberal democracy, is inherently dangerous, being more apt to end in outright authoritarianism, inasmuch as the distance from "tyranny of the majority"[41] to simple tyranny is not as great as one might suppose.

This brings me to the question of timing. In endeavoring to introduce liberal democracy in a country which has known neither liberalism nor democracy, one can opt for any of three alternative strategies:

Liberalism first, democracy later;
Democracy first, liberalism later;
Both at once.

I have already explained why the second strategy is unlikely to succeed; to repeat, illiberal democracy is an illegitimate system and, as such, cannot provide the foundation for building a legitimate system.[42]

Of the other two strategies, both have advantages. The third strategy has certainly worked well in states under occupation (e.g., post-war Germany and Japan[43]) where the occupying powers were willing to invest their resources heavily, and in most of the post-communist societies of East Central Europe, it may be the only realistic option. Still, it is worth remembering that the first strategy (liberalism first, democracy later) was historically the strategy adopted in Great Britain,[44] while in the United States, the Founding Fathers declared broad liberal values but established a limited democracy in which suffrage was limited by race, gender, and property ownership, feeling, as Alexander Hamilton once put it, that "the people is a Great Beast" and cannot be trusted with the responsibility of nurturing a liberal order.

As for the wisdom of trying to "do it all at once," without outside assistance, the French Revolution stands as a sobering lesson on the dangers of attempting too much too rapidly and failing to develop a clear *liberal* program, as well as on the dangers of the sudden mobilization into politics of large numbers of people hitherto deprived of the practice of citizenship.

But "Great Beast" or not, the people are, of necessity, included in the project of building liberal democracies following the third strategy, throughout most of Eurasia. There are, in fact, only two states in the region where the restoration of royal monarchy might play a salutary role in the "traversion", as I am calling it, to a liberal order, viz., Russia and Serbia. Both have had a troubled transition with authoritarian practices and widespread corruption hiding behind the trappings of parliamentary democracy. Both societies have been involved, at least in part, in local wars (Russian forces most prominently in Chechnya, but also in Tadjikistan and in Ossetia; Serbian forces and supplies in Croatia, Bosnia, and Kosovo). Both societies have seen the development of a large local mafia and the impoverishment of broad sectors of society. And both have local dynasties available, which enjoy at least some popularity and/or credibility. Whether we shall actually witness the restoration of the Romanov and Karadjordjevć dynasties, in Russia and Serbia respectively, is beside the point. The point is rather that, at this writing, such restorations could serve a legitimating function, helping these societies to build constitutional monarchies on the British, Norwegian, or Spanish models.[45]

Reversions

I do not agree with Shklar when she writes that "morality and knowledge can develop only in a free and open society."[46] That authoritarian systems may obstruct the dissemination of information and growth of knowledge is conceded; in communist Romania, for example, it was necessary to obtain a license just to keep a typewriter in one's house and, needless to say, such licenses were hard to obtain. But, as any student of communism knows, the communist party was rarely able to wipe out entire areas of knowledge (Stalin and Mao came the closest to achieving this dire goal, while Pol Pot achieved the same result by simply wiping out people) and, in fact, knowledge became a highly prized commodity in communist systems, being much more highly valued than in the open societies of the West.

On the other hand, there is an argument to be made that it is precisely in conditions of repression that courage and moral commitment may obtain their most lofty expressions. James Joyce would have seen the point. Certainly, the examples of Jan Vaculík, Václav Havel, Jerzy Turowicz, and Jacek Kuroń,[47] to name just a few, serve as suggestive counter-examples to Shklar's linkage of morality with democracy. Ultimately, insofar as I place morality at the center of political life, I prefer to think of moral challenges and the opportunities for moral growth as being equally present in all societies.

That said, I find myself in full agreement with Shklar, and here also with Henri Ruiz-Peña,[48] that the cynical relativism which worries that the liberal tradition may be specifically 'Western' and not 'exportable' (the wrong word, of course) to non-Western societies is blindly complacent and profoundly apathetic. To declare that non-Western societies might do 'better' without the rule of law, without respect for human rights or for the harm principle, founding their systems, instead, on bigotry of various kinds, on inequality, and on the conjunction of Church and state smacks of hauteur and contempt for foreign lands. As Shklar has written, "It may be a revolting paradox that the very success of liberalism in some countries has atrophied the political empathies of their citizens."[49]

The spreading commitment to liberal values in the post-communist world holds the promise of creating legitimate systems which, in turn, is the guarantee of stability. But a new emergent homogeneity should by no means be presumed. There are, as I indicated at the outset, three competing heirs to the classical liberal tradition, and the societies of East-Central Europe and Eurasia may find themselves highlighting insights and features from one or another rival legacy, hybridizing these variations on the theme of rights and duties, with variations in the economic sphere and in political institution-building.

Endnotes

[1] In her influential essay, "The Liberalism of Fear", Judith Shklar offers a definite definition of liberalism, viz, that it is an ideology aiming to "secure the political conditions that are necessary for the exercise of personal freedom" and, on the basis of that understanding, concludes that Hobbes stands outside the liberal tradition. I include Hobbes among classical liberals for fou easons: (1) my definition and understanding of liberalism are different from Shklar's and do notexclude Hobbes; (2) Hobbes' stress on individual rights to life, limb and property place him within the liberal tradition as it has generally been understood; (3) Hobbes has had enormous influence on liberal thinkers, above allin America; and (4) the American system is, in any event, more Hobb'sian than Lockean in some critical areas, and is counted by Shklar herself as a liberal society. See Judith N.Shklar, Political Thought and Political Thinkers (Chicago: University fo Chicago Press, 1998), pp. 3, 6. AlsoFrank M. Coleman, Hobbes and America: Exploring the Constitutional Foundations (Toronto: University of Toronto Press, 18977); and James R. Hurtgen. "Hobbes's Theory of Sovereignty in Leviathan", in Reason Papers, No. 5 (Winter, 1979), pp. 55-67

[2] Richard Hooker, *Of the Laws of Ecclesiastical Polity: Preface, Book I, Book VIII*, ed. Arthur Stephen McGrade (Cambridge: Cambridge University Press, 1989); Thomas Hobbes, *Leviathan,* selected by Richard S. Peters, ed. Michael Oakeshott (New York: Collier Books, 1962); Thomas Hobbes, *Behemoth: The History of the Civil Wars of England* (London: [s.n.], 1679); John Locke, *Two Treatises of Government,* ed. by Peter Laslett (Cambridge: Cambridge University Press, 1988); and Immanuel Kant, *The Metaphysics of Morals,* trans. from German by Mary Gregor (Cambridge: Cambridge University Press, 1991).

[3] Hooker, *Of the Laws of Ecclesiastical Polity,* pp. 77, 80.

[4] Locke, *Two Treatises of Government,* II, p. 271.

[5] On this and related points, see Nancy L. Rosenblum (ed.), *Liberalism and the Moral Life* (Cambridge, Mass.: Harvard University Press, 1989).

[6] On this point, see Norberto Bobbio, *Thomas Hobbes and the Natural Law Tradition,* trans. from Italian by Daniela Gobetti (Chicago: University of Chicago Press, 1993).

[7] Locke, *Two Treatises of Government,* II, p. 415.

[8] James Madison, "No. 51", in Alexander Hamilton, James Madison, and John Jay, *The Federalist Papers* (New York: Mentor Book, 1961), p. 322.

[9] See Sterling P. Lamprecht, "Hobbes and Hobbism", in Isaac Kramnick (ed.), *Essays in the History of Political Thought* (Englewood Cliffs, N.J.: Prentice-Hall, 1969).

[10] Madison, "No. 51", p. 324.

[11] Madison, "No. 57", in Hamilton et al., *The Federalist Papers*, p. 350.

[12] Hobbes, *Leviathan*, pp. 41, 42.

[13] Coleman, *Hobbes and America*, p. 107.

[14] Samuel P. Huntington, *Political Order in Changing Society* (New Haven, Conn.: Yale University Press, 1968). Of course, on the basis of this notion, Huntington could have had no idea that the communist governments were in any particular difficulty, let along on the road to dissolution. To have suspected that result would have required that he would have been able to identify a fundamental difference between democratic and communist systems, i.e., look at issues of legitimacy; but to have done so would have entailed his abandonment of his unrealistic 'realist' views and his embrace of the more realistic position of liberal 'idealism'.

[15] Hobbes, *Leviathan*, p. 99.

[16] See, for example, Jeremy Bentham, *A Fragment on Government and an Introduction to the Principles of Morals and Legislation*, ed. Wilfrid Harrison (Oxford: Basil Blackwell, 1948); and Jeremy Bentham, *"Legislator of the World": Writings on Codification, Law, and Education*, ed. Philip Schofield and Jonathan Harris (Oxford: Clarendon Press, 1998).

[17] See, for example, John Stuart Mill, *On Liberty and Other Writings*, ed. Stefan Collini (Cambridge: Cambridge University Press, 1989); John Stuart Mill, *August Comte and Positivism* (London: Kegan Paul, Trench, and Tübner, 1907); and John Stuart Mill, *Considerations on Representative Government*, ed. Currin V. Shields (New York: Liberal Arts Press, 1958).

[18] L. W. Sumner, *The Moral Foundation of Rights* (Oxford: Clarendon Press, 1987).

[19] Russell Hardin, *Morality within the Limits of Reason* (Chicago: University of Chicago Press, 1988).

[20] Sabrina P. Ramet, *Whose Democracy? Nationalism, Religion, and the Doctrine of Collective Rights in Post-1989 Eastern Europe* (Lanham, Md.: Rowman & Littlefield, 1997), pp. 65—66.

[21] Quoted in Michael S. Moore, "Good Without God", in Robert P. George (ed.), *Natural Law, Liberalism, and Morality: Contemporary Essays* (Oxford: Clarendon Press, 1996), p. 231.

[22] Mill, *On Liberty*, p. 14.

[23] For an example from Germany, see Jürgen Elsässer (ed.), *Nie wieder Krieg ohne uns. Das Kosovo und die neue Deutsche Geopolitik* (Hamburg: Konkret, 1999).

[24] Steven L. Burg and Paul S. Shoup, *The War in Bosnia-Herzegovina: Ethnic Conflict and International Intervention* (Armonk, N.Y.: M. E. Sharpe, 1999), p. 10.

[25] Susan L. Woodward, *Balkan Tragedy: Chaos and Dissolution after the Cold War* (Washington D.C.: The Brookings Institution Press, 1995), p. 106.

[26] On this point, see my essay, "The So-Called Right of National Self-Determination and Other Myths", in *Human Rights Review*, Vol.II, No.1 (October-December, 2000).

[27] Woodward, *Balkan Tragedy*, p. 215. Note that she uses the word "claims", casting the net wider, by allowing the reader to conflate Croatia's historic *jurisdiction*, under the four socialist constitutions, over areas claimed by Serb insurrectionaries, with Croatian President Tudjman's megalomanic fantasies about territorial expansion into Bosnia-Herzegovina. This conflation is not innocent in its effect.

[28] See Lamprecht, "Hobbes and Hobbism".

[29] For an intelligent discussion of this theme, see John Hoffman, *Sovereignty* (Minneapolis: University of Minnesota Press, 1998); see also Sabrina P. Ramet, "Evil and the Obsolescene of State Sovereignty", in *Human Rights Review*, Vol. 1, No. 2 (January/February 2000).

[30] Kant, *Metaphysics of Morals*, p. 44.

[31] *ibid.*, p. 51.

[32] On the problem of evil in the world, see Joan Copjec (ed.), *Radical Evil* (London: Verso, 1996).

[33] See Richard Hofstadter, *Anti-Intellectualism in American Life* (New York: Vintage Books, 1962).

[34] Allen W. Wood, *Kant's Ethical Thought* (Cambridge: Cambridge University Press, 1999), p. 57.

[35] *Ibid.*

[36] See J. Budziszewski, *True Tolerance: Liberalism and the Necessity of Judgment* (New Brunswick, N.J.: Transaction, 1992); and Susan Mendus (ed.), *Justifying Toleration: Conceptual and Historical Perspectives* (Cambridge: Cambridge University Press, 1988).

[37] Shklar, *Political Thought and Political Thinkers*, p. 19.

[38] Fareed Zakaria, "The Rise of Illiberal Democracy", in *Foreign Affairs*, Vol. 76, No. 6 (November—December 1997).

[39] Marc F. Plattner, "Liberalism and Democracy: Can't Have One without the Other", in *Foreign Affairs*, Vol. 77, No. 2 (March—April 1998).

[40] For discussion and explanation, see my *Whose Democracy? Nationalism, Religion, and the Doctrine of Collective Rights in Post-1989 Eastern Europe:* introduction, chapter 3 and conclusion.

[41] Mill, *On Liberty,* p. 8. Regarding Kant's concerns about tyrranical democracy, see Matthew Levinger, "Kant and the Origins of Prussian Constitutionalism", in *History of Political Thought,* Vol. 19, Issue 2 (Summer 1998), p. 245.

[42] I believe that Giuseppe Di Palma would agree with me on this point. See G. Di Palma, *To Craft Democracies: An Essay on Democratic Transitions* (Berkeley: University of California Press, 1990), p. 80.

[43] See Jutta-B. Lange-Quassowski, "Coming to Terms with the Nazi Past: Schools, Media, and the Formation of Opinion", and Arthur E. Tiedemann, "Japan Sheds Dictatorship" – both in John H. Herz (ed.), *From Dictatorship to Democracy: Coping with the Legacies of Authoritarianism and Totalitarianism* (Westport, Conn.: Greenwood Press, 1982).

[44] See Edmund S. Morgan, *Inventing the People: The Rise of Popular Sovereignty in England and America* (New York: W. W. Norton, 1988).

[45] For discussions of the Spanish case in a comparative context, see Juan J. Linz and Alfred Stepan, "Political Identities and Electoral Sequences: Spain, the Soviet Union, and Yugoslavia", in *Daedalus,* Vol. 121, No. 2 (Spring 1992); and Oriol Pi-Sungar, "The Spanish Route to Democracy: A Model for Eastern Europe in Transition?", in Hermine G. DeSoto and David G. Anderson (eds.), *The Curtain Rises: Rethinking Culture, Ideology, and the State in Eastern Europe* (Atlantic Heights, N.J.: Humanities Press, 1992).

[46] Shklar, *Political Thought and Political Thinkers,* p. 9.

[47] For discussion, see Sabrina Petra Ramet, *Social Currents in Eastern Europe: The Sources and Consequences of the Great Transformation,* 2nd ed. (Durham, N.C.: Duke University Press, 1995), esp. chaps. 4—5; and Vladimir Tismaneanu, *Reinventing Politics: Eastern Europe from Stalin to Havel* (New York: Free Press, 1992).

[48] See his fine contribution to this volume.

[49] Shklar, *Political Thought and Political Thinkers,* p. 17.

- Chapter 4 -

The Political Significance of Media Literacy

Andrew Calabrese

I see a new Athenian Age of democracy forged in the fora the Global Information Infrastructure will create.
U.S. Vice-President Al Gore to the International Telecommunications Union . Buenos Aires, March 21, 1994

In this new land, education will be every citizen's most prized possession. Our schools will have the highest standards in the world, igniting the spark of possibility in the eyes of every girl and every boy. And the doors of higher education will be open to all. The knowledge and power of the Information Age will be within reach not just of the few, but of every classroom, every library, every child.
President William J. Clinton, Second Inaugural Address, Washington, D.C., January 20, 1997

Is the ability to make effective use of new and emerging communication and information technologies essential to the realization of competent citizenship? By what standards do we judge the importance of this connection between technology and citizenship? This essay analyzes contemporary discourse about how the new means of communication are vital to democratic citizenship, focusing particularly on underlying assumptions about a proper role for a democratic state in fostering civic competence through the promotion of *media literacy*, a term discussed below. This analysis enables me to draw connections between the aforementioned body of thought and *the media,* a term I define to include traditional mass media as well as new communication and information technologies (particularly the Internet) and their uses.[1] Despite the tendency of most social and political theory to treat communications media as an afterthought, I argue that no meaningful definition of contemporary citizenship should fail to account for how the modern media are technological and institutional means for citizens to obtain information about the world in which they live, and for engaging in democratic deliberation. I will aim in this essay to provide an original, and, I believe, necessary way of conceptualizing the connections among communication policy, welfare politics, and the ideal of the competent citizen in an information society.

Literacy, Geography, and National Identity

What it means to be media literate is subject to a wide range of interpretation, and for this reason it is necessary to offer a working definition that could serve as the focus of a study about the political significance of media literacy. Any concept of media literacy must be founded on a working definition of literacy more generally. As Harvey Graff demonstrates in his valuable historical study, the idea of literacy is politically significant not only in terms of issues pertaining to citizens' ability to acquire instrumentally "useful knowledge," but also through the relationship between literacy and political judgement and action.[2] Following the introduction of the movable-type printing press by Gutenberg in 1455, the spread of this technological innovation was rapid, and its political impact was significant. Historians of that period have recognized the importance of the printing press — through which Bibles and religious tracts were made widely available — as a means of communication that was indispensable to the Protestant Reformation. Indeed, Martin Luther once waxed rhapsodically, "Printing was God's highest act of grace."[3] By many accounts, the "press of protest" on which Protestant reformers relied represented a marriage of technological and religious revolution.

Printing and literacy are historically and politically significant not only for their role in spreading the word of God, but also for the forging of early modern European nation states. By the end of the sixteenth century (roughly 150 years after Gutenberg), the market in Europe for texts published in Latin, the universal language of print, was more or less saturated. Gradually, publishers sought to create new markets for books by consolidating linguistically similar geographic areas into single markets for publications printed in standardized vernacular languages. Thus, through a slow process of defining the geographic boundaries of linguistically unified markets, national literatures and elements of national cultures came to be reinforced and territorialized.[4] While no claim is being made here of which is cause and which is effect, as the printing press spread throughout Europe, the number of literate people grew, and what began as a strategy for developing new publishing markets became in effect a means of unifying the reading publics of national bourgeoisies. For example, the *Catechism* (1555) and *Grammar* (1584) published by Primo Trubar began the process of the standardization of the Slovenian language and, arguably, were among the most significant formal developments to consolidate the idea of Slovenian cultural identity.

Literacy was profoundly important for the circulation of political ideas in the decades preceding the French revolution. As Habermas and others have shown, the availability of political newsletters and broadsheets was vital to the emergence and consolidation of political power by the French bourgeoisie.[5] Literacy also divided the bourgeoisie from the lower classes, which became a social issue that led to state intervention. For example, in mid-nineteenth century Britain, a state-supported literacy movement emerged that was, according to Graff, "derived from the need for social order and morality in a time of unprecedented social and economic transformation. Education was a Victorian obsession."[6] This observation illustrates a recurring theme in the history of literacy, namely, the tendency for literacy movements to serve as means of consolidating rather than challenging a given social order. Immediately following World War II, the British adult education movement promoted literacy beyond a very basic and functional level. Most famous among the participants in this movement was literary critic Raymond Williams, whose involvement was mainly through his work for Oxford University's Extramural Delegacy, which began in 1946 and continued to 1961. Despite the difficulties and frustrations of the work, Williams was a committed teacher who felt that he had an important political mission to fulfill in helping to elevate the critical capacities of the working class. As one biographer writes, "Williams wanted to assert the democratic imperative of a discriminating working class."[7] By 1950, Williams was introducing popular culture, specifically film, as a legitimate topic for serious analysis and discussion, an area of inquiry he promoted not out of an attempt to elevate the status of popular culture, but rather to promote understanding about the political significance of the popular arts. Moreover, he was doing so despite the guilt and pressure from peers and administrators who were disapproving of the few teachers who felt that popular forms of cultural expression are no less worthy of serious scrutiny and criticism simply because they are entertaining.[8] In his writing and his teaching, Williams returned to this vein throughout the remainder of this career out of an explicit commitment to promoting political awareness within the arenas in which the working class engaged with culture. In this regard, Williams's contribution to the study of culture can be said to also be a contribution to the development of a particular, and explicitly political, concept of media literacy.

Today, the term media literacy is used widely, most commonly in the fields of media and communication studies, and in education. One quickly gets a sense of how diffuse the meaning of the term is when one realizes that it can range from dealing with concerns about how children are being affected in their television viewing habits to issues regarding the teaching of computers in the school. High school and undergraduate classes designed to teach students critical television viewing skills can fall under the same general heading as instruction designed to teach students how to surf the Internet or build a web site. A media-literate person might be one who has the ability to use the local cable access center's video equipment to produce a documentary on local environmental issues, or one who has the capacity to provide an insightful and rigorous analysis of the prioritization of political issues in a network newscast. Teaching technological skills is, in this sense, roughly equivalent to imparting political understanding. Of course, these differences illustrate the anemia inherent in the vocabulary used to describe the activities involved in various sorts of media education, vocabulary which presents a serious problem to the extent that technical capacities are seen as equivalent to civic competence in all of its social, cultural, and political dimensions. To complicate the matter further is the degree to which media education is focused on the provision of professional skills to future media industry practitioners, which is indeed the main reason for which college students are attracted to media education. However, this very large category of media education, and its corollary definitions of media literacy, are not the central focus of the remainder of this paper. Rather, the focus is on the cultivation of knowledge among citizens to enhance their capacities for participation in cultural understanding and political communication of a variety of forms of discourse.

The Competent Citizen

Since its beginnings, there been fundamental disagreement in Western political philosophy about what role citizens can and should play in public debate and governance. Within the specific context of early 20th century United States, Walter Lippmann argued in *Public Opinion* and subsequent work that the "omnicompetent citizen" is a myth, and that public debate should be left to more level-headed experts of various kinds. [9] Among those who vigorously disagreed with Lippmann was John Dewey, whose *The Public and Its Problems*, was written as a response that aimed to depict the average citizen as one whose civic competence is worthy of cultivation and trust rather than of suspicion and under-estimation.[10] In Dewey's view, the ability to participate as listener and speaker in public debate, both literally and figuratively, is essential to competent citizenship. This unsettled debate poses fundamental issues about educational policy, media policy, and the connection between the two.

Moving the discussion about the capacities of ordinary citizens forward into the late twentieth century, Carole Pateman begins with a critical explication of a position that echoes Dewey's, namely, she challenges the assumptions that participation is impractical and unwarranted, and that it should be limited to voting for representatives.[11] As Pateman notes, there is a powerful tendency in political thought to treat the public as a "mass" that is "incapable of action other than a stampede" (Schumpeter), that is apathetic (Berelson), whose lower socio-economic groups tend toward authoritarianism (Dahl), and whose increased participation would threaten to undermine political stability (several authors). Little needs to be said about the low regard that this perspective, and the political action it informs, holds for average citizens. This view of citizens is mirrored in many ways by the dismissive manner in which citizens are regarded in "mass society" theory[12] from which much of mass media theory is derived.

Drawing from Tocqueville's *Democracy in America,* Pateman argues that the capacity for competent public judgement is derived experientially, and the feasible opportunity to participate in public life is a necessary precondition to that end. Tocqueville saw participation in local public affairs as a means of enabling individuals to become effective participants in a national polity: "Town meetings are to liberty what primary schools are to science; they bring within it the people's reach, they teach men how to use and how to enjoy it."[13] Pateman's argument can be summarized as stating that participation in political and non-political settings at local levels, where greater opportunities for participation are available, engenders a competent citizenry at representative levels. As she argues,

> "The ordinary man might still be more interested in things nearer home, but the existence of a participatory society would mean that he was better able to assess the performance of representatives at the national level, better equipped to take decisions of national scope when the opportunity arose to do so, and better able to weigh up the impact of decisions taken by national representatives on his own life and immediate surroundings. In the context of a participatory society the significance of his vote to the individual would have multiple opportunities to become an educated, public citizen."[14]

Pateman's analysis emphasizes the value of local participation in the name of both participatory and representative democracy. What Pateman does not emphasize, however, is what I term *translocalism*: the direct communication that increasingly takes place between and among active participants in organizations, coalitions and social movements which may or may not have significant memberships in a single locale, but whose collective membership across potentially great distances makes for an increasingly important form of participation. Amid all of the discussion of global culture, the information highway, and the globalization of the mass media, little is said about the persistent and increasing problems experienced at the local level by communities struggling to sustain political, economic, and cultural autonomy as capital deprives them of it with the tacit and active assistance of government at all levels. An examination of the opportunities and limitations for greater access to communications media is one of value in that regard.[15]

A complementary approach to the idea of the competent citizen that is valuable for a political interpretation of media literacy is the critical theory of *communicative competence* presented by Jürgen Habermas.[16] This theory centers on the argument that communication can be systematically distorted by relations of power and domination, which necessitates that actors, listeners, and speakers develop the capacity to recognize when such forms of repression are happening. Thus, as Thomas McCarthy has noted, the pedagogical function of such a theory is to offer a guide for the critique of systematic ideological distortion and for the institutionalization of more democratic forms of discourse.[17] Of course, Habermas has been taken to task for idealizing the conditions under which systematic distortion, assuming it can be identified, can be overcome.[18] Despite this, Habermas's efforts to further develop a theory of *communicative action* continue to be based on the ideal of the public use of reason rather than on instrumental rationality grounded in power relations.[19] Most important about Habermas's view on communicative competence is its grounding in historical materialism, which he argues is essential if we are to be able to recognize the deviations in discourse that can threaten democratic public communication:

I would propose to make two empirical assumptions: firstly, that these deviations increase in proportion to the degree of repression which characterizes the institutional system within a given society; and secondly that the degree of repression depends in turn on the developmental stage of the productive forces and on the organization of authority, that is of the institutionalization of political and economic power.[20]

Although Habermas's concept of communicative competence offers a valuable conceptual orientation to democratic education, its great deficiency is its abstractness, which leaves much to the imagination as far as what sort of interventions are possible, both in terms of a critique of systematically distorted communication, and of the institutionalization of forms of democratic communication. While Habermas does not appear to have abandoned the general normative goal of a practical concept of communicative competence within a broader theory of communicative action, his more recent work is preoccupied with the legal preconditions of democratic deliberation. Accordingly, the pedagogical preconditions for deliberative democracy remain unanswered, except in very general terms.[21]

In contrast, such preconditions are at the forefront of the work on democratic education by Amy Gutmann,[22] whose various writings address the relationship between political education and public deliberation. For Gutmann, political education in the modern age necessitates state patronage, because in no other way can minimal guarantees be provided for universal democratic access to such an education. In taking this position, she links welfare politics to the politics of citizenship rights, a connection that has more than a few critics.[23] Gutmann views education as a means to equip citizens with the capabilities to deliberate on what constitutes a good society. In her book, *Democratic Education*, she presents two core principles, or limits, which she argues need to be placed on political and parental authority over education, namely, "nonrepression" and "nondiscrimination":

"The principle of nonrepression prevents the state, and any group within it, from using education to restrict rational deliberation of competing conceptions of the good life and the good society."[24]

"*Nondiscrimination* extends the logic of nonrepression, since states and families can be selectively repressive by excluding entire groups of children from schooling or by denying them an education conducive to deliberation among conceptions of the good life and the good society . . . . The effect of discrimination is often to repress, at least temporarily, the capacity and even the desire of these groups to participate in the processes that structure choice among good lives. Nondiscrimination can thus be viewed as the distributional complement to nonrepression . . . . No educable child may be excluded from an education adequate to participating in the political processes that structure choices among good lives."[25]

Based on these two principles, we can see that Gutmann is committed to the idea of a welfare state that is aimed at securing what she characterizes as a fundamental precondition for enabling citizens to engage in democratic deliberation, namely, *democratic education*. While this perspective does not dispute the fundamental contradictions of the welfare state, Gutmann reflects the liberal tradition that characterizes such institutional forms as the outcome of a progressive movement toward democratic citizenship.[26] In her case, the highest aim is to enable citizens to become competent interlocutors in democratic deliberation and decision making about what constitutes a good life. While it may be idealistic for us to think that such a burden can realistically be placed on welfare states, it is difficult to think that citizens can develop such capacities to recognize the sorts of political and economic distortions described by Habermas, and the forms of repression and discrimination described by Gutmann, without having access to educational resources that are not commodified by market relations. In Gutmann's own work, she examines how the media are means of social learning, for better and for worse, and she makes a case for state support of media that can best serve to enlighten citizens rather than appeal to them simply as consumers.[27] However, she neglects to delve into the value, if not the necessity, of a system of formal education that can reinforce such values with respect to the citizens' use of the media. To that end, I advocate a more central place for media studies as a part of the core of the *liberal arts*.[28]

The important alternative to the academic treatment of media education as a subject for professional training is media education as a core subject of a liberal education. That is easier said than done. Some educators assert that "Computers are a tool, not a subject."[29] Computers are indeed tools, but to ignore computers and other tools of communication and information storage and retrieval that are central to major structural transformations in the world is to ignore how those tools are being developed and used to test the possibilities and limitations of democratic citizenship. To view media education as a subject of liberal education is to see it as a means to further the development of capacities for critical reflection about the ways in which communication and information technologies shape and are shaped by social and cultural forces. Seen in this light, media literacy fits within a broader concept of *cultural literacy*, a form of literacy that is better reflected in the aims of Raymond Williams than of E.D. Hirsch.[30]

There is no shortage of futuristic speculation about how democracy will be strengthened as a result of technological innovation. However, a research and teaching agenda ought to go beyond platitudes about how "the digital citizen" of today has become a coveted target in terms of political marketing in modern democracies.[31] It ought to promote discussion and inquiry about why it is important to understand media institutions as civic institutions, and about the realities and potential for making technological innovation a means to enhance democratic citizenship. Assuming that the traditional ideals of liberal education should not be abandoned, and that they include a view of liberal education as civic education, how can such ideals be adapted to treat the study of communication and information technology in terms that can inform the practices of citizenship in modern democracies?

Media Literacy as Political Necessity?

The idea of the information society has sparked the popular imagination, and visions of such a society vary widely. For nearly thirty years, scholars,[32] futurists,[33] inventors,[34] captains of industry[35] and world political leaders have speculated on and debated about the meaning of such a society. The currently popular discourse on so-called electronic democracy is aesthetically pleasing, but these visions of empowerment are illusory or manipulative if they do not rest on the foundation of a clearly articulated vision of government.[36] Of course, it is possible that the vision of government that is operant will be one that is entirely swept away by the ideology of the information age, and the bandwagon of computer literacy is one that has become a very powerful symbol of this age. While we cannot afford to ignore the facts of there being material consequences to going without becoming "computer-literate" (a mostly ill-defined term) we also must be careful of the seductions of a fetishized vision of the information society.

Today, a convergence of political, economic, technological, and cultural changes have made the idea of the information society a reality, albeit a contested one.[37] This contest should be understood as a struggle over the balance between instrumental reason and autonomous citizenship, which can be seen readily by carefully examining the politics of media literacy. In the United States and other affluent countries, telecommunication policies and educational strategies and policies are being harmonized to promote more competitive workforces and more prosperous economies overall. Often, it is implied that more democratic communication and participation will follow, which is a matter of contention, as is the proper role of the state in promoting such ideals.[38] In this vision, digital literacy is a means to political and cultural autonomy, an emancipatory aim premised on equipping people with the tools to be competent citizens and to participate effectively in democratic culture and politics. On the other hand, digital literacy is a means to equip people with the skills necessary to work and consume effectively and efficiently. Either way, such increasingly familiar academic slogans as "to be hypermedia-literate is to be liberated"[39]

- 78 -

reflect how sold many educators are on a rarefied, sanitized, and friction-free vision of the information society that is not complicated by social relations, cultural differences, economic conditions, or any other form of encumbrance. In fetishizing the mastery of technique, the idea of civic competence being based on political consciousness becomes an afterthought at best.

One quickly gets a sense of how vague the term media literacy is when one realizes that it can range from dealing with how children are being affected in their television viewing habits, to issues regarding computers in the schools, from teaching critical television viewing skills to teaching students how to surf the 'Net, build a web site, or operate a video camera. Should media studies be seen as advanced vocationalism and nothing more? Should it be seen as a proper focus of civic education? These questions highlight the Procrustean nature of the term media literacy, and they pose a category problem to the extent that the exercise of technical capacities is seen as equivalent to the practical expression of civic competence, that is, to the extent that *techne* is seen as equivalent to *praxis*, as the Greeks defined these terms. Thus, as Habermas asserts, "The modern thinkers no longer ask, as the Ancients did, about the moral conditions of the good and exemplary life, but about the actual conditions of survival."[40] Even Lyotard, who in so many ways has been a major antagonist of Habermas's theory of politics, argues: "The question (overt or implied) now asked by the professionalist student, the State, or institutions of higher education is not longer "Is it true?" but "What use is it?"[41] Such is the condition of the academic study of the media.

Along with the vitally important and interesting questions raised in media studies, an ethical and intellectual challenge inherent in the institutional legitimation in the university of this field has come with the ever-present temptation among scholars to lose a critical distance and function mainly as industry handmaidens and lose sight of the tensions between market imperatives of the media industries and political needs for relatively uncommodified public communication. A critical discussion of private media ownership and control, and conditions of commercial competition among media industries, cannot continually be sustained in courses in which students are taught to become professional journalists. At some level, teachers and students in professionally related courses have no choice but to work within the constraints which market and political conditions impose on news story selection and presentation, and such conditions are for pragmatic reasons accepted as the order of things. Thus, it is all the more important that there be an emphasis elsewhere in the curriculum to stimulate critical self-reflection through theory and research. While the need for practical knowledge is important for researchers, I tend to think that the more serious educational challenge in the future will be to prevent professional education from becoming so instrumentalized that it will foster anti-intellectualism and relative ignorance of the political, economic, and cultural forces which shape the possibilities and limitations for professional practice.

To reduce the scope of media studies to an agenda that is bounded by administrative concerns would defeat the historical mission of liberal education. Such agendas often envision the proper role of the liberal arts as one of fostering appreciation, if not the celebration, of technological power, rather than as a valuable resource that can broaden and deepen our understanding of the decisions we make about the development and uses of technology. Under instrumental agendas, specific technological innovations and vested interests often are granted a degree of unassailability that is expedient from a bureaucratic perspective, but is not necessarily in the interest of the public. As one author argues, "[b]ureaucracy's double feat is the moralization of technology, coupled with the denial of the moral significance of non-technical issues."[42] By dismissing or marginalizing the actual and potential contributions that the liberal arts—including all branches of the arts, the humanities and the social sciences—can bring to bear in terms of research, reflection, debate, and imagination about the possibilities of media education, the university will have set very limited sights for what it can contribute to society, and it will have trouble defending why such a narrow orientation should not be pursued somewhere other than at a university.

Conclusions

Although I am mainly focused on the state of media education in higher education in the United States, there is a growing tendency in many countries for external forces to pressure universities to emphasize the vocational/professional aspects of education for "useful knowledge," increasingly at the expense of a wider range of cultural, historical, and political knowledge that generally is understood to constitute a liberal education. Certainly, it is tempting to view the primary mission of media education in such narrow terms, and in the process to neglect the opportunity, if not the necessity, to recognize the media as civic institutions, and a broadly based education about those institutions as being fundamental to civic competence. The viewpoint that pushes for a restrictive treatment of media education is short-sighted because, taken to its extreme, it calls into question the reasons why universities should be involved in communication education, if not to train well-rounded, intellectually flexible, and critical thinkers. It is easy enough for faculties to assess the skill demands in the media industries today in order to be able to train the students needed to fill those jobs. It is more difficult, and a more fundamentally important challenge for faculties to recognize communication education in less instrumental, more ethically and philosophically grounded terms, and to design and maintain a curriculum which, while it cannot afford to ignore instrumental needs, also aspires to satisfy higher needs, particularly the historical requirements of a liberal education.

The more important question today is what sort of agenda for media education we can and should develop. While the priorities of media education are geared primarily toward professionalism, does it not make sense to also promote a deeper understanding of media institutions as social, cultural, and political institutions? Of course, to do so means that we must revisit the Lippmann-Dewey debate about the possibilities and limitations of citizenship in modern and complex democratic societies. Recently, significant financial investments in civic journalism, deliberative opinion polls, and electronic democracy initiatives testify to renewed interest in developing the means to involve citizens in public deliberation, thus lending support for Dewey's aspirations that participation in modern democracies not be out of the reach of average citizens. While the effectiveness and authenticity of these particular social experiments are matters of dispute, the optimistic conviction that underlies them is that professional expertise and technological innovation can serve as means to empower citizens to engage in democratic processes, rather than as obstacles.

Today, talk of a global information society challenges cultural and political conceptions of citizenship that are based principally on the idea of the nation-state, and it leads to new speculation about the deterritorialization of literacy, including *media literacy.* Manuel Castells, a sociologist who has for many years focused on the impact of telecommunications on urban and regional development, has made the following useful observation: "The new territorial dynamics . . . tend to be organized around *the contradiction between placeless power and powerless places,* the former relying upon communication flows, the latter generating their own communication codes on the basis of an historically specific territory."[43]

I would argue that this is a valid description of today's reality in terms of the relationship between a world of highly mobile flows of capital, on the one hand, and worlds of territorially distinct and relatively immobile cultures and communities. The challenge to aspirations for democracy in a world of "placeless power" and "powerless places" is that the nature of territorial integrity—political sovereignty, statehood, cultural autonomy—is widely considered to be under siege. According to this view, we live in a world of virtuality — virtual communities, virtual culture, virtual democracy — an assertion which, while in many ways being true, also provides a very convenient mechanism for governments to renege on their responsibilities to citizens. Without wanting to appeal to any sort of atavistic sense of nationalism, or to reject the validity of arguments in favor of all citizens becoming more culturally knowledgeable, tolerant, and capable of respect for cultural differences, I subscribe to the view that the value of democratic state institutions is radically underestimated in the context of the celebratory discourse about cultural and economic globalization.

To argue that we live in a world of post-national identity can be aesthetically pleasing, and to some degree accurate, particularly for those who are in the highest socio-economic strata and whose cosmopolitan life experiences and prospects have prepared them for such a world. However, the appeal to post-national identity can also be devastatingly harmful to the vast majority of individuals and communities in the world who depend on their governments, rather than on their personal wealth and life chances to survive the vagaries of the global market. For now and for the foreseeable future, the nation state is one of, if not the, best means for delivering democracy.[44] From this perspective, I would defend the necessity of our treating media literacy as social, cultural, and political literacy, and a competent understanding of the global media as an absolutely vital frontier in redefining what we mean by civic education in modern democratic societies.

Endnotes

[1] The term "media" is used here to refer to the fullest range of industries providing information and communication technologies, networks, and content. This includes the entertainment industries of Hollywood; cable, satellite and broadcast networks; the publishing industries, the music recording industry, software suppliers, and the various online information industries (including content providers and ISPs). It includes the providers of telecommunications infrastructure, specifically, the various local and long-distance telephone companies. It also includes the suppliers of the many types of hardware used in the production, distribution and retrieval of information and entertainment. A casual glance at weekly news magazines and daily newspapers tells one that all bets are off as far as any of these industries conforming to historical distinctions and separations from one another. The popular terms "synergy" and "convergence" pervade media industry news as mergers and acquisitions, and innovative movement into new market opportunities, transform the previously stable and familiar landscape of media and communication.

[2] Harvey Graff, *The Legacies of Literacy: Continuities and Contradictions in Western Culture and Society* (Bloomington: Indiana University Press, 1987).

[3] Quoted in Elizabeth L. Eisenstein, "Some Conjectures About the Impact of Printing on Western Society and Thought: A Preliminary Report," *Journal of Modern History* 40 (March 1968), 34.

[4] Lucien Febvre and Henri-Jean Martin, *The Coming of the Book: The Impact of Printing, 1450-1800*, trans. David Gerard (London: New Left Books, 1976).

[5] Jürgen Habermas, *The Structural Transformation of the Public Sphere*, trans. Thomas Burger (Cambridge, MA: MIT Press, 1989); Elizabeth Eisenstein, *Print Culture and Enlightenment Thought* [The Sixth Hanes Lecture] (Chapel Hill, NC: University of North Carolina Rare Book Collection, 1986); and R. Censer and Jeremy D. Popkin, eds., *Press and Politics in Pre-Revolutionary France* (Berkeley, CA: University of California Press, 1987).

[6] Graff, *The Legacies of Literacy*, 313.

[7] John McIlroy, "Teacher, Critic, Explorer," in *Raymond Williams: Politics, Education, Letters*, ed. W. John Morgan and Peter Preston (New York: St. Martin's Press, 1993), 36.

[8] ibid., 32-35.

[9] Walter Lippmann, *Public Opinion* (New York: Free Press, 1922). See also Walter Lippmann, *The Phantom Public* (New York: Harcourt Brace, 1925).

[10] John Dewey, *The Public and Its Problems* (New York: Henry Holt & Co., 1927).

[11] Carole Pateman, *Participation and Democratic Theory* (Cambridge: Cambridge University Press, 1970).

[12] Patrick Brantlinger, *Bread and Circuses: Theories of Mass Culture as Social Decay* (Ithaca, NY: Cornell University Press, 1983).

[13] Alexis de Tocqueville, *Democracy in America*, vol. 1, eds. & trans. H. Reeve & F. Bowen (New York: Random House, 1945), 63.

[14] Pateman, 110.

[15] Andrew Calabrese, "Why Localism? Communication Technology and the Shifting Scale of Political Community, in *Communication and Community*, eds. Gregory Shepherd and Eric Rothenbuhler (Mahwah, NJ: Lawrence Erlbaum Publishers, forthcoming).

[16] Jürgen Habermas, "On Systematically Distorted Communication," *Inquiry* 13 (1970): 205-18; Jürgen Habermas, "Toward a Theory of Communicative Competence," *Inquiry* 13 (1970): 360-365; and Jürgen Habermas, *Communication and the Evolution of Society*, trans. Thomas McCarthy (Boston: Beacon Press, 1979).

[17] Thomas McCarthy, "Translator's Introduction," in *Legitimation Crisis*, by Jürgen Habermas (Boston: Beacon Press, 1975), vii-xxiv.

[18] Robert C. Holub, *Jürgen Habermas: Critic in the Public Sphere* (London: Routledge, 1991).

[19] Jürgen Habermas, *The Theory of Communicative Action*, vol. 1, *Reason and the Rationalization of Society*, trans. Thomas McCarthy (Boston: Beacon

Press, 1984); and Jürgen Habermas, *The Theory of Communicative Action,* vol. 2, *Lifeworld and System: A Critique of Functionalist Reason,* trans. Thomas McCarthy (Boston: Beacon Press, 1987). See also Georgia Warnke, "Communicative Rationality and Cultural Values," in *The Cambridge Companion to Habermas,* ed. Stephen K. White (Cambridge: Cambridge University Press, 1995), 120.

[20] Habermas, "Toward a Theory of Communicative Competence," 374.

[21] The contributions by the late Paulo Freire to an understanding of the relationship between literacy and civic education are not incompatible with the agenda Habermas has pursued. Indeed, Freire has offered much more than Habermas in the way of demonstrating practical understanding of political education and its role in the cultivation of a critical consciousness, and he rightfully holds a more central place among educational researchers and activists who are engaged in political practice at a grassroots level. See Paulo Freire, *Pedagogy of the Oppressed,* trans. Myra Bergman Ramos (New York: Continuum, 1990); and Paulo Freire, *The Politics of Education: Culture, Power, and Liberation,* trans. Donaldo P. Macedo (New York: Bergin & Garvey, 1985).

[22] Amy Gutmann, *Democratic Education* (Princeton, NJ: Princeton University Press, 1987); Amy Gutmann, "Distributing Public Education in a Democracy," in *Democracy and the Welfare State,* ed. Amy Gutmann (Princeton, NJ: Princeton University Press, 1988), 107-130.

[23] Andrew Calabrese, "Creative Destruction? From the Welfare State to the Global Information Society," *Javnost/The Public* 4 (1997), 7-24.

[24] Gutmann, *Democratic Education,* 44.

[25] *Ibid.,* 45.

[26] Most notable among the proponents of that tradition is sociologist T.H. Marshall, "Citizenship and Social Class," in *Citizenship and Social Class and Other Essays* (Cambridge, UK: Cambridge University Press, 1950), 1-85. For more recent expositions on this perspective, see Bryan S. Turner, *Citizenship and Capitalism: The Debate Over Reformism* (London: Allen & Unwin, 1986); and J.M. Barbalet, *Citizenship: Rights, Struggle and Class Inequality* (Minneapolis: University of Minnesota Press, 1988).

[27] Gutmann, *Democratic Education,* 232-255.

[28] The following definition of "liberal arts" is taken from the 1998 *Encyclopaedia Britannica* (CD-ROM edition): "college or university curriculum aimed at imparting general knowledge and developing general intellectual capacities in contrast to a professional, vocational, or technical curriculum. In the medieval European university the seven liberal arts were grammar, rhetoric, and logic (the trivium) and geometry, arithmetic, music, and astronomy (the quadrivium). In modern colleges and universities the liberal arts include the study of literature, languages, philosophy, history, mathematics, and

science as the basis of a general, or liberal, education. Sometimes the liberal-arts curriculum is described as comprehending study of three main branches of knowledge: the humanities (literature, language, philosophy, the fine arts, and history), the physical and biological sciences and mathematics, and the social sciences.

[29] William M. Bulkeley, "Hard Lessons," *Wall Street Journal* (17 November 1997).

[30] Hirsch's version of cultural literacy seems aimed at an instrumental agenda for education that ultimately serves the purpose of offering readers a sense of what they need to know in order to do a bit of pseudo-sophisticated name-dropping at cocktail parties. See E.D. Hirsch, Jr., *Cultural Literacy: What Every American Needs to Know* (New York: Vintage, 1987). By comparison, Williams' concept of culture, particularly as it is manifest in his approach to workers' education, places emphasis on how individuals might become more capable of critically examining their own lived experiences, social institutions, and cultural formations. See Raymond Williams, *Politics and Letters: Interviews With the New Left Review* (London: Verso, 1979); and Raymond Williams, *Problems in Materialism and Culture* (London: Verso, 1980). See also W. John Morgan and Peter Preston, eds. *Raymond Williams: Politics, Education, Letters.*

[31] Jon Katz, "The Digital Citizen," *Wired* (December 1997).

[32] Alain Touraine, *The Post-Industrial Society: Tomorrow's Social History* (New York: Wildwood House, 1971); William Kuhns, *Post-Industrial Prophets: Interpretations of Technology* (New York: Weybright and Talley, 1971); Daniel Bell, *The Coming of Post-Industrial Society: A Venture in Social Forecasting* (New York: Basic Books, 1973); Boris Frankel, *The Post-Industrial Utopians* (Madison, WI: University of Wisconsin Press, 1987); Jennifer Daryl Slack and Fred Fejes, eds., *The Ideology of the Information Age* (Norwood, NJ: Ablex, 1987); Jorge Reina Schement and Leah Lievrouw, ed., *Competing Visions, Complex Realities: Social Aspects of the Information Society* (Norwood, NJ: Ablex, 1987); and Frank Webster, *Theories of the Information Society* (London: Routledge, 1995).

[33] Alvin Toffler, *The Third Wave* (New York: Bantam, 1980); John Naisbitt, *Megatrends: Ten New Directions Transforming Our Lives* (New York: Warner Books, 1982); and Howard Rheingold, *The Virtual Community* (Reading, MA: Addison-Wesley, 1993).

[34] Stewart Brand, *The Media Lab: Inventing the Future at MIT* (New York: Viking Penguin, 1987); and Nicholas Negroponte, *Being Digital* (New York: Alfred A. Knopf, 1995).

[35] Bill Gates, *The Road Ahead* (New York: Penguin, 1996); Andrew S. Grove, *Only the Paranoid Survive* (New York: Currency Doubleday, 1996). While Gates needs no introduction, Andy Grove, the president of Intel, is less well

known. By 1997, Grove had led Intel to being supplier of over eighty percent of all personal computer chips. See Ken Auletta, "Only the Fast Survive," *The New Yorker* 20 & 27 October 1997, 140.

[36] Andrew Calabrese and Mark Borchert, "Prospects for Electronic Democracy in the United States: Re-thinking Communication and Social Policy," *Media, Culture and Society* 18 (April 1966): 249-268.

[37] Webster; and Manuel Castells, *The Information Age: Economy, Society, and Culture*, vol. 1, *The Rise of the Network Society* (Oxford, UK: Blackwell Publishers, 1996); Castells, *The Information Age: Economy, Society, and Culture*, vol. 2, *The Power of Identity* (Oxford, UK: Blackwell Publishers, 1997); and Castells, *The Information Age: Economy, Society, and Culture*, vol. 3, *End of Millenium* (Oxford, UK: Blackwell Publishers, 1998).

[38] Len Masterman, *Teaching the Media* (London: Routledge, 1985); Kevin Robins and Frank Webster, *The Technical Fix: Education, Computers and Industry* (New York: St. Martin's Press, 1989); Peter McLaren, Rhonda Hammer, David Sholle, and Susan Reilly, *Rethinking Media Literacy: A Critical Pedagogy of Representation* (New York: Peter Lang, 1995); Len Masterman, "Media Education Worldwide: Objectives, Values and Superhighways," *Media Development* 42(2) (1995): 6-9; Ivor F. Goodson and J. Marshall Mangan, "Computer Literacy as Ideology," *British Journal of Sociology of Education* 17(1) (1996): 65-79; Robert Kubey, ed. *Media Literacy in the Information Age* (New Brunswick, N.J.: Transaction Publishers, 1997); John Katz, "The Digital Citizen," *Wired* (December 1997): 68-82, 274-275; and Paul Gilster, *Digital Literacy* (New York: Wiley, 1997).

[39] Bent B. Andresen, "To be Hypermedia-Literate is to be Liberated," *Educational Media International* 33 (September 1996): 110-113.

[40] Jürgen Habermas, "The Classical Doctrine of Politics in Relation to Social Philosophy," chap. in *Theory and Practice*, trans. John Viertel (Boston: Beacon Press, 1973), 50.

[41] Jean-Francois Lyotard, *The Postmodern Condition: A Report on Knowledge*, trans. G. Bennington & B. Massumi (Minneapolis: University of Minnesota, 1984), 51. (Original work published 1979)

[42] Zygmunt Bauman, *Modernity and the Holocaust* (Ithaca, NY: Cornell University Press, 1989), 160

[43] Manuel Castells and Jeffrey Henderson, "Techno-Economic Restructuring, Socio-Political Processes and Spatial Transformation: A Global Perspective," in *Global Restructuring and Territorial Development*, ed. Manuel Castells and Jeffrey Henderson (Beverly Hills, CA: Sage, 1987), 7.

[44] Andrew Graham, "The Importance of the 'Familiar' for the Information Superhighway." Paper presented at the International Conference of the Burda Academy of the Third Millennium on "The Internet and Politics: The

Modernisation of Democracy through Electronic Media," held at the European Patent Office, Munich, 19-21 February 1997.

- Chapter 5-

Media Education: The Need for Curriculum Development in Slovenia

Karmen Erjavec, Zala Volèiè

Introduction

What kind of knowledge, attitudes and skills are essential for being a citizen in a media age? How does one create opportunities for young people to develop their interests in democracy? What role can the media, teachers and parents play? The participants of The National Leadership Conference on Media Literacy (USA) agreed that media literacy is the ability "to access, analyze, evaluate and communicate messages in a variety of forms (Aufderheide 1997, 79). They further agreed that most conceptualizations include the following elements: media are constructed and construct reality; media have commercial implications; media have ideological and political implications; form and content are related in each medium, each of which has a unique aesthetic codes and conventions; and receivers negotiate meaning in the media (Aufderheide 1997, 80).

Media literacy is the ability to understand how mass media work, how they produce meanings, how they are organized, and how to use them wisely, in a creative way. The media literate person can describe the role that the media play in his or her life. The media literate person understands the basic conventions of various media, and enjoys their use in a deliberately conscious way. The media literate person understands the impact of music and special effects in highlighting the drama of a television program or film... this recognition does not lessen the enjoyment of the action, but prevents the viewer from being unduly credulous or becoming unnecessarily frightened. The media literate person is in control of his or her media experiences.

Why are some teacher and media scientists attracted to Media Education?

⟹   Some see *media literacy* as a tool to build relevance into contemporary education, building links between classroom and the culture, so that students see how themes and issues resonate in popular culture as they do in the study of literature, history or social studies.

⟹   Some see *media literacy* as a kind of protection for children against the dangers and evils engendered by excesses of television, and see *media literacy* as an antidote to manipulation and propaganda.

⟹   Some see *media literacy* as a citizenship survival skill, necessary to be an thoughtful consumer and an effective citizen in a superhighway-driven media age.

⟹   Some see *media literacy* as a new kind of language education, learning to appreciate and analyze ads and sitcoms and films - some of which are destined to become the 'classics' of the next century - with the same tools used to study the traditional genres of poetry, short story and the novel.

⟹   Some see *media literacy* as a way to give children the opportunity to tell their own stories and better understand the power of those who shape the stories of our culture and our times.

Why teach *Media education*?

Media bring the world into our homes. Almost everything we know about people, places, and events that we cannot visit first-hand comes from the media. We also rely on media for entertainment and pleasure. The cumulative impact of mass media is to unconsciously shape our vision of ourselves. Mass media can teach us what it means to be a woman, what it means to grow old, and so on. Children are among our nation's heaviest but least sophisticated viewers. We must help them to develop media literacy skills, which will allow them to analyze critically what they see and read and to develop theirs own vision of themselves.

The case for *Media Education* in politically and economically transitional countries has never been more urgent. The global spread of a few media empires and their ability to influence the terms of public discourse have stymied the advancement of the right to communicate. The liberalized media environment, aided no doubt by development in transmission technology, is a symptom of a new world order in which regulation and public control have been replaced by the law of the market. This law equates communication with information and information with commodities to be bought and sold. Furthermore, it naturalizes the flows, authorities and centers of knowledge and power. *Media Education* attempts to work towards the establishment of an environment for public communication through an active, negotiated understanding of contemporary media practices and its politics of representation.

Especially in postsocialist countries like Slovenia, citizens are not equipped with the skills and knowledge of how to critically assess the media sphere. The processes of commercialization on one hand, and on the other, the lack of democratic public tradition have had a deep influence on the current situation, particularly on the blind perception of media messages.

We offer here one of the most important reasons for arguments on the development of *Media Education* that must be given the most urgent priority: to change passive viewers and consumers to active citizens. For this matter, the answer is not to stop watching the television or not being exposed to the media at all, but to change the way of consumption of the media.

Barry Duncan (1989, 6-8) suggests there are several key concepts that provide a framework for understanding mass media and popular culture, including:
1. The media construct reality.
2. The media have their own forms, codes and conventions.
3. The media present ideologies and value messages.
4. The media are businesses that have commercial interests.
5. Audiences negotiate meaning in media.

Each of these trends and tendencies demands a commensurate expansion in critical consciousness, and coherent development of education programs which will encourage critical autonomy.

What are Media Education and Media Literacy?
Before we go any further, let's be clear about what exactly we mean by *Media Education and media literacy*. The powerful concept of literacy was driving the force that led leaders in the *Media Education* movements to adopt a comprehensive definition of *media literacy* as "the ability to access, analyze, evaluate and produce communication in a variety of forms" in a conference sponsored by the Aspen Institute. Put simply, *media literacy* includes the skills of literacy extended the wide variety of messages that we are exposed to in contemporary society. *Media literacy* includes reading and writing, speaking and listening, accessing new technologies, critical viewing, and the ability to make your own messages using a wide range of technologies, including cameras, camcorders, and computers. *Media literacy* is not a new subject area and it is not just about television: it is literacy for the information age.

Media literacy is an informed, critical understanding of the mass media. It involves an examination of the techniques, technologies and institutions that are involved in media production, the ability to critically analyze media messages, and a recognition of the roles that audiences play in making meaning from messages.

Media Education is not teaching 'through' media. It is teaching 'about' media. *Media Education* is through linked analytic and production activities. As with traditional literacies, 'reading' and 'writing' are learned together. Although many think about television when they consider the media, *Media Education* takes as its field all the media - TV, radio, film, print, rock music and less obvious forms like fashion, children's toys and dolls, or T-shirts. The notion that popular culture is a debased version of high culture has its roots in a class-based society which elevates a particular canon of literature or art to a privileged position. However, instead of concerning ourselves with abstract considerations of aesthetics, we should examining issues of ownership, control, representation and ideology. It should be sufficient to point out that the traditional canon is currently under attack in many quarters as the creation of a white, male Eurocentric culture. Surely it is time we learned to develop our own standards, make our own choices, to understand ourselves and our culture through those choices.

For better or worse, media culture is our culture and we cannot hope to own it without understanding it. Apart from philosophic reasons, there are some excellent practical reasons for teaching media literacy. First, it is highly motivating, because it starts from interests and knowledge that students already have.

Because students often have more knowledge about the media being studied than their teachers do, *Media Education* tends to democratize the classroom and turn lessons into exploration. Our classrooms must shift from a focus on content transmission to information management and evolution. The critical thinking that lies at the heart of *media literacy* is the real lesson of the *Media Education* class.

As the process of globalization continues, concerns about the representation of those whom we seen as 'others' will only increase in importance. Dealing with equity issues is a natural and integral part of *media literacy,* not an incidental addition as is so often the case in other subject areas. *Media Education* also makes the classroom more equitable by validating and building on the visual and integrative skills of those we identify for 'special education'.

Finally, *Media Education* is natural integrator, involving virtually all areas of the curriculum. Whether involved in production or analysis, children will make extensive use of language arts skills. Comparing media consumptions with reality is central to social and environmental studies, particularly given extensive use of vital material in such programs. Values and attitudes are always embedded in media texts, which also model behaviors and social structures for children. All this needs to be dealt with very critically. Even mathematics is a natural presence in the *Media Education* classroom, whether through surveys and demographic studies or through the limiting of production work. Students also learn about technology, both its use and a critical understanding of its role in our society.

It is vital that we create an educational framework which encourages intelligent and active responses to the new media and enables us to grasp the nature of knowledge itself. We need both skills and understanding in visual and aural communication as well as in the traditional areas of speaking, reading and writing. When we are able to evaluate media messages with confidence and respond critically to them, we are much likely to become autonomous rather than automatons. In learning how meaning is made in the media, we can gain more understanding of the world in which we live. We can be determined not to be determined.

How to practice Media Education?

Proponents and practitioners of *Media Education* often fail to identify the distinct components of *Media Education*, and as a result, *Media Education* practices often vary widely, as many different approaches to building *media literacy* skills are proliferating. But these different practices can be conceptualize along a continuum with four phases, as articulated by Elizabeth Thoman (1997, 34-36):

1. Awareness of time and choice in media consumption. This phase of *Media literacy* involves gaining consciousness and

sensitivity regarding the extent and magnitude of individuals' exposure to different kinds of media messages, from billboards to T-shirts, from newspapers and television to videogames and the Internet. Activities often involve counting and measuring one's use of media, exploring different pleasures and satisfactions people receive from a range of media messages, and learning strategies from managing media use in the home.

2. Critical reading/viewing skills and media production activities. This phase of media literacy involves developing skills for analyzing and producing media messages, explicitly extending the traditional skills of literacy to include 'critical reading' and 'writing' for the mass media. Producing media messages has long been understood as one of the most valuable methods to gain insight on how messages constructed. Critical analysis examines specific techniques involved in constructing messages by looking inside the frame of media messages to study specific patterns in the representation of social reality in range of genres - books, magazines, sitcoms, ads, public service announcements, websites, documentaries, films, newsletters, comics, and editorial columns. 'Looking inside the frame' includes examining the range of choices made by the author about the 'text,' including asking questions about the author's motives, purpose and point of view, the techniques used to attract attention, the use of image, sound and language to convey meaning, and the range of different interpretations which are likely for different individuals.

3. Analysis of political, economic, social and cultural contexts of the media environment. This phase of *media literacy* involves gaining knowledge about the ways in which media institutions are shaped by the historical, political, economic and social forces. For example, students can learn about the historical and economic conditions which, during the 19th and early part of the 20th century, led to the concept of 'journalistic objectivity'. They can examine the economic

relationships between advertising and a consumer culture; study the patterns of representation of masculinity, power and violence in sport reporting; examine how advertiser preferences shape TV programming; understand government's role in subsidizing the technologies which comprise the Internet; or learn about the historical dimension of broadcast de-regulation and reform and advocacy initiatives.

4. Media advocacy, media action and social change. This phase of *media literacy* involves active participation in 1) efforts to mobilize public opinion towards a specific policy of media reform, or 2) using specific media strategies to attract press interest, build coalitions, shape policy decision-making, and change offensive or problematic practices on a number of social issues. For example, students can write letters to advertisers about programs they dislike; they can support campaigns which raise awareness of the need to protect freedom of speak in cyberspace. They can create their own media campaigns to promote concern about particular social health issues, like violence, alcohol abuse or smoking.

Media Education in the rest of the world

Media education's status in many countries has gradually grown all over the world during the past two decades, although only a few countries have integrated it into the curriculum of the school (von Feilitzen 1999). Until recently, debate about the role of *Media Education* was often rather moralistic. The framework of *Media Education* has often been the informative, book-oriented culture that has been the culture of the school.

In a modern society characterized by an increasing amount of communication, there is no doubt that children and young people lead day-to-day lives in which communication and media have ever greater importance. A rather new phenomenon is the growing commercialization of the media all around the world and not least the new integration of politics and media ownership. From the commercialization trends of recent years, it is becoming increasingly evident that television is no longer produced for the enlightened citizens, but that a great deal of TV output has an overriding aim of reaching the consumer. Media becomes a 'parallel school'.

The debate about *Media Education* and about media as a parallel school is not new. As early as 1964, UNESCO supported *'Media Education'* as an important area. The Finnish researcher Sirkka Minkkinen offered a systematic introduction to *Media Education* in 1978. According to Minkkinen, *Media Education* aims at developing skills in cognitive, ethical, philosophical and aesthetic matters. Inspired by the Lasswell formula, she has divided *Media Education* into the following subject headings: (a) the history of communications; (b) the production of communication; (c) the content of mass communication; and (d) the impact of mass communication (Minkkinen 1978, 53-54). Her approach is very much related to early theories of communication.

Newer media research and recent trends within the area of communication-pedagogical research focus on the audiences, the 'receiver' of the messages. Where the media some years ago were seen as big bad wolves influencing children and youngsters with lies and propaganda, today there is a twofold trend: mass media are still seen as a powerful, but on the other hand the audiences is also seen as strong to a limited extent, only remembering information/media messages which are relevant to their daily lives. One of the consequences of this philosophy is that media teaching is seen as a relationship between producers, texts and audiences. Perceiving pupils as active producers of meaning who are also vulnerable in their reception of messages is a way of thinking which has implications for *Media Education*: it can no longer be seen as a one-way process. The new trend emphasizes a relaxed, pluralistic and integrated curriculum approach to media.

Early *Media Education* in Europe (Tufte 1999, 215-218) could be called an aristocratic approach, trying to teach pupils about 'good taste' and cultural capital of education. Some of the newer media experiments are rather populistic, for instance accepting youth culture without criticism. Another new aspect in the media education ethic is gradually gaining foothold in various countries: the combination of the students' own media production and media analysis.

In the European countries, the first approach was 'screen education' i.e. film teaching, and France especially has a strong tradition (*Media Education Around the World* 1998, 10-11). Great Britain is one of the leading countries in Europe regarding *Media Education*. The British Film Institute has played an important role in getting *Media Education* into the educational system and introducing *Media Education* into the National Curriculum (Bazalgette et al. 1992, 77). *Media Education* appears to be a growing area in Germany (Halloran and Jones 1984, 66). In Sweden, media education has been compulsory since 1980. In Norway, *Media Education* is a compulsory part of all school subjects. As for Denmark, several pilots projects have been carried out recently with the support of the state schools' development council, which deal with media analysis and production (Tufte 1999, 205-218). In other European countries, there are interesting *Media Education* projects going on, and in many countries, such as Spain and Austria, *Media Education* pioneers are working to introduce it into school curricula at al levels.

The case for *Media Education* in politically and economically transitional countries has never been more urgent. The global spread of a few media empires and their ability to influence the terms of public discourse have stymied the advancement of the right to communicate. The liberalized media environment (aided no doubt by development in transmission technology) is a symptom of a new world order in which regulation and public control have been replaced by the law of the market. This law equates communication with information and information with commodities to be bought and sold. Furthermore, it naturalizes the flows, authorities and centers of knowledge and power. *Media Education* attempts to work towards the establishment of an environment for public communication through an active, negotiated understanding of contemporary media practices and their politics of representation. Especially in postsocialist countries, like Slovenia (but also in developed, capitalist states), citizens are not equipped with the skills and knowledge to critically assess the media sphere. The processes of commercialization on the one hand and the lack of democratic public tradition on the other have had a deep influence on the current situation; that is, on the blind perception of media messages.

There are **three major ways** in which *media literacy* can contribute to strengthening the future of Slovene democracy:

First, *media literacy* practices help strengthen students' information access, analysis and communication skills and build an appreciation for why monitoring the world is important. *Media literacy* can inform students about how the press functions in a democracy, why it matters that citizens gain information and exposure to diverse opinion, and whom people need to participate in policy decision-making at the community, state and federal levels.

Secondly, *media literacy* can support and foster educational environments in which students can practice the skills of leadership, free and responsible self-expression, conflict resolution and consensus-building, because without these skills, young people will not be able to effectively engage with others in the challenges of cooperative problem-solving that participation in a democratic society demands.

Third, *media literacy* skills can inspire young people to become more interested in increasing their access to diverse sources of information. The trends towards increased centralization of ownership of mass media and technologies industries may promote an 'illusion of diversity' that limits people's access to ideas which are different from their own. *Media literacy* can raise awareness of the vital role of being exposed to a rich array of diverse opinions and ideas.

As the *media literacy* movements gains momentum in Slovenia, our increasingly diverse community of educators have a lot of issues to debate, because *media literacy* can take many different forms. Moreover, the techniques of media analysis can be relevant to almost every major policy issue - both domestic and international - and media production makes it possible for people to contribute their voices to the complex, deep and important issues which face us we enter the 21st century.

Conclusion

Mass media are pervasive in contemporary society. In recent decades, print and motion pictures have been supplemented by radio and television as dominant forms of communicating information and entertainment to mass public. Mass media continually grow in their influence on individuals' and society's use of leisure time, on their awareness of political and social reality, on their forming of personal values in culture and ethics.

Just as the development of widespread literacy skills has always seen as a necessary prerequisite of successful democracy, so it is clear that media literacy skills are essential to the democratic health of contemporary media-saturated societies. The danger to democratic values lies precisely in the gap which has opened up between the relative sophistication and power of media producers and media audiences. Media education is one of few weapons any culture possesses for at least addressing - and hopefully beginning to close - the gap.

The media occupy a central role in this society. *Media Education* will fulfill most of the objectives of an integrated curriculum. The question is really not whether we should have *Media Education* in ours schools, but why it is taking us so long to get on with it.

References:

Aufderheide, Patricia 1997. *Media literacy: From a report of the National Leadership Conference on Media Literacy.* In Robert

Kubey (Ed.) *Media literacy in the information age.* New York: Transaction Press, 79-86.

Bazalgette, Cary, Bevort, Evelyne and Savino, Josiane 1992. Teacher training: Introduction. In Carry Bazalgette, Evelyne Bevort and Josiane Savino (Eds.) *New Directions: Media education Worldwide,* London: British Film Institute, 77-78.

Duncan, Barry (Ed.) 1989. *Media Literacy Resource Guide.* Ministry of Education of Ontario, Canada. Publications Branch, the Queen's Printer.

von Feilitzen, Cecilia 1999. Media education, Children's Participation and Democracy. In Cecilia von Feilitzen and Ulla Carlsson (Eds.) *Children and media Image, Education, Participation.* Götenborg: The UNESCO International Clearinghouse on Children and Violence on the Screen, 15-30.

Halloran, D. James and Jones, Marsha 1984. Learning about the Media: Media education and Communication Research. *Communication and Society,* no. 16. Paris: UNESCO.

Media Education around the World
http://www.screen.com/mnet/eng/med/bigpict/worlmtxt.htm.

Minkkinen, Sirkka 1978. *A General Curricular Model for Mass Media Education.* Paris: UNESCO.

Thoman, Elizabeth 1997. *Media & values.* Los Angeles: Center for Media Literacy.

Tufte, Birgitte 1999. Media education in Europe. In Cecilia von Feilitzen and Ulla Carlsson (Eds.) *Children and media Image, Education, Participation.* Götenborg: The UNESCO International Clearinghouse on Children and Violence on the Screen, 205-219.

Part II Governance: Citizens, Citizenship, and Education

- Chapter 6-

Civic Education Between Human Rights And The Public Good

Mojca Peček

In Slovenia, the discussions about the concept of civic education are connected with, or have been reduced to, the question of values to be taught in school. This is reflected first in the controversy around the primary school subject "Ethics and Society", the task of which is to train pupils in a systematic way to become good citizens[1]; and secondly, in the controversy around the overall educational concept of the public primary school. In these discussions two expressions are frequently used when individuals try to express their attitudes and opinions about the subject and educational goals in general: "izobraževanje" and "vzgoja". In English, both expressions are usually translated by the word "education". This leads us to the specific understanding of the professional educational field in Slovenia. The former expression refers to the intellectual and instructional aspect of education. It is used when we focus on the process of acquiring a certain body of knowledge. The latter includes everything else. It encompasses above all the process of the development of emotions, motives and wishes, the relationship between oneself and other people, with an emphasis on the moral and value aspects of education. The key question connected to civic education and educational goals in general is what should be the ratio of one aspect with regard to the other. Should a school focus more on instruction and learning of curriculum syllabi or on the moral and value aspects of education? Such discussions do not take place only at the professional level but are frequently politically coloured. The purpose of my paper is to present part of these discussions and through them analyse the concepts predominant in the field of civic education in Slovenia.

Illusions About Systematic Teaching of Values

The 1995 White Paper[2] on education in Slovenia states that in conceptualizing our school system we should lean on the "common European heritage of political, cultural and moral values recognisable in the human rights, legal state, plural democracy, tolerance and solidarity."[3] The above statement arises from the conviction that the modern public school should not and cannot be based on a particular value system as the only true and acceptable one, which would enforce one value code and thereby deny the differences among people which arise from their own world view, their values, and from what they believe to be a good life for them. On the contrary, the starting point should represent the highest possible point of agreement of all citizens, taking into account all the different traditions, beliefs and common civic principles which have been developed through history and which represent the basis of a modern society. The question here is: What is the common core for all citizens, or which are the values needed for a life together in a collective state that are universally valid and desirable in a democratic society? This core is represented by human rights that come from the key documents designed by the international community and promoted also by the European Union, which advises its members to make human rights the organising principle of the school concept. Whenever we touch upon an area of values, human rights should always be our point of reference.[4]

The definition of moral education in our public primary schools refers to the notion of citizenship which focuses on the rights of the individual. Its central idea is the emphasis on the equality of all individuals who have, independent of their obligations and respect, inalienable rights which cannot be invalidated or suppressed by any social institution, especially not by the state. The notion harbours three major sets of human rights - civil, political and socio-economic. It must be mentioned, however, that the notion of human rights is constantly evolving and new rights are founded not only in the principle of the basic equality of all individuals but also in the recognition of differences among them. In spite of these common rights, some groups feel excluded not only because of their socio-economic position but because of their social and cultural identity. Therefore, there is a need to acknowledge the special particularities of these groups.

I am not saying that anyone involved with the questions of moral education would not want to place common human rights at the core of moral education in our schools. However, this does not in any way lessen the conflicts connected with moral education in the public school and with civic education alongside it. In this connection, a growing moral vacuum can be observed here, which is the result of the increased efficiency oriented interests of our schools, which only teach while forgetting about the transfer of moral values. It is claimed that the moral education of our schools is not efficient enough, and also that the values upon which the fundamental moral education in the primary schools are based are not appropriate. There are even claims that the school is neutral with regard to values. Let us take a closer look at these statements.

The origin of the claim that our school is forgetting about the individual's moral education goes back to the seventies. Ever since the end of the eighties, such statements have even become part of daily discussions. A frequently cited author states: "If we are to compete successfully with other nations, it will definitely not suffice to develop only the intellect of our children and youth but one should be equally concerned with their physical and emotional development (a healthy and strong vitality, healthy emotional equilibrium and culture, cultivated ethical and aesthetic, social and psychological abilities and characteristics). These characteristics all belong in the domain of moral education. A school lacking good moral education would be forming emotional cripples...incapable of a healthy human life in the future."[5] Within this context, each school concept based on the needs of the society is being criticised. The proper concept should namely be founded on the children and their abilities, interests and talents. When conceptualising such moral education it is, however, frequently overlooked that in this way we are creating just another pedagogical illusion, which does not allow the individuals any more freedom for realising their potentials than does the one being criticised. According to the authors of such concepts, the task of the school is to form a new kind of personality which they either call "a total or an all-round human being" or a "real, harmonious and genuine human being." For our purpose, the actual name is quite irrelevant. What is relevant is the fact that in this way a certain personality image is introduced as the only universally valid one, overwhelming all others. It becomes the norm and the ideal of the total effort invested in this direction, in the name of which anybody or anything not fitting this ideal can be disqualified.

Within the framework of pedagogical argumentation these concepts reveal a strong faith in a planned and systematic teaching of values. It is the belief that the individuals, provided all obstacles in their development are removed, can realise their natural potential all by themselves. Herein lies the conviction that human nature is subject to certain exactly determined and observable laws, in accordance with which the educational process, exactly determined in advance, can be brought to its goal. The goal is the realisation of one's nature. This would mean, paradoxically, that human nature can only be realised through moral education, which does not leave anything to pure chance and treats the individual as a whole. Here we can clearly recognise the enlightenment concept of the all-powerful moral education, advocated by Rousseau: the teacher is not allowed to do anything at all, he has to be able to wait for nature to reveal itself. For this to happen, we should remove any obstacles in the path of an individual's development, which, however, can only be achieved if the child is never left on its own, is constantly under control as are all the possible influences on the child, and the learning situations are all organised in advance. Education which forms the child in accordance with its nature, thus has to be able to embrace all and not leave anything uncontrolled, while the family, if necessary, can be removed from the process since, claims the same author: "It cannot be rationally expected from the parents to be capable of offering the children all the demanding knowledge about interpersonal relations and about the proper relations with one's inner world, of teaching them how to establish one's inner personal equilibrium and set off on the path of inner growth towards genuine human values which are not provided by the modern school although they are of major importance to the whole life of the individual and the society."[6]

We are therefore dealing with education which cannot be considered free at all. It has goals, which represent at the same time the ideal and the norm of educational activities, exactly determined in advance. Because it fears all other educational effects, it must be an all-embracing, total education, and must encompass all the aspects of the individual's personality development, cover all the areas of his or her life and not leave anything to coincidence. Such education completely absorbs individuals and does not leave room for any initiative on their part.

A question naturally follows of how moral education should be carried out according to some declared goals and aims, and whether in education this is not already happening, namely, through the effects triggered by the teacher's personality, through the mechanics of school discipline, and whether everything else is nothing but a pedagogical illusion and an ideology.[7] The arguments involve the subjects of History and Mother Tongue. For example, these can only be understood once we comprehend their purpose, which is the transfer of specific knowledge; their undeniable side effect, however, is the teaching of moral values, which can be even more powerful than the subjects specifically declared to be moral education subjects because we are frequently not even aware of the moral effects of the former. These moral effects are the result of the way certain facts are connected, which ones are emphasised or which left out, or which context they are placed in, and how they are taught. All of the above, and probably more, could be learned from our most recent history. Teaching subjects which were expressly ideologically-oriented did not succeed in stopping either the criticism of our former political order or finally not even the social and political upheavals that came about. In this connection, a major role was played by influences outside of school. The events also reveal the weak moral power of those subjects, the purpose of which was, after all, to at least neutralise those moral influences of the society which were considered negative.

- 107 -

Which Values Are The Right Values?

When we are discussing the lack of moral education in school, one is forced to ask what kind of education and which moral values should be taught. The strongest advocates of determining the content are the advocates of the Christian value system, who emphasise the importance of "teaching young people to value and respect the individuality, personal freedoms, rights and obligations and the responsibility for a common good."[8] These values appear to bear a strong resemblance to the ones advocated by the recently-passed school legislation, but this is only seemingly so. The criticism of the proponents of the Christian value system that our public primary school lacks moral education, that "young people are left without any value system and that the person not acknowledging ethical values and norms originating from them is not capable of responsible action," and that "the family, school and the society should all be based on a firm and clear value system which has to be taught to the young people"[9] all reveal a very different understanding of human rights in spite of the common terminology in advocating them.

The last few decades have witnessed an expressed acknowledgement of human rights by the Roman Catholic Church although "authentic Christianity and the doctrine of human rights are two distinctly separate worlds, which might have some (seemingly) common points, not however, the same orientation or content identity."[10] The analysis of M. Cerar reveals that the recognition of the existence of human rights by the modern Roman Catholic Church expresses the political urgency of this institution, which has to adapt to a certain degree to the current, basically liberal social streams. One can, nevertheless, detect certain basic controversies between the Church and the secular doctrine and practice. Thus, the Roman Catholic Church does not accept certain human rights, unquestioned by international law. For example, it cannot accept the freedom of thought, association, and expression at all. According to the doctrine of human rights, these are the fundamental freedoms and the starting point for the assertion of the majority of human rights. The Church wants to manage this freedom in accordance with the absolute laws of God, while the doctrine and practice of human rights does not encroach upon this sphere of man, and allows for a variety of possibilities at the level of thought, expression, and association. This view allows us to understand the accusations of the Roman Catholic Church that our school is neutral with respect to values and that it cannot provide an all-round development. It exposes the fear of a vacuum between human rights and values of the individual and the fear of the possibility that individuals might fill in this space by themselves. It demands that the state should very clearly and exactly determine the value system for its citizens.

The above criticism of the Roman Catholic Church can also be discussed alongside the comments expressed in Parliament when the new school legislation was in the process of passing, such as: The school plays an important role in safeguarding the national identity and should, therefore, emphasise national belonging and a proper relationship to the fatherland. Although these goals have been explicitly stated in the new legislation, they have not stilled the criticism of the value orientation of our schools. After an agreement had been reached by the political parties of the coalition government concerning the renewal of the school system, the beginning of 1998 saw this thought surface prominently. The agreement states that the primary school subject of "Ethics and Society" be renamed and become "Civic Education and Ethics": "The teaching should follow the educational goals of the White Paper document and the School Law and should acquaint students with the fundamental knowledge and skills necessary for effective and responsible participation of the individual in the cultural, economic and political development of the Republic of Slovenia." Why, one is tempted to ask, had the realisation of the goals stated in the Law be separately and specifically determined by a political agreement and why should this field not be governed by professional debate rather than be predominantly subjected to political decisions? In spite of the fact that the concept of the subject was the result of two three-year research studies and although even foreign experts in this field as well as teachers of the subject have all positively evaluated this concept, the curriculum has, according to the above agreement, become the subject of further reconsideration.

The idea of a state which has to decide for the individual what is good for him in the sense of exactly determining his value system goes well together with the above requirement of the accentuation of the nation and of the national element in public primary schools. The value system most frequently advocated within this context is Catholicism, which, as emphasised by its proponents, is the foundation of the whole of the European and world culture, a fact that does not need direct exposure, but can be safely referred to by stressing the national element. The origin of the national tradition in this context is again Catholicism. Its advocates claim that unless these values are nurtured, individuals will be formed who will not be capable of responsible action, and that a school which does not educate students according to these values lacks the moral dimension of education and thus assists in the upbringing of developmentally handicapped individuals. Of course, arguments in defence of a specific value system cannot but exhibit the desire of the system to become a universal one in the public schools. The question of the relevance of such a standpoint for those to whom a specific value system might be foreign has not been raised, as if such people did not exist at all. Finally, the idea is in contradiction with the most fundamental human rights – the freedom of thought, conscience and faith.

Within this context one can speak about two types of states. The first finds justification for its legitimacy in myths originating from the national tradition, while the other is justified by laws governing the state. In the former the starting point is the nation, in the latter a group of people living in a certain territory, which makes them the subject of analysis in the research of the history of the state. The latter does not equate nationality with citizenship, while the former completely denies the concept of citizenship in today's sense of the word, and denies the individual in it the sovereignty over his moral world. Belonging to a certain nation is considered as part of one's nature which thwarts the choice of one's identities: "In nationalism the identity of the individual is provided for in advance.

It excludes the concept of citizenship because a citizen in the modern world is defined by the absence of any kind of positive social determination, which is nothing but an empty abstraction with regard to identity. The actor of nationalistic politics is defined first and foremost as a member of the national community. Such an actor might also be a citizen, which is, however, of secondary importance and a deduced characteristic – because first, one must belong to a real nation."[11]

The concept of citizenship originating from a nation and possessing a clearly determined value system is very close to the republican definition of citizenship, which developed from the quest for an answer to the question whether one can discuss good education at all if one does not know exactly what a just society and a virtuous individual might be. According to this tradition, the state has to exercise authority over education in order to establish harmony between the individual and the common good. Its proponents endeavour to form uniform thinking and a level of friendly relations among the citizens, which is most frequently found, or which one would like to encounter, in the family. For this reason A. Gutmann calls such a form the family state.[12]

Contrary to the notion of citizenship originating from the individual, his rights and freedoms (which has been mentioned in connection with the legalised concept of the public primary school in Slovenia) this notion emphasises the characteristics of the individual as a member of a political society stressing the feeling of belonging to the political community, where citizenship means participation in collective life, loyalty to the homeland which presupposes loyalty to the legal foundations of the society; and the dominance of citizen's duties over individual interests, which allows individual rights to be subjugated to social duties.

The experience and thinking of Ancient Greece offer strong arguments for the conviction that a political community cannot exist without an active attitude among its citizens. This bears an even stronger rational relevance at the time of democratic leadership of today than in the past. It also offers strong arguments for the belief that the interests of the individual are subordinate to social ones and that the educational authority should rest with the centralised state, which joins the knowledge of what is good with political power. Such a belief contains limitations, observable in any society, where the state takes over the right to define what is good for its citizens. The question rather is what is good for the society and what for each individual separately. This involves the possibility of someone possessing the wisdom with which he could concoct a definition of good for himself and for everybody else. Even if we were to accept this possibility, the question remains how and with what right do we convince people to live according to this concept and to accept it for their own. The problem in such a society would not only be the creation of a value system which at least some people, most frequently its leaders, would believe to be the best one, but also the enforcement of the system upon others and non-acceptance of any other notion of what might be good. In this point our former political system bore resemblance to other systems based on an ideology. It does not make any difference whether the ideology be Marxism or Christianity, which is the case nowadays, when Christian values are being put forward, sometimes quite aggressively and with great authority, as the fundamental values to be accepted by the school system. Although the proponents of the Christian value system criticise the Marxist tradition, their arguments only too strongly resemble it. Neither of the two traditions see an ideologically biased educational system as problematic. For them the only problematic educational system is a system which does not fit in the orientation advocated by them.

Deficiencies of Human Rights

On the basis of what has been discussed so far, we can say the fundamental task of the school is the transfer of knowledge, tradition and culture and not the formation of some kind of an ideal personality or the enforcement of an exactly defined set of values. Such education would namely be in contradiction with the basic requirements of the modern understanding of interpersonal relations, which cannot prescribe what is good for everybody or anybody. This certainly does not suggest that a public school should or could remain neutral with regard to value orientation of individuals, and that it does not need a well-defined educational concept and with it the concept of civic education. A. Gutmann believes that the neutrality of a school cannot be accepted because of the demands of living together. While we might not agree as to value orientation, and to what the nature of the good life or the elements of a moral character might be, we are committed to recreate together the society that we share. Although we are not collectively bound to any particular set of values, we do have to reach a consensus in matters of common interest, as for example in educational goals. The core of such an obligation is conscious social reproduction, from which it follows that the society has to educate all its children so as to be capable of participating in collectively shaping their society. [13]

A. Gutmann does not only claim that the society cannot and should not remain neutral with regard to the moral orientations of its citizens but also that the limits of non-neutrality are a matter of democratic agreement and a constituent part of the reflections about what is public good. This way of thinking presupposes the right of the state to establish a certain vision of public life, but definitely not in the form of a new educational doctrine with an image of the personality clearly determined in advance, offering a limited set of values which the student would acquire "with conscious, planned and consistent development and consolidation"[14], which is advocated by the proponents of Christian ideology. Neither can the vision of public life take the form of a political system based on the trust in its leaders. Such power is namely based on morality which can never protect itself from its opposite, that is, immorality; it is therefore so much more important to institutionalise democracy, save it from a predominantly subjective state of being, and objectivize it in such a way that its existence and function would not be left to the mercy of good or bad intentions of its momentary leaders, and not only to their intentions, even more to their mentality and psychology, universality and the limitless personal aspect.[15] In this sense democracy does not mean neutrality but a search for the fairest ways for reconciling our disagreements and for enriching our collective life through discussion.[16] It means "enforcing" a dialogue "where the excluding attitudes need to agree on the legitimacy of plurality and tolerance among the opposing views and standpoints."[17]

Limits of non-neutrality should therefore become the subject of a democratic dialogue the starting point of which may well be human rights, since they represent a far greater degree of universality than any other particular moral system. At this moment social consensus on a more concretely determined moral ideal probably cannot be reached in a morally acceptable way. However, all the deficiencies inherent in human rights also have to be taken into account,[18] because the rights are not at all universal. A consensus even on the fundamental ones could namely only be reached at an extremely abstract level, and only among the proponents of these rights. The doctrine of human rights justifies these rights by claiming that in each individual there exists the same or equal nature, from which certain rights directly originate. Yet the researchers have not succeeded in determining an exhaustive and commonly valid list of fundamental, natural and universal human needs justifying in their turn the corresponding rights. Neither are the human rights neutral in the sense of being independent of the subjective judgement of norm givers in individual states or of the concrete social context. They are in a way coercive for those not accepting them or understanding them differently. An example in this context would be the already mentioned understanding of human rights by the proponents of the Roman Catholic religion. The ideal of human rights nevertheless remains at this moment as one of the more influential ones in comparison with other relatively appropriate means of improving the quality of interpersonal relations. This can be supported by the fact that regarding the human rights there exists a high degree of international normative consensus.

The starting point taken by our new legislation to define the educational concept of the public primary school and of civic education is in my opinion the only acceptable one at this moment. Of course one has to consider the deficiencies of the human rights, which can be observed in school itself, sometimes as a contradiction between the rights of children and their parents, teachers and pupils, and also as a contradiction between the rights of the individual and the rights of groups, since individual rights are sooner or later expressed in some form of collective group rights. "This implies that the acknowledgement of common characteristics and their safeguarding actually prescribes what is 'good' for the followers of a certain group. In this way protecting a common culture changes into terror over individual's decision."[19] The above contradictions should be articulated by the school, thus offering an insight into the complexity of social relations and simultaneously developing the necessary skills for a tolerant living together, where tolerance is not an excuse for ignorance, passivity or some kind of a manoeuvre, behind which a lack of arguments why a certain form of behaviour cannot and should not be tolerated is safely tucked away. This represents the understanding of and the discrimination between acceptable and unacceptable forms of behaviour. The school should also attend to other problems connected with human rights. While human rights have been created by the human mind, we know we learn about the world in other ways as well - by using our feelings and intuition. In spite of our rational thinking our behaviour is constantly characterised by a series of prejudices and stereotypes which force us into situations not at all in accordance with our rational mind. This makes education on the basis of human rights all the more difficult.

Conclusion

Conceptualisation of the public primary school and civic education on the basis of human rights does not allow for a neutral position of the school with regard to the value orientation of the individual, nor does it represent an instant solution to all the questions concerning its educational function, which would result in greater efficiency. While human rights can only be defined at an abstract level, they are being realised at a concrete one, a situation which again triggers numerous new problems. However, the school system can become more effective if it succeeds in implementing a dialogue where its students will have the opportunity not only to learn about the value orientation of others but also to identify their own position. Such a dialogue will make them aware about the urgent need of creating and respecting the rules for a life together and the need of institutionalising the mechanisms of their formation and change based on the principles of nonrepression and nondiscrimination of opposing attitudes and viewpoints. The dialogue represents the search for the most honest ways of developing our values and harmonising our misunderstandings. It is therefore the form of the educational process, and not the inventions of new educational ideals and particular values, which should be the first and foremost idea in our endeavours to ensure the realisation of the educational goals of the school as well as of civic education.

Bibliography

Cerar, Miro, *Večrazsežnost človekovih pravic in dolžnosti.* (Ljubljana: Znanstveno in publicistično središče, 1996.)

Challenger, Douglas F., "Attending to the Positive Potential in Public Life: Active Citizenship and Civic Education in Karl Destovnik" Irena Matovič (ed.), *Izobraževanje učiteljev ob vstopu v tretje tisočletje.* (Ljubljana: Pedagoška fakulteta, 1997) pp. 450-461.

"Civic Education" in *Education International*, Vol. 3, No. 1 & 2, 1997, pp. 15-26.

"Državljanska vzgoja" in *Časopis za kritiko znanosti*, Vol. 22, No. 172-173, (Ljubljana, 1994), pp. 5-176.

Gutmann, Amy, *Democratic Education.* (Princeton: Princeton University Press, 1987.)

Krek, Janez (ed.), *Bela knjiga o vzgoji in izobraževanju v Republiki Sloveniji.* (Ljubljana: Ministrstvo za šolstvo in šport, 1995.)

Kymlicka, Will and Wayne Norman, "Return of the Citizen: A Survey of Recent Work on Citizenship Theory" in Ronald Beiner (ed.) *Theorizing Citizenship*, (Albany: The State University of New York Press, 1995.)

Mastnak, Tomaž, *Vzhodno od raja.* (Ljubljana: DZS, 1992.)

Močnik, Rastko, "Strpnost, sebičnost in solidarnost" in *Časopis za kritiko znanosti*, Vol. 22, No. 164-165 (Ljubljana, 1994) pp. 143-163.

Ocvirk, Drago (ed.), *Slovenska šola in njen čas* (Ljubljana: Družina, 1995)

Osler, Audrey and Hugh Starkey, *Teacher Education and Human Rights* (London: David Fulton Publishers, 1996)

Platon, *Država*. (Ljubljana: Mihelač, 1995.)

Platon, *Poledni dnevi Sokrata* (Ljubljana: Slovenska matica, 1955)

Reeher, Grant and Joseph Cammarano (eds.), *Education for Citizenship* (Lanham, Rowman & Littlefield Publishers, 1997)

Starkey, Hugh (ed.), *The Challenge of Human Rights Education* (London: Cassell, 1991)

Svetina, Janez, *Slovenska šola za novo tisočletj* (Radovljica: Didakta, 1990)

Štrajn, Darko (ed.), *Družbene spremembe in izobraževanje* (Ljubljana: Pedagoški inštitut, 1998)

"Toleranca", *Časopis za kritiko znanosti*, Vol. 22, No. 164-165. (Ljubljana, 1994) pp. 5-258.

"Včem je razlika med vzgojo in izobraževanjem", *Problemi - šolsko polje*, Vol. 26, No. 11. (Ljubljana, 1988) pp. 3-146.

Endnotes

[1] Before and during the Second World War, that kind of education was ensured by religion. After the war, religion was first a voluntary subject; in 1952 it was abolished and replaced by a school subject which dealt with civic education from a socialist point of view. Various complaints about the subject, the changed political situation, the foundation of the independent state in 1991 and the first democratic elections resulted in the reform of the subject. According to the new educational legislation, which was passed at the beginning of 1996, the school subject Ethics and Society is taught in the 7th and 8th grade of primary school.

[2] The White Paper contains the professional basis for the legislation in the field of education in Slovenia.

[3] Slavko Gaber, "Beli knjigi na pot" in Janez Krek (ed.), *Bela knjiga o vzgoji in izobraževanju v Republiki Sloveniji* (Ljubljana: Ministrstvo za šolstvo in šport, 1995) p. 5.

[4] "Recommendation No. R (85) 7, The Council of Europe Recommendation on Teaching and Learning about Human Rights Education", in Hugh Starkey (ed.), *The Challenge of Human Rights Education* (London: Cassell, 1991, pp. 256-259)

[5] Janez Svetina, *Slovenska šola za novo tisočletje* (Radovljica: Didakta, 1990) p. 8.

[6] *Ibid*, p. 13.

[7] Zdenko Kodelja, "Ali je vzgoja predmet pedagoške znanosti" in *Problemi - šolsko polje*, Vol. 26, No. 11 (Ljubljana, 1988) p. 61.

[8] "Spomenica o vzgoji" in Drago Ocvirk (ed.), *Slovenska šola in njen čas* (Ljubljana: Družina, 1995) p. 8.

[9] *Ibid*, pp. 7-8.

[10] Miro Cerar, *Večrazsežnost človekovih pravic in dolžnosti* (Ljubljana: Znanstveno in publicistično središče, 1996) p. 90.

[11] Tomaž Mastnak, *Vzhodno od raja* (Ljubljana: DZS, 1992) p. 206.

[12] Amy Gutmann, *Democratic Education* (Princeton: Princeton University Press, 1987) pp. 22-28.

[13] *Ibid*, p. 39

[14] "Spomenica o vzgoji" (1995), p. 7.

[15] Tomaž Mastnak, *Vzhodno od raja* (1992) p. 168.

[16] Amy Gutmann, *Democratic Education*, (1987) p. 12.

[17] Darko Štrajn, "Družbene spremembe in izobraževanje" in Darko Štrajn et al (eds), *Družbene spremembe in izobraževanje* (Ljubljana: Pedagoški inštitut, 1998) p. 44.

[18] See further: Miro Cerar, *Večrazsežnost človekovih pravic in dolžnosti* (1996)

[19] Rastko Močnik, "Strpnost, sebičnost in solidarnost" in *Časopis za kritiko znanosti*, Vol. 22, No. 164-165 (Ljubljana, 1994) pp. 160-161.

- Chapter 7 -

The Church and the Liberal Project: The Case of Poland

Sabrina P. Ramet

Introduction: Definitions and a Framework

It is necessary to begin by distinguishing liberalism from democracy, in order to avoid confusion, as well as to establish, at the outset, what is at stake. By liberalism, following Joseph Raz, I shall mean a philosophy, value-system, ideology, or culture which places supreme value on toleration, respect for fundamental human equality, and abiding by the harm principle[1] (to be defined presently). Insofar as these three elements are strictly moral in nature, I understand liberalism to be coterminous with moral universalism, which is to say, to be a moral, rather than a political orientation, albeit having definite programmatic political consequences. By democracy, on the inspiration of John Stuart Mill, I shall understand a system premised on the maximization of tolerance and political choice. [2] The value tolerance appears also as an essential component of democracy. Thus, democracy is to be understood, in the first place, as a political system, and only secondarily, insofar as all politics is ultimately moral in nature (as Plato, Aristotle, Locke, Kant, and Hegel -- among others -- all taught), as also entailing a moral orientation.

A few further definitions are in order. The harm principle, a principle well known in philosophic literature,[3] refers to the stricture that one's freedom of action is limited by the need to avoid unnecessary harm to other living beings, "unnecessary" being an allusion to issues of self-defense and survival. Moral universalism is the moral orientation which holds that there are universal moral guidelines, discernible by the light of Reason (by the light of unaided Reason, in the secular version of this orientation), so that one may say, for example, that cruelty is always wrong, kindness is always good. A specific corollary to this is that the failure to oppose genocide (as in Bosnia or Kosova) represents a species of moral decrepitude. The major alternatives to this orientation, at least in the contemporary West, are moral consequentialism, which holds that no action is good or evil in itself and can be judged only by its specific results, and moral conventionalism, which holds that there is nothing good or evil except as declared by fiat. In other words, for moral conventionalists, morality has purely nominal meaning, and all morality is only positive (in the sense of being created by positive law) and hence relative rather than natural. Moral conventionalism is, thus, compatible with nationalism. The universe of moral alternatives is complete with the mention of moral contractarianism (which affirms a mythical model of collective choice and explains morality in terms of tradition and custom), theocracy, and nihilism; these latter three alternatives are distinctly less important in the contemporary West.[4]

Only moral universalists are able to provide a firm anchor for absolute human rights. For contractarians and conventionalists, rights, like duties, are mere matters of custom, convention, or law. For theocrats, there is no such thing as the Good-in-itself, because morality derives from and is dependent upon divine revelation and divine command. For nihilists, such as the nineteenth-century solipsist Max Stirner, nothing has value, and hence neither have rights nor duties.[5] As for the consequentialists, whether the classic expostulators Jeremy Bentham and John Stuart Mill or the creed's more modern advocates Russell Hardin and L. W. Sumner, in spite of the sophistication of their theory, they remain unable, as John Finnis has argued, to ground morality in any fixity and hence, for utilitarians, "there are no absolute human rights" – not life, not liberty, not the pursuit of happiness, and certainly not property.[6] Moral universalism can, on the other hand, provide such a grounding, as I have argued elsewhere. [7]

Liberalism and democracy

In the communist era, the terms "liberalization" and "democratization" became commonplace, but only with bastardized meanings. After all, if liberalization -- the movement toward a moral liberal culture -- means only an easing of repression and the granting of some limited forums for self-expression, then toleration, equality, and the harm principle disappear down the rabbit hole on the tails of the White Rabbit. And if democratization -- the movement toward a more democratic arrangement -- could be construed as compatible with the preservation of the communist one-party monopoly, then the democracy toward which such a process was pulling society certainly could not be thought to involve a maximization of political choice.

The danger of misunderstanding has not disappeared with the collapse of the communist organizational monopoly. While I consider it self-evident that neither toleration nor the aspiration to maximize political choice should bestow any form of legitimacy or functional legality on groups, parties, organizations, or ideologies which repudiate or show disrespect for the harm principle and/or equality (such as groups which preach racial hatred, intolerance of gays and lesbians, transophobia, or religious intolerance), one encounters political currents of a right-wing orientation in Central and Eastern Europe today which want to exclude from office or influence persons of a social democratic persuasion on the mere pretext of their having had some connection with the communist party monopoly prior to 1989/90 as well as avowedly chauvinist groups of sundry hues. Where sexual intolerance is concerned, the Romanian Orthodox Church has waged a steadfast war to prevent the government in Bucharest from adopting European standards on the treatment of sexual minorities -- a prerequisite for Romania's inclusion in broader trans-European institutions -- on the argument that any departure from heterosexual relations is sinful and that transsexualism tampers, allegedly, with "God's handiwork". [8] The motivations here may vary. Certainly for Romanian Orthodox churchmen there is a conviction that conservative ways enjoy divine favor, combined with a deep-seated distrust of anything new and anything sexual -- anything new in the realm of sexuality being hence twice damned. Where lustration is concerned, some of its advocates are probably motivated by sheer opportunism, while others, blinded by self-righteous fury, allow themselves to believe that some people can never reform their views, can never play a useful role in society. That this orientation is more dangerous than the danger it purports to address should be clear to any who take the liberal project literally.

Now, if liberalism and democracy are not the same thing, two corollaries follow. First, liberal democracy must, in that case, be a hybrid phenomenon, so that one can speak of a society being liberal but not democratic (as in the case of eighteenth-century Prussia) and of a society being democratic but not liberal (as in the case of post-communist Poland). [9] Second, the processes of establishing the predominance of liberal values and of establishing and consolidating a working democratic system are not necessarily co-terminous; one may precede the other in time. The question is whether this makes any difference or whether, on the contrary, it is entirely immaterial. I, for one, am of the view that the order in which these tasks are undertaken is of fundamental importance both for the path in which values emerge and are transformed and for the ultimate success in the project of establishing liberal democracy. In the West, as C. B. McPherson has pointed out [10], liberal values (including religious toleration, as advanced by John Locke in the face of some initial resistance) were well entrenched long before universal suffrage was introduced and before the emergence of the notion that government existed to protect all of its citizens, and not just "men of property". In post-communist Eastern Europe, by contrast, a rather different path is being followed. Here democratic or nominally democratic arrangements have been introduced, even though liberal values have not been secured anywhere in the region. One may grant that Slovenia and the Czech Republic show the greatest sensitivity to liberal values in the region, but even here, there are limits. Without suggesting, by any means, that the United States has reached an impregnable promontory of sublime liberalism from which no serious challenges can be assayed (the recent clamor for introducing quasi-mandatory Protestant prayers in all public schools and repeated clerico-fascist efforts to pass laws which would dramatically escalate the systematic discrimination against gays and lesbians in the United States being sufficient to lay to rest any such optimistic fantasies), one may point out, for example, that in the Slovenian case, the repeated rumblings from the clerical right about introducing Catholic religious instruction in public schools and about legislating a Church-inspired ban on abortion indicate that the right is willing, at the most, to agree to a markedly narrow interpretation of what should and should not be tolerated, while reconstructing the harm principle to fit Church doctrine and moral teachings. The case of Poland is particularly instructive, for it is here where the Roman Catholic Church has been most energetic in exploiting democratic mechanisms to serve theocratic ends, so as to produce a hybrid state formation which one might call -- not without irony -- theocratic democracy. Poland certainly still qualifies, at least under a minimal definition, as democratic, though one may point out that the less tolerance manifested in the Polish system, the less democratic one should judge its performance. But one would be hard pressed to defend Poland as an example of a state which embodies, secures, and protects liberal values. Nor does it come as any surprise that for Pope John Paul II, the "Polish pontiff" who still casts a long shadow over the Polish state, liberalism appears to be a twin to capitalism, with both being ultimately illegitimate. [11] At the core of the liberal project, as regards religion, is the claim, even the insistence, that the state be neutral in matters of religion and not allow its legislation, infrastructure, and coercive apparatus to advance programs and policies specific to one or another religious association. [12] It is precisely this claim which John Paul II, the Catholic episcopate in Poland, the Romanian Orthodox Church, and the religious right in both Europe and North America reject. To this, I should like to make two preliminary replies. First, capitalism, understood as an economic formation, is not necessarily coterminous with liberalism, a moral orientation, any more than is democracy. On the contrary, one may find in the moral universalism of the liberal project the basis for a critique and repudiation of

- 123 -

capitalism as an illegitimate formation.[13] And second, the theocratic program entails, of necessity, the dual principle, explicitly enunciated and defended by Cardinal Ratzinger in his controversial interview book of 1985, that one cannot submit Truth to a debate and that there can be no toleration for error, which, of necessity, scuttles reference to the harm principle as the exclusive source of limits to tolerance, replacing this with divine revelation as interpreted by clerics. [14] The result can be neither liberal nor democratic. Moreover, equality likewise soon falls by the wayside. Pope Pius XI (1857--1939; reigned 1922--39) was quite clear on the subject of equality, declaring in 1937 that "It is not true that all have equal rights in civil society. It is not true that there exists no lawful social hierarchy." [15] By lawful social hierarchy, Pope Pius XI was defending both the established class system and the political authorities, construed as in accord with some 'divine plan', but in denying the existence or even possibility of 'equal rights', Pius XI certainly presumed further that the Catholic Church, on its understanding of itself as God's own institutional creation and institutional representative in this 'vale of tears', enjoyed rights to dictate moral codes which were beyond debate, beyond challenge, beyond qualification or revision. Joseph de Maistre, the eighteenth-century French Catholic apologist, took these clerical claims to their logical conclusion in rejecting altogether the notion that one might refer moral questions or matters of divine revelation to reason. To this Mill replies, "If all mankind minus one, were of one opinion, and only one person were of the contrary opinion, mankind would be no more justified in silencing that one person, than he, if he had the power, would be justified in silencing (the rest of) mankind." [16]

The Functional Minima of Liberalism

I have suggested above: (a) that classical liberalism is the repository of moral universalism, (b) that only moral universalism (and hence also, only liberalism) can provide an ideological and cultural bedrock for absolute human rights and for equality of human dignity (which is not the same thing as declaring that any liberal society automatically achieves utopian levels of dignity and equality, however), and (c) that democracy is one thing, liberalism is another. Indeed, one may speak of liberal monarchies and illiberal democracies. It is because of democracy's easier claim to legitimacy in the modern and post-modern world that democracy may serve as the most suitable vehicle for realizing liberal values, but, to my mind, it is liberal values which are the point and purpose of the liberal-democratic amalgam.

The question, then, is: What are the functional minima of liberalism? What must a society or system assure, if it is going to be liberal, and how does it go about achieving these functional minima? Pride of place goes to education. Hugh Seton-Watson, in his classic study of interwar Eastern Europe, emphasized the centrality of education in liberal values,[17] and the point remains likewise valid today. Unlike air, upon the presence of which one can depend without having to take any special precautions,[18] liberal values require cultivation, and the key to such cultivation is the assurance that such values are fostered in the educational system, both explicitly (through the reading of works by Kant, Locke, Hobbes, Mill, and others) and implicitly (through the way in which humanities and social science classes are presented), and protected from rampant violation in the media, whether cinematic film or television or the medium of rock music. Lyrics which advocate murder or racial hatred represent an assault on liberal values, for example, and resignation may not be the most effective way in which to counter such assaults, at least when they cease to be trivial in their potential effect.

Second, the liberal project requires and entails the rule of law. Ironically, in spite of many solemn avowals to the contrary, democracy does not have this requirement, which is one reason why a democracy which is not liberal risks turning into a heinous creature of willful social tyranny, as Mill himself warned. The expression "rule of law" means that all laws are published and available to the general public, that all citizens are treated equally under the law, that the government and its officials are themselves subject to the law on an equal basis with other citizens, that the government obeys the law and carries out the laws, and that there be legal recourse for violations of positive rights whether by agencies of the government or by other agencies or individuals. The rule of law also presumes that the laws are secular in derivation; when the parliament caters to a Church or faith and tailors the laws to suit the programmatic interest of that Church, the result is, at best, the "rule of divine law" as interpreted by clerics, i.e., a species of theocracy. On the other hand, the concept "rule of law" does not presume that the laws (least of all, all the laws) be good and just, only that such laws as exist be enforced as indicated above. But "rule of law" is only one of five functional minima for a liberal order, and the content of the laws is prescribed by other preconditions.

Third, the concepts of free speech and free association may well obtain an unlimited interpretation by advocates of illiberal democracy or of that debased alloy, "whatever democracy". The advocates of "whatever democracy" lack even such a compass as Hua Guofeng (of the "two whatevers" fame) could boast, in that they are prepared to let people do precisely what they want when they want, regardless of consequences. Contemporary whateverists (who subscribe to a dizzy variant of moral consequentialism, aka moral hedonism) are all too happy to defend the alleged right to own and use guns (including in the court, as recent events in a major American city sadly record), to defend hate speech, to defend the alleged right to publish slanderous misrepresentations of the works of liberal-minded scholars in journals, to defend the so-called 'right' of racists and chauvinists to organize parties for the purpose of spreading hatred, and to defend the access by groups dedicated to the promulgation of bigotry and hatred to radio and television. The steps taken by the Czech Republic and Bulgaria to ban hate speech and to proscribe ethnically-based parties represent not a retreat from liberalism, but, on the contrary, a concerted effort to protect liberal values. As the Baron de Montesquieu urged in 1748, "...political liberty does not consist in an unlimited freedom. In governments, that is, in societies directed by laws, liberty can consist only in the power of doing what we ought to will." [19] Or, as Kant would say, there can be no freedom and no right to increase the tally of human suffering in the world or to otherwise practise or perpetrate evil. [20]

Not everyone who professes to respect the liberal tradition is willing to embrace the harm principle, though I would argue that to minimize or abandon the harm principle is to quit the liberal tradition itself in favor of the moral nominalism of Thrasymachus, Socrates' adversary in Book I of Plato's Republic. [21] To abandon the promontory of the harm principle is to abandon Madison and Mill for Adam Smith (with his exhortation to trust in an "invisible hand") and Herbert Spencer (with his advice that the solution to poverty is to let the poor starve to death). But Adam Smith's "invisible hand", which cast its shadow also over Social Darwinism, in giving rich and poor nominally equal political prerogatives without limiting their exercise, allows the rich to ride roughshod over the poor. Indeed, one might say that without respect for the harm principle, the would-be 'democrat' ends up abandoning the substance of equality and embracing oligarchy. Is it any wonder that at the turn of the century, income differentials are greater in "the land of the free" than anywhere else on the planet at any time in history?

But political solipsists want us to believe that courtesy, observance of the moral law in public affairs, and respect for the harm principle all limit freedom. In fact, such claims are phoney. On the contrary, as liberals from Locke to Raz have argued, the harm principle maximizes freedom by providing the only effective defense against those who deny a right to defy the mainstream religious views or the right to be what one is sexually (gay/lesbian/transgendered) on the fallacious claim that sexual attraction is freely chosen (suggesting that those arguing this took time to consider the options from a standpoint of complete neutrality and then to make their choice), or the right to dress differently or paint one's house strange colors or to develop one's own political views. Without the harm principle to safeguard one, all these rights and others are left defenseless and exposed to the ravages of choleric and intemperate foes of liberalism.

Were we to resurrect Thrasymachus from the dead, he would surely reproach me for my idealist praise of the moral law (which, adopting a conventionist position, he equated with whatever the ruling class decreed), much as he reproached Socrates for the same thing. Indeed, Thrasymachus was incapable of understanding either justice or the moral law as anything other than either opportunism (insofar as the legislators would draft laws to suit their own class interests) or self-defeating blindness in the event that the "just man" actually aspired to integrity and something higher than the pursuit of self-interest. [22] The reason that Thrasymachus would be eager to construe the moral law as merely some further species of opportunism is precisely that he himself understands the "clever man" as "utilizing circumstances or opportunities to gain one's ends" -- which is the very definition of opportunism. [23]

For Thrasymachus, there was no higher law than the written law, and no higher standard to which the state's laws should conform. This classic conventionalism opens the door to 'total freedom', in the spirit of whatever is not expressly forbidden is permitted. But Thrasymachus is not so foolish as to fail to recognize this for what it is. On the contrary, he admits quite openly that this total freedom can only redound to the interest of the strong and the rich. As Thrasymachus explained, "...governments use their power to make tyrannical, democratic, or aristocratic laws, as suits their interests...[Therefore,] justice is what advantages the interest of the ruling class. Since the ruling class is also the strongest class, the conclusion should be evident to anyone who reasons correctly: justice is the same in every case -- the interest of the stronger." [24]

Thrasymachus' argument would not be dangerous if it remained at the empirical level. But latter-day Thrasymacheans such as Hans-Hermann Hoppe and other libertarians carry the argument to the normative level. Reviling the centralized state as "a territorial monopolist of force" which threatens to "reduce market participation and the formation of wealth," [25] Hoppe advances that a proliferation of secessions, down to the level of the household, will push the overall standard of living upwards -- at least for the well-to-do, who would be the most likely to want to take advantage of Hoppe's invitation to secede from income tax, property tax, and the obligation to assist the less well-to-do. [26]

Fourth, the liberal project requires the effective protection of human rights (understanding, by this term, both individual rights and the rights of the entire community of people living in a given society, regardless of language, nationality, religion, or sexual orientation, qua community). Moreover, these rights must be understood in the broadest sense -- to include the right not only to life, free thought, free expression (within limits set by the harm principle), and free association, but also the right to an education, to medical care, and to economic justice.[27] It is these latter rights which are challenged by neo- Thrasymachean libertarians and other advocates of privilege for wealth.

And fifth, a liberal program must, of necessity, involve neutrality on matters of religion and conscience, including in areas which have remained controversial. Moral universalism refers moral judgment to Universal Reason, i.e., to such conclusions as may be reached by all sane persons, but when reasonable people disagree, as in the case of abortion, the best approach -- in the sense of most compatible with liberal values -- is to abstain from legislating. The hanging of crucifixes in classrooms, which has proven divisive in post-communist Poland and in post-unification Germany, may gratify Catholic believers' desire to bring their Church into the classroom; but it violates, at the same time, the ideological safety of the classroom, every bit as much as if the words "Allah is Great" were displayed in Polish and German classrooms.

Voltaire, an early champion of the confessional neutrality of the state, held that the civil government "has no right to use coercion to lead men to religion," noting that the use of coercion to achieve virtue is self-defeating, in that virtue presupposes free will and free choice. Accordingly, for Voltaire, "obedience to ecclesiastical order must...always be free and voluntary;...submission to civil order, on the other hand, may be compulsory and compelled." [28]

For classical liberalism, thus, the purported 'right' of religious communities to practise their faith to the fullest to the point of prescribing the laws of the state itself, violates the harm principle, much as a theoretical 'right' of cannibals to 'maintain their folk traditions' would violate that self-same principle. It also violates the principle of equality since it is self-evident that only one religion can control and dictate to any given state, all other religious associations thereby becoming the objects of discrimination, even if they happen to agree with the precepts being dictated by the established Church to the state.

The Clerical Challenge in Poland

The Roman Catholic Church has challenged all five of these functional 'minima' for a liberal system. [29] To begin with, the Holy See has tended to conflate liberalism with capitalism, thereby implicating liberal values in its attacks on capitalist economics. Moreover, insofar as liberalism champions a secular morality, based in Universal Reason and not in divine revelation, the Church has perceived in liberalism a dangerous rival to the inheritance of the Natural Law tradition which both uphold. On the second point, the Church's challenge to secular-based law has been fundamental and unflagging. From the beginning, the Polish prelates insisted that the preamble to the eventual constitution begin with the words, "In the name of God", even at the expense of suggesting to non-believers that their values and beliefs are not respected equally by the Polish state,[30] and framed their entire campaign for outlawing abortion on the claim that the practice is contrary to divine law, as revealed and explained by the Vicar of Christ and his ministers. [31] The Roman Catholic Church in Poland thereby violated John Rawls' dictum that, in advocating legislative alternatives in a liberal society, "...we are to appeal only to presently accepted general beliefs and forms of reasoning found in common sense, and the methods and conclusions of science when these are not controversial." [32] Among the reasons for Rawl's prescription is the desirability of avoiding the polarization of society. The fact that this principle has been flagrantly violated by the Catholic Church has contributed to the sharp polarization of Polish society along confessional lines since 1989, and indeed, even before then. [33]

As to the third functional minimal condition for liberalism -- that freedom of speech and freedom of association be limited by observance of the harm principle, i.e., that neither speech nor actions on the part of either individuals or organized groups be allowed to infringe on the basic rights of any residents (whether citizens or not) of a given society -- Polish prelates violated this condition during the 1995 presidential race. It was on that occasion that Archbishop Jozef Glemp denounced SLD presidential candidate Aleksander Kwasniewski as a "neo-pagan" and that Archbishop Ignacy Tokarczuk described the thinking and behavior of Kwasniewski's party as "hysterical and traumatic, the result of an anti-religious and anti-God complex going back to the seeds of Marx and Lenin." [34] The use of similarly abrasive vocabulary by Polish prelates and their adherents to describe the decision taken by some Polish women to have abortions, without acknowledging that they may have taken such decision in good conscience, again violated this condition. On the other hand, even while asserting their own right to indulge in hate speech, Poland's Catholic prelates harnessed the power of the state in 1993 by pressing to have clauses inserted into a law on broadcasting which effectively barred any discussion over the air of topics considered taboo by Poland's Catholic hierarchy.[35]

The fourth functional minimum of liberalism, which some writers might prefer to list in first place, and not without reason, is the effective protection of human rights, embracing both individual and societal rights. Here it is quite clear that the Roman Catholic Church hierarchy in Poland does not recognize a right of children in public schools (even of non-Catholic children) to absent themselves from Catholic religious instruction,[36] or a right on the part of a pregnant woman to act in accordance with her conscience (unless, of course, her conscience follows the programmatic preferences of the prelates), or a right to discuss homosexuality or transsexualism on television and radio, or a right on the part of bereaved Protestant families in remote areas to bury their dead in a Catholic cemetery (as provided by Polish law but as excluded by the Concordat), or a right, in a confessionally mixed marriage, to bring the offspring up in another faith other than Catholic, or a right to have one's children obtain the basics of sex education at the school (as opposed to Church-approved classes on how to be a good parent[37]). Referring to those challenging the Church's agenda on these and other points, Cardinal Glemp, the Polish Primate, warned of "...those leftist tendencies which the Church would like to see outside public life."[38]

And finally, as to neutrality on matters of religion and conscience, the entire activity of the Polish Catholic Church has been directed toward undermining this principle. Poland's leading clerical figures have repeatedly declared that church-state separation is entirely "unacceptable" to the Church,[39] even though, without church-state separation, one cannot speak of a liberal project, the equality of citizens, tolerance, or even adequate protection of human dignity in modern conditions. In 1994, Bishop Tadeusz Pieronek, Secretary-General of the Polish Episcopal Conference, allowed that the state might be neutral as long as it is not secular.[40] But his argument was specious, since if a state is not secular, that can only signify that it is confessional, and if it is confessional, then it can scarcely be neutral in matters of faith, conscience, and ritual. Indeed, Pieronek came close to conceding as much when he urged, on the same occasion, that "the Constitution should include a provision on the autonomy of, and cooperation between, the Church and the state, and not on [the] separation from each other."[41] Long before the new constitution was finally adopted and at a time when the communist system was still fresh in its grave, Bogdan Tranda called attention to the quasi-theocratic prominence of the Roman Catholic Church in the public life of Poland:

> "On radio, on television, you hear and see Catholic priests. If there is a Solidarity meeting, it starts with a mass. If there is a national festival, the official program includes a mass. If a new party organizes a congress, it starts with a mass. If there is a military celebration, there is a mass in the program, and all the soldiers in their ranks with guns and bayonets receive communion one after another. Anyone who wants to achieve an important position in the country tries to get the support of a bishop, of the Primate or of the Pope, or at least tries to act together with a priest."[42]

Now, on the insistence of the Bishops' Conference, (Catholic) religious instruction was introduced in schools and kindergartens.

It may be conceded that the question of abortion, which has figured as the rallying issue for the Church in the post-communist era, is a morally grey area, and that, in successfully blocking recourse to a nationwide referendum as to whether abortion ought to be legal, Church prelates were acting 'in good conscience'. One would, for that matter, be well advised in urging that not everything should be put to a referendum, certainly not programs which would subvert the fundamental principles of the liberal order -- unless one wishes to champion 'totalitarian democracy', of course. But at the same time, one may note that Church prelates have not been willing to concede that their liberal competitors have similarly acted in good conscience or that there might be reasonable doubt about the morality or immorality of abortion in at least some circumstances or even that a television commentator might refer to the proscriptive 1993 law as the "antiabortion law". [43] The attitude prevalent among Poland's overwhelmingly conservative hierarchy and clergy was aptly summed up by Bishop Pieronek in 1994 when he told a plenary conference of the Episcopate held in Niepokalanow near Warsaw that "the Church would not object to a democratic Constitution," pointing out, however, that "there are also the people who have the right to voice their opinion (about that) in a referendum...."[44] Although unwilling to submit the question of abortion to democratic referendum, Pieronek seemed quite willing to submit the entire question of (liberal) democracy to a referendum, thereby championing an alleged democratic right to reject democracy. Without insisting that democratic forms are necessarily the only means whereby to establish and protect liberal values -- a proposition which, as I have already indicated, I consider open to debate[45] -- there is something inherently self-contradictory in arguing that democratic methods might be legitimately employed in order to disestablish democracy. Yet this statement by Pieronek is neither accidental nor incidental, but reveals the essence of the Catholic Church's attitude toward the state in Poland.

Conclusion

Sociological research has confirmed that organized religion may play a constructive role in deterring deviance from mainstream moral precepts and in fashioning what might be called "moral communities".[46] But one may question whether religion, let alone one specific religious association, may claim, on this basis, to enjoy a right (or duty) to impose moral precepts specific to itself on an entire society, using the apparatus of state for this purpose. This latter aspiration smacks of religious fundamentalism, which I shall define (on nominalist grounds) as the elevation of divine authority over morality, thereby excluding certain persons outside the given religious association from enjoying fully equal rights with those inside the religious association, releasing association members from the association's own moral precepts when association interests are served, and authorizing the association to take steps to impose its own confessional and moral agenda on the entire society. When, thus, an American religious activist sees fit to murder physicians and patients or to participate in group action to prevent patients from reaching a given medical facility, that person is releasing self from the moral precepts accepted by most religious associations, including all bona fide Christian Churches, for the purpose of preventing non-members from exercising positive rights granted under the laws of the society. The fundamentalist currents present in Polish Catholicism may figure as a response to the normative erosion and social demoralization which have been associated, in Central and Eastern Europe, with the collapse of the social order imposed after the Second World War, as Melanie Tatur has suggested.[47] Sociologists have disagreed among themselves as to whether such religious fundamentalism represents "the ultimate direction of (post)-modern societies," with Willfried Spohn, for example, disputing this contention,[48] but there is a general understanding that fundamentalism, at least as I have defined it, if not also under other definitions, is fundamentally at odds with the presuppositions of the liberal order.

The University of Notre Dame Press recently published a book entitled *Religion and Contemporary Liberalism*, which has direct bearing on the foregoing discussion. [49] Bringing together scholars of diverse views, the volume makes an important contribution to understanding the issues at stake and the emotions and presuppositions associated with specific points of view. Defending the liberal viewpoint, Robert Audi, a professor at the University of Nebraska at Lincoln, enumerated three principles which he considers basic to the liberal project: the libertarian principle (that religious practice be permitted within certain limits), the equalitarian principle (that the state not favor one religion over another), and the neutrality principle (that the state either advance nor hinder either religion in general or any specific incarnation(s) of religion). Audi also urges that the "liberal state might be held to be the only kind that preserves freedom and provides adequate scope for individual autonomy."[50] Another contributor to the same volume, Timothy Jackson, stakes out his position by making the confused assertions that liberalism frames social discourse "in nonmoral or minimally moral terms", thus fostering moral relativism and stating that "the Holocaust was at least partially the product of scientific rationality and democratic governance."[51] Having thus identified himself as critical of liberalism and democracy alike and having, at the same time, ignored the fact that liberalism is ontogenetically bound up with moral universalism, as tough a moral code as one may identify, Jackson nonetheless concedes that there are varieties of liberalism, but then errs in associating what he calls the "liberalism-as-morally-basic" variant with utilitarianism, whereas utilitarianism is a branch of liberalism associated with moral consequentialism[52] which, I have argued elsewhere,[53] is associated, on the contrary, with hedonism, short-range thinking, and the abandonment of Natural Law as the source of moral certainty, giving rise to situational ethics. Unfortunately too, when Jackson does finally allude to (but not discuss) Kant, whose views were anything but utilitarian or consequentialist, it is only in the context of attacking "reductive objectivity" which, allegedly, "avers that the only good thing is the good will"[54] -- a statement which Kant scholars can trace to Kant's metaphysical writings[55] but which, as rephrased by Jackson, is entirely foreign to Kant's intention and

- 135 -

thinking. Jackson's purpose in debunking liberalism in all its varieties is, in his own words, to argue that "...some politically relevant truths can only be grasped in religiously sonorous terms,"[56] an argument he does not, however, elaborate.

Taking a position equally hostile to Audi and elaborating specific theses having direct relevance for present-day Central and Eastern Europe, Philip Quinn, in what originated as his presidential address to the American Philosophical Association in 1995, disputes Audi's contention that debating public policy issues in religious terms can be unnecessarily divisive in a democratic society and makes the improbable claim that citizens who reject utilitarian suppositions can be expected, by that virtue alone, to have contempt for policies which offer benefits in terms of utility or convenience. Moreover, to Audi's Rawlsian exhortation that proponents of specific policies (such as the prohibition of abortion) offer secular rationale for their policy preferences, in order to remain within a lingua franca comprehensible to all parties to the debate as well as to preserve the confessional neutrality of the state, Quinn replies that "...religious believers will rightly regard Audi's principle of secular rationale as making an unfair demand on them unless it is coupled with corresponding principles that make similar demands on people whose secular reasons are no better off than their religious reasons..."[57] and criticizes Rawls' concept of liberalism because it "...privileges liberal conceptions of justice over their rivals by including the substantive principles, guidelines of inquiry, and political values of a liberal conception of justice, or a family of such conceptions, but not those of competing, nonliberal conceptions, within the bounds of public reason."[58] To this suggestion that liberal tolerance is flawed by its refusal to tolerate the illiberal, Budziszewski has provided an appropriate response, in contending, "Tolerance is a virtue indeed; but if it is the only virtue, it can hardly be anything more than good conscience in our continuing lack of convictions." [59] In order words, to question liberalism's grounds for excluding illiberal political conceptions is to falsely equate liberalism with moral relativism and to ignore its grounding in the Natural Law tradition. Significantly, Quinn closes his address/chapter with a confession that he does not recognize that Americans have an obligation to uphold the first amendment to the U.S. constitution (regarding religious liberty) or to refrain from seeking to repeal the constitutional exclusion of ecclesiastical establishment.[60] In other words, Quinn upholds the notion that there is a right to strive to introduce a theocracy, i.e., a right to seek to relegate some citizens to second-class status; nor does he deny citizens the right to seek to declare the United States a "Christian nation"[61].

But such a statement may be either empirical or prescriptive. If it is intended as an empirical statement, then it would be simply false, since there are non-Christians who are U.S. citizens. But if intended to be prescriptive -- and I believe that this is, in fact, the purpose of any attempts in such direction -- then such a statement would be tantamount to declaring that non-Christians are not Americans, non-Catholics are not Poles or Slovenes or Croats, Orthodox are not Romanians or Russians, and so forth; in other words, the purpose of such a statement in law is to lay the groundwork for discrimination along confessional lines. Against Quinn, I would contend, as Budziszewski did, that liberalism does not allow any tolerance of intolerance or of "seeking" to relegate other citizens to second-class status, and that, to the extent that Quinn defends these positions, he relinquishes any claim to be considered a "liberal".

It may be useful, before closing, to make a few remarks concerning one last contribution to the aforementioned book, viz., the chapter by Nicholas Wolterstorff.[62] Wolterstorff believes that "liberalism formulates its political conception of justice entirely in terms of rights"[63] -- a belief which could not be applied to Kant, for example, and which is not even adequate as a description of Locke's beliefs. As Peter Laslett has noted, "Natural law, in [Locke's] system in Two Treatises, was at one and the same time a command of God, a rule of reason, and a law in the very nature of things as they are, by which they work and we work too."[64] Wolterstorff goes further, however, blaming liberalism for repudiations of its own tenets, and equating liberalism with the moral relativism which is the

- 137 -

earmark of the erosion and subversion of the liberal project.[65] Curiously, he ascribes to liberal scholars the belief that "religion plays no explanatory role in human affairs"[66] -- a view which, I confess, I am unable to associate with any scholar. He continues by dissecting a statement by Rawls concerning the necessary competence implied in citizenship -- "the ideal of citizenship imposes a moral...duty...to be able to explain to one another...how the principles and policies they advocate and vote for can be supported by the political values of public reason"[67] -- and mocking Rawls with the sarcastic paraphrase, "The ideal imposes a duty to be able to explain, not to explain." [68] As a result of this confusion, Wolterstorff loses sight of the importance which Rawls was attaching to the duty to inform oneself and to be intelligent about issues and portrays Rawls as if he were advocating hypocrisy.[69] Wolterstorff's purpose, rather transparently, is to legitimate a public, political role for churches and other religious associations on the argument that only religion can hold back the rising tide of moral "debasement" and obsessiveness with individual, materialistic self-gratification.[70] In advancing this recipe, however, Wolterstorff mistakenly implies an equation of liberalism and utilitarianism[71] -- evidently a favorite canard among liberalism's foes -- and throws the doors wide open to hate speech, intolerance, and discrimination, with the misleading exhortation, "Why not let people say what they want, but insist that they say it with civility?"[72] One can imagine a representative of the Aryan Brotherhood discussing his views on racial differences in a civil manner and appreciate how meaningingless such civility of expression would be. Closer to home, one has the example of the Christian Coalition's strategy (in the U.S.) of expressing sexually intolerant views in misleadingly civil tones, with the intent of beguiling listeners into accepting hatred and intolerance as legitimate views.

Unlike some analysts, I do not subscribe either to pure voluntarism or to pure determinism. In my view, there is no necessary or inevitable future, even though one may identify forces pushing in certain directions, even in contrary directions. If the classical liberal ideas developed largely in the eighteenth and early nineteenth centuries represent the bedrock of the project to protect human dignity and equality, then the rising fundamentalisms or religious nationalisms of the late twentieth century are not merely the principal threat, but may possibly constitute the predominant default syndrome of the age, as well as of the age to come.[73] Post-modernism may be neither secular nor liberal (the moral foundations of liberalism having been eroded to a considerable extent by consequentialism and misguided efforts to marry liberalism to veiled tablishmentarianism), but the challenge is to push history beyond post-modernism toward what I call liberal solidarism: a system based on liberal mores, economic justice, and political legitimism.[74]

Endnotes

[1] Joseph Raz, "Autonomy, Toleration, and the Harm Principle", in Susan Mendus (ed.), *Justifying Toleration: Conceptual and Historical Perspectives* (Cambridge: Cambridge University Press, 1988), esp. pp. 157, 165.

[2] See John Stuart Mill, "On Liberty" (1859), in J. S. Mill, *On Liberty and other writings*, edited by Stefan Collini (Cambridge: Cambridge University Press, 1989), pp. 8--9, 11, 13, 16, 20, 22.

[3] Regarding the harm principle, see J. W. Harris, *Legal Philosophies*, 2nd ed. (London: Butterworths, 1997), pp. 23, 131--136.

[4] But on these six moral orientations, see L. W. Sumner, *The Moral Foundation of Rights* (Oxford: Clarendon Press, 1987); Russell Hardin, *Morality within the Limits of Reason* (Chicago: University of Chicago Press, 1988); and Robert P. George (ed.), *Natural Law, Liberalism, and Morality: Contemporary Essays* (Oxford: Clarendon Press, 1996). Regarding Thomas Hobbes' relation to moral
universalism, see Norberto Bobbio, *Thomas Hobbes and the Natural Law Tradition*, trans. by Daniela Gobetti (Chicago: University of Chicago Press, 1993).

[5] Max Stirner, *The Ego and His Own*, trans. by Steven T. Byington, ed. James J. Martin (New York: Libertarian Book Club, 1963). See also John Henry Mackay, *Max Stirner: Sein Leben und Sein Werk* (Freiburg: Mackay-Gesellschaft, 1977); and R. W. K. Paterson, *The Nihilist Egoist: Max Stirner* (London: Oxford University Press, 1971).

[6] John Finnis, "Absolute Human Rights", in Peter Singer (ed.), *Ethics* (Oxford: Oxford University Press, 1994), p. 256.

[7] Sabrina P. Ramet, *Whose Democracy? Nationalism, Religion, and the Doctrine of Collective Rights in Post-1989 Eastern Europe* (Lanham, Md.:

Rowman & Littlefield, 1997), especially the introduction, chapter 3, and the conclusion. See also Immanuel Kant, The Metaphysics of Morals , trans. by Mary Gregor (Cambridge: Cambridge University Press, 1991).

[8] More details in Sabrina P. Ramet, *Nihil Obstat: Religion, Politics, and Social Change in East-Central Europe and Russia* (Durham, N.C.: Duke University Press, 1998), pp. 197--199.

[9] I find myself here in agreement with Fareed Zakaria. See his essay, "The Rise of Illiberal Democracy", in *Foreign Affairs* , Vol. 76, No. 6 (November/December 1997), pp. 22-43. For an alternative point of view, see Marc F. Plattner, "Liberalism and Democracy: Can't Have One Without the Other", in *Foreign Affairs* , Vol. 77, No. 2 (March/April 1998).

[10] C. B. McPherson, *The Real World of Democracy* (New York: Oxford University Press, 1972), p. 5, as cited in Dijana Plestina, "Democracy and Nationalism in Croatia: The First Three Years", in Sabrina Petra Ramet and Ljubisa S. Adamovich (eds.), *Beyond Yugoslavia: Politics, Economics, and Culture in a Shattered Community* (Boulder, Colo.: Westview Press, 1995), p. 126.

[11] *Sollicitudo rei socialis* (1988), as excerpted in *New York Times* (20 February 1988), p. 4.

[12] Robert Audi, "The State, the Church, and the Citizen", in Paul J. Weithman (ed.), *Religion and Contemporary Liberalism* (Notre Dame: University of Notre Dame Press, 1997), pp. 40--42.

[13] See the argument in Sabrina P. Ramet, "Liberalizam, moral i drustveni poredak: Slucaj korumpiranog populistickog pluralizma u Hrvatskoj", in *Erasmus* (Zagreb), No. 24 (May 1998), pp. 2--14.

[14] Joseph Cardinal Ratzinger (in interview) with Vittorio Messori, *The Ratzinger Report* , trans. from German by Salvator Attanasio and Graham Harrison (San Francisco: St. Ignatius Press, 1985), pp. 61--61.

[15] *Encyclical Letter of Pope Piux XI on Atheistic Communism* (19 March 1937), Official Vatican text (Boston: St. Paul Editions), p. 21.

[16] Mill, "On Liberty", p. 20

[17] Hugh Seton-Watson, *Eastern Europe between the wars, 1918 -1941*, 3rd ed. (Hamden, Conn: Archon Books, 1962), p.266.

[18] Of course, if one wants fresh air, that is another matter.

[19] Baron de Montesqueiu, *The Spirit of the Laws* (1748), excerpted in Isaac Kramnick (ed.), *The Portable Enlightenment Reader* (New York: Penguin Books, 1995), p. 412.

[20] Kant, *Metaphysics of Morals* , p. 52. See also Mary Gregor, "Kant on 'Natural Rights", in Ronald Beiner and William James Booth (eds.), *Kant & Political Philosophy: The Contemporary Legacy* (New Haven, Conn.: Yale University Press, 1993), pp. 52--53, 59--60, 66.

[21] The debate between nominalists and essentialists remains, of necessity, unresolved to the present day. For Thomas More's essentialism, see T. More, *Utopia*, trans. and edited by Robert M. Adams (New York: W. W. Norton, 1975), pp. 39, 69, 84. For Thomas Hobbes' nominalism, see Thomas Hobbes, *A Dialogue between a Philosopher and a Student of the Common Laws of England*, ed. by Joseph Cropsey (Chicago: University of Chicago Press, 1971), pp. 69-70.

[22] Plato, *The Republic*, trans. by Richard W. Sterling and William C. Scott (New York: W. W. Norton, 1996), p. 41.

[23] *The Cassell Pocket English Dictionary* (London: Arrow Books, 1991), pp. 564-565.

[24] Plato, *The Republic*, p. 36.

[25] Hans-Hermann Hoppe, "The Western State as Paradigm", in *Society*, Vol. 35, No. 5 (July/August 1998), pp. 21, 22.

[26] *Ibid.*, pp. 23-24. See my rebuttal to Hoppe: Sabrina P. Ramet, "Profit Motives in Secession", in *Society*, Vol. 35, No. 5 (July/August 1998), pp. 26-29. For an effective demolition of cultural-moral relativism, see John J. Tilley, "Cultural Relativism, Universalism, and the Burden of Proof", in *Millennium*, Vol. 27 (1998), No. 2, pp. 275-297.

[27] For an elucidation of my thinking here, see Ramet, *Whose Democracy? Nationalism, Religion, and the Doctrine of Collective Rights in Post-1989 Eastern Europe*, introduction and chapter 3.

[28] François-Marie Arouet de Voltaire, "Reflections on Religion" (1764), in Kramnick (ed.), *Portable Enlightenment*, pp. 116, 117.

[29] E.g., *Sollicitudo rei socialis* (note 11).

[30] *Gazeta Wyborcza* (11 August 1994), p. 1, trans. in *FBIS, Daily Report* (Eastern Europe), 11 August 1994, p. 26.

[31] See Rebecca Pasini, "Piety amid Politics: The Roman Catholic Church and Polish Abortion Policy", in *Problems of Post-Communism*, Vol. 43, No. 2 (March--April 1996); and Małgorzata Fuszara, "Legal Regulation of Abortion in Poland", in *Signs*, Vol. 17, No. 1 (Autumn 1991).

[32] John Rawls, *Political Liberalism* (New York: Columbia University Press, 1993), p. 224.

[33] Bogdan Tranda, "The Situation of Protestants in Today's Poland", *in Religion in Communist Lands*, Vol. 19, Nos. 1--2 (Summer 1991), p. 40; and Bogdan Tranda, "The Great Change and the Protestants", in *Religion in Eastern Europe*, Vol. 13 (April 1993), p. 32.

[34] Both quotes from Ramet, *Whose Democracy? Nationalism, Religion, and the Doctrine of Collective Rights in Post-1989 Eastern Europe*, p. 106.

[35] Dziennik Ustaw (Warsaw), 29 January 1993, pp. 62--72, trans. in U.S. Department of Commerce, *Central and Eastern Europe Legal Texts* , 29 January 1993, on Nexis . See also Ramet, *Nihil Obstat* , pp. 299--300.
[36] See *The Independent* (London), 8 July 1990, p. 13.
[37] PAP (10 June 1996), on Nexis .
[38] Rzeczpospolita (3 January 1995), p. 2, trans. in *Polish News Bulletin* (3 January 1995), on Nexis .
[39] See, for example, *Ibid* .
[40] *Gazeta Wyborcza* (24 October 1994), p. 1, trans. in *Polish News Bulletin* (24 October 1994), on Nexis
[41] Quoted in Ibid .
[42] Tranda, "Situation of Protestants", p. 40.
[43] Anna Sabbat-Swidlicka, "Church and State in Poland", in *RFE/RL Research Report* (Munich), 2 April 1993, p. 47.
[44] Quoted in *Gazeta Wyborcza* (note 40), my emphasis.
[45] In my *Whose Democracy*, I argued that hereditary monarchy might figure as an alternative guarantor of liberal values.
[46] See, for example, Rodney Stark and William Sims Bainbridge, *Religion, Deviance, and Social Control* (New York and London: Routledge, 1997), chapters 4--5.
[47] Melanie Tatur, "Catholicism and Modernization in Poland", in *The Journal of Communist Studies* , Vol. 7, No. 3 (September 1991), pp. 342--344.
[48] Willfried Spohn, "Protestantism, Secularization, and Politics in Nineteenth-Century Germany", in Sabrina Petra Ramet and Donald W. Treadgold (eds.), *Render unto Caesar: The Religious Sphere in World Politics* (Washington D.C.: American University Press, 1995), p. 173.
[49] Weithman (ed.), *Religion and Contemporary Liberalism* (note 12).
[50] Audi, "The State, the Church", pp. 38, 39.
[51] Timothy P. Jackson, "The Return of the Prodigal? Liberal Theory and Religious Pluralism.", in Weithman (ed.), *Religion and Contemporary Liberalism*, pp. 182, 183.
[52] *Ibid* ., p. 187.
[53] *Whose Democracy* , pp. 64--66.
[54] Jackson, "Return of the Prodigal", p. 193.
[55] Cf. Kant: "A good will is not good because of what it effects or accomplishes -- because of its fitness for attaining some proposed end: it is good through its willing alone -- that is, good in itself." -- Immanuel Kant, *The Moral Law: Groundwork of the Metaphysics of Morals* , trans. by H. J. Paton (London and New York: Routledge, 1991), p. 60.
[56] Jackson, "Return of the Prodigal", p. 212.

[57] Philip L. Quinn, "Political Liberalisms and Their Exclusions of the Religious", in Weithman (ed.), *Religion and Contemporary Liberalism* (note 12), pp. 143, 144.

[58] *Ibid.*, pp. 145, 148

[59] J. Budziszewski, *True Tolerance: Liberalism and the Necessity of Judgment* (New Brunswick, N.J.: Transaction, 1992), p. xiii.

[60] Quinn, "Political Liberalisms", p. 160.

[61] *Ibid*.

[62] Nicholas Wolterstorff, "Why We Should Reject What Liberalism Tells Us about Speaking and Acting in Public for Religious Reasons", in Weithman (ed.), *Religion and Contemporary Liberalism*, pp. 162--181.

[63] *Ibid.*, p. 165.

[64] Peter Laslett, "Introduction" to John Locke, *Two Treatises of Government: a Critical Edition* (New York: Cambridge University Press, 1963), p. 95.

[65] Wolterstorff, "Why We Should", p. 165.

[66] *Ibid.*, p. 168

[67] Quoted in *Ibid.*, p. 173, Wolterstorff's emphasis removed: dangling preposition in original

[68] *Ibid*, p. 173, Wolterstorff's emphasis removed

[69] Again, see Wolterstorff's sarcastic paraphrase of his own misunderstandings: "I'm ready and able to offer such reasons, but I don't in fact do so." -- *Ibid*, p. 174.

[70] *Ibid.*, pp. 177--178.

[71] *Ibid.*, p. 178.

[72] *Ibid.*, p. 180.

[73] Mark Juergensmeyer, *The New Cold War? Religious Nationalism Confronts the Secular State* (Berkeley and Los Angeles: University of California Press, 1993).

[74] I have explained the components of my vision in: *Whose Democracy*, especially pp. 1--16, 59--66, 163--177; and "Liberalizam, Moral i Drustveni Poredak", pp. 2--3, 12--14. 31

- Chapter 8 -

Civic Education And The Liberal Arts

Ralph Ketcham

Introduction

In many parts of the world, especially in nations seeking to institute more democratic governments, there has been widespread and useful attention to the growth of what Vaclav Havel and others have called "civil society": the associations, habits, economic practices, non-governmental organizations, varieties of public media, worker unions, social clubs, and neighborhoods that give citizens opportunities to talk with each other and learn to act together. Civil society nurtures the attitudes and skills of self-government necessary for making democracy genuine and effective rather than a farce or a charade; a civil society acknowledges that good democratic government requires more than freedom of expression, political parties, popular elections, the rule of law, and other formal mechanisms. Schools open to all and the free inquiry there, as well as the growth of local, deliberative forums on public policy are also viewed as essential to healthy democracy.

We must, however, also pay serious attention to the content of the materials and studies designed to foster civil society. For example, in planning the courses of study that encourage responsible citizenship, to the consideration of the processes of government, the modes of policy analysis, and the ways of effective participation, we must add instruction in the ideas of human potential, of social accord, and of justice that must in the long run undergird the practice of democratic citizenship. We must attend, that is, to the values, the aspirations, the world-view that citizens of a self-governing society need to encounter and deliberate about together if they are to fulfill their responsibilities wisely and profoundly. Without such attention and study, the processes and analyses of self-government are likely to lack direction and purpose, or even be manipulated and distorted for all sorts of selfish, nefarious, or tyrannical schemes and intentions. Citizens must be enabled to understand and judge and aspire as well as to participate.

Obvious and important as these may seem for relatively new democracies, they are equally urgent for older democracies whose political cultures, despite the persistence of all the formal mechanisms of popular representation, have become so unfulfilled, dysfunctional, and hostage to special interests that they affront the idea of good government. The alienation, dissatisfaction, and injustice common in democratic polities from North America to New Zealand and from Japan to Jamaica may also rest on a failure of their political cultures to nourish in their citizens the values, judgments and aspirations needed to give guidance and good direction to their participation. We need to acknowledge that there may be ideals and moral purposes and principles that need to be encountered and understood as a critical dimension of responsible democratic citizenship. It may be not enough to build the institutions of civil society and to teach and practice modes of participation. We need citizens who are capable of making self-government be good government, who possess humane, just and principled understandings that can furnish direction and aspiration. These come from a liberal education.

Liberal Education

We must admit that freedom is our ideal and we should have no hesitation in making it the touchstone of our education, of free inquiry, and of diverse studies long traditional in our universities. Common precepts go under many names – Walter Lippmann called them "the tradition of civility," Thomas Jefferson, following the Scottish philosophers, called them "the moral sense, a conscience," while other schools of philosophy have called them "natural law". The United Nations have made them into a "Universal Declaration of Human Rights." All have the capacity, more or less, to gain the general assent of humankind.

Perhaps the best way to grasp the essence of liberal education and its connection with *civic* education is to think of it not so much as a certain substance or content, but as possessing three characteristics: it must be *profound*, it must be *integrated*, and it must be *radical*. In this way liberal education will always be in tension with at least the more pretentious claims of specialized, vocational, and critical studies, because such claims tend, in their preempting of attention, to obscure the wider meaning of the word education itself (to educe; draw forth). What does it mean to be profound? Educationally, at least, it means to read and be exposed to the good, deep knowledge that challenges and then enriches and enlarges the most important concerns one has about oneself and the world one lives in. Its essence is found in the best works of art and literature and history and philosophy the world around.

The requirement that liberal education be *integrated* is of heightened concern in our age of specialization and of reductionist or deconstructionist studies. One prominent executive made the point in remarking that in his world of specialized scholars and sophisticated think tanks and elaborate bureaucracies, there were far too few "experts in the situation as a whole." The deficiency of this lack is apparent enough in the realms of scholarly inquiry and public policy, but in a way it is even more poignantly harmful to young minds seeking meaning in the world they live in and to young citizens seeking to understand their role in government. We must recognize that no matter how important and challenging and brilliantly-presented any specialized courses might be (and thus worthy in their own right), random assemblages of them will seldom amount to more than that.

Elective, specialized studies, of course, are open-ended, diverse, creative, with everyone free to pursue individual interests. But a serious flaw is at least as apparent; there is neither pattern nor effective guidance to help students "get it together." There are no systematic, required courses to give students foundations, and therefore no big pictures into which they might then fit specialized pieces. Large, integrative works are likely to be neglected as attention focuses on the results of "the latest research." Connections between things are likely to receive less emphasis than the examination of the parts. Even less likely is the explanation of pattern and purpose and cosmology, not with the idea of imposing orthodoxy, of course, but simply to give students and citizens-in-training the repeated experience of confronting and considering such integrations.

Finally, liberal education must be *radical*, in that it opens up to young minds something of the range of potential and alternative humankind has attempted, explored and envisioned for itself through time and across space. Only thus can one be free of the confines of one's own (small, narrow, stultifying) world and begin to imagine and pursue a brighter, more beckoning one, however practically difficult its realization might be (awareness of such obstacles, of course, is part of intelligent radicalism). Such radicalness as much searches the present as the past, as much the distant as the close at hand, and as much humankind's inward as outward journeys in pursuit of aspirations that might liberate and ennoble life. In advising a young nephew about religious and philosophic studies Jefferson urged him first to "divest yourself of all convention and prejudice and instead favor novelty and singularity of opinion...Fix reason firmly in her seat, and call to her tribunal every fact, every opinion...Neither believe nor reject anything, because other persons, or description of persons, have rejected or believed it. Your own reason is the only oracle given you by heaven, and you are answerable, not for the rightness, but uprightness of the decision."[1] Unless students experience the exhilaration that goes with such honest inquiry, with such openness to "novelty and singularity of opinion," they risk forever being confined within their biases, limitations, and short-sightedness. Such experience, of course, is the highest purpose of multicultural as well as canonical studies.

Peter Kropotkin wrote in his "Letters to the Young" that they should "ask what kind of world do you want to live in? What do you need to know? What are you good at and want to work at to build that world? Demand that your teachers teach you that." The young, that is, must, if they are to be truly liberated, have had visions set before them, and paths pointed out toward their realization, of fuller, better ways to live. "No idea does more to lift the human spirit and to fan its enthusiasm," Immanuel Kant wrote near the end of his life, "than the very idea of a pure moral character...If constant use of this view were made a principle of private and public education, the state of human morality would improve in short order."[2] Thus, to read the likes of Plato and Marx and M.L. King and Gandhi and C. Milosz, great envisioners of ideals that can challenge orthodoxies and open minds to alternatives, is also an essential part of true liberal education. We see the scope of this need when we recall that the English words "theory" and "theater" both derive from the Greek "thea," which means *the act of seeing*. In the company of Aristotle and Shakespeare, of Hannah Arendt and Milan Kundera, students can be led to "the act of seeing" dimensions and depth previously unknown to them.

Liberal education means, then, to bring students to a liberating sense of the nature of the world they live in and of their own potential as human beings. It would thus seem self-evident that it would have to be profound, integrating, and radical: to be shallow, fragmented, and conventional is to miss the nature of the world and of our human potential and to have trivial answers to the big questions "who am I, what is the world like, what might it be like, and why am I here?" In addition to any specificities – in vocation, in life-style, in nationality as well as of race, class, or gender – we must as well be full, liberated human beings, and citizens of one's country and of the world. Indeed, we might say that any rich understanding of what those categories really amount to must rest on the qualities that infuse genuine liberal education. In a kind of secular version of the Puritan general and personal callings, liberal education provides the generality and purpose within which our more particular identities and nationalities find meaning and direction. In the Puritan case, as explained by a sixteenth-century English theologian, William Perkins, "a personal calling is the execution of some particular office, arising [from diversity of talents among people], as for example the calling of a magistrate to execute the office of government,...the office of a minister is to execute the duty of teaching his people, [and] the office of a physician is to put in practice the good means whereby life and health are preserved." Perkins explains further, though, that "the final cause or end of every calling...is for the common good; that is, for the benefit and good estate of mankind...The common good of men stands in this, not only that they live, but that they live well, in righteousness and holiness, and consequently in true happiness."[3] The language may be a bit strange to modern ears, but the point is clear: we all have our particular vocations and niches and need to learn and be them with skill and faithfulness, but we must also fit these particular tasks and identities into larger patterns of meaning and purpose and citizenship. The particular calling is the special province of the vocational or professional school, but the general calling, the placing of these particulars in a wider context, a wiser understanding, and a richer imagination, is the function of liberal and civic education. Human nature requires the fulfillment of both callings.

The point about liberal (liberating, freeing) education meaning not merely the absence of restraint on a student's inquiries, but more profoundly requiring that the student's mind be *furnished* with deep and integrating and radical questions and aspirations was made with poignant force in 1996 by the reformer/revolutionist Daw Aung San Suu Kyi shortly after her partial release from six years of house arrest in Burma-Myanmar. Asked whether she was finally truly free, she replied:

> "Well, I am acting as though I'm free. I do what I think I should, but to be free? What does that mean?...I think to be free is to be able to do what you think is right [Confucius, Jesus, and Hegel, among others, have made the same point], and in that sense I felt very free – even under house arrest. Because it was my choice. I knew I could leave anytime. I just had to say, 'I'm not going to do politics anymore.' But it was my choice to be involved in the democracy movement. So, I was perfectly free."[4]

"To be free is to be able to do what you think is right." So, a truly liberal and liberating education gives one a sense of high ideals drawn from a wide exposure to them, and then a sense of efficacy about how to be involved in the real world.

Civic Education

This idea of liberal education as informing a "general calling" has a special meaning in the public life of a liberal democratic society. It means the sort of education required by *all* people in such a society, whatever their particular skills or group identity or walks of life, in order for them to perform their *public office as citizens*. Jefferson put it simply in his first proposal, in 1779, for a system of universal primary education suited to the United States' new independent status: all citizens thus "would be qualified to understand their rights, to maintain them, and to exercise with intelligence their parts in self-government." Such education, he explained to John Adams after each had served as President of the United States, "would raise the mass of the people to the high ground of moral respectability necessary to their own safety, and to orderly government...Worth and genius would thus be sought out from every condition of life, and completely prepared by education for defeating the competition of wealth and birth for public trusts." To skeptics who thought this too high an idealism Jefferson replied, "if we think [the people] not enlightened enough to exercise their control [over government] with a wholesome discretion, the remedy is not to take it from them, but to inform their discretion through education."[5]

Horace Mann, an early theorist of public education in the United States, picked up Jefferson's argument when he pointed out to the people of Massachusetts in 1845 that "one of the highest and most valuable objects, to which the influence of a school can be made conducive, consists in training our children in self-government." "A republican form of government, without intelligence in the people," Mann continued, "must be, on a vast scale, what a mad-house, without superintendent, or keepers, would be, on a small one...The very terms, *Public School*, and *Common School*, bear upon their face, that they are schools which the children of the entire community may attend. Every man...is taxed for their support...on the same principle that he would be taxed to defend the nation against foreign invasion,...because the general prevalence of ignorance, superstition, and vice, will breed Goth and Vandal at home, more fatal to the public well-being, than any Goth or Vandal from abroad." Mann argued as well that the development of rational intelligence, the training of young people so that they might rise from poverty and ignorance, the instruction in the processes of American government, and the inculcation of a morality suited to public enlightenment were all vital parts of a system of universal public education. "Is it obvious," Mann asked, "for the high purpose of training an American child to...become a constituent part of a self-governing people...that...the law by which he is bound should be made intelligible to him; and as soon as his capacity will admit, that the reasons on which it is founded, should be made as intelligible as the law itself?"[6]

Mann's theory of *public* education thus was an idea guided fundamentally by its *public purpose*. He advocated in Massachusetts a system of education funded by the state (thus public in one sense), and he intended these schools be open to every child (thus public in yet another sense), but even more, he was intent on the stake the public had in them to prepare young people to be good citizens. Public education, then, whether conducted in state-supported, or privately or religiously operated schools, was essential for every child because each would become a member of the public and thus require education for that role. It is therefore the *public* and not the *private* benefits of universal education which loom largest.

To the concern of Jefferson and Horace Mann for "training our children in self-government," what can we add about education for citizenship in 2000? I would suggest, following the distinguished philosopher Joseph Tussman,[8] that we begin by regarding the citizen in a democracy as an office-holder in government. That is, in discussing, voting, and acting in a self-governing society, the citizen is part, actually one of the ultimate parts, of the government itself. Thus, the role differs only in degree from that of any elected or appointed official, or even from that of a monarch in a society ruled by one person. The essential obligation this entails, as we expect (though don't always receive) from all office holders, is a perspective and habit that puts the public interest, the good of the country as a whole, above private, selfish, dynastic, class, race, gender, or any other partial interest. In educating young people for the office of citizen, then, we must start and end with nourishing the essential, public-spirited stance expected of any public official. The skills of data collection, policy analysis, and communication taught by social scientists are important and useful, and the nourishment of cultural and group identities can be vital and constructive, but standing by themselves they leave the political decision-maker, the citizen, without guidance at crucial points. That guidance can only properly come from an enlarged and disciplined way of looking at public affairs, best understood as part of liberal education.

A cynic is inclined, at this point, to ask for a definition of "public spirit," or "the public interest," or even to question whether such an idea can have an objective meaning. The public interest is often defined simply as the resultant of the self-interested forces at work in the political arena. Hence, in a free society it receives its definition from the interplay of a multitude of special interests. It neither assumes nor requires that any public interest objectively understood either exist or be sought directly by anybody. This view is beguiling because it allows, even encourages, individuals and groups to pursue their own interests, and because it relieves everyone – citizens as well as higher officials – from having to think about the common good. Indeed, such thought is often held to be delusive nonsense at best and the sure path to totalitarian bigotry – the closed society – at worst. Deconstructionist thought is similarly subjectivist and cynical: all expression of value is conditional, reflecting relation to political dominance, and all claims to objectivity or universality are merely self-serving delusions or masks.

Eighteenth century political discourse took the idea of public interest seriously and defined it as the opposite of corruption, which meant any form of self-seeking or bribery or partiality or factional spirit that opposed or ignored or defiled the well-being of the nation as a whole. Thus, the public good consisted of the intention first to discern, through rational discourse, the idea of the interest of the whole, and second to work together to give effect to that idea. Though the assumption existed that there was such an objective good (sometimes thought of as natural law or natural right), more directly on the agenda was the need to *seek* it, deliberately, reasonably, and disinterestedly. Of course it was recognized that human beings were flawed and in part indelibly selfish, but it was also widely believed that people – ordinary people at least as much as the learned and the powerful and the wealthy – has some potential, at least, for more noble thought and conduct. There *is* a potential capacity in human beings, that is, for in some degree rising above narrow and self-serving states of mind which can be nourished, *educed*, drawn forth in our public schools and our universities. If that's not true, then democracy is not likely in the long run to make a constructive contribution to human history. Making such a point, furthermore, calls for the sort of profundity, integration, and radicalism fundamental to liberal and civic education.

The drawing forth of this capacity requires initially a proper perspective. The public interest can be said to begin with an interest in the public, the taking seriously of the existence of a political community of which one is a part and the possibility of participating usefully in its common affairs. Such a perspective also allows potentially for a result greater than the sum of the parts arising from the public intentions of the members. Thus, the central need in educating for the office of citizen is to encourage an interest in the public as an objective reality and as an approach both within human potential and capable of yielding unpredictable benefits. Through such a process, a trust and capacity for mutual aid are nourished which have the potential to transform an individual or a group member into a citizen.

Such an idea of citizenship, of course, has an ancient and honored lineage and thus offers teachers of history and philosophy inspiring opportunities. It was central to Aristotle's argument that good government depended on the public virtue of those who ruled (all the citizens in a constitutional polity) and to the Renaissance "civic republican" model requiring an independent, reasonable, and responsible citizenry. It was also central to Jefferson, Horace Mann, John Dewey, and other American proponents of democratic citizenship. All attended primarily to the quality of the parts, the nourishment of the vital public spirit as well as the practical skills of those who would take part in self-government. In our day, despite the pre-occupation of generations of social scientists with research skills and policy analysis and the useful application of them to public life, the need for public spirit and proper perspective remains as strong as ever.

Lest this approach seem unduly utopian about the capacity of human beings to achieve a public-spirited posture, let us remember first the possibly even greater utopianism of supposing that all is fine in democratic societies when *no one* is expected or even encouraged to achieve such a perspective, when it is supposed sufficient to simply open up the political process to all people, groups, and interests, and then deconstruct and analyze various policies. Such a dynamic *might* work well, or at least be the best we can do in a free and pluralistic society, but in our interdependent world, one suspects this is less and less likely to suffice. Problems of economic development and global ecology and world peace may in our day require the forethought, reasoned approach, and concern for the good of the whole central to the office of the citizen – and may *not* be amenable to a "sum of the parts" approach. Instead, that is, of being naïvely optimistic about human nature, the encouragement of the human potential for a vision beyond the merely subjective and the narrowly selfish may, in the twenty-first century, be the only practical thing left for us – or at least more practical than the very dubious optimism of supposing everything will be all right if we simply pursue our own special interests in free and open political arenas. Even more problematic are the assumptions or assertions that such higher ideas of human potential are delusive.

The American philosopher Reinhold Niebuhr noted in 1944 that "man's capacity for justice makes democracy possible; but man's inclination to injustice makes democracy necessary."[9] Though attention usually focuses on the hard-headed insight that the human tendency to abuse power makes its dispersal the most effective way to prevent corruption and tyranny (bad government), as a one-person one-vote government best exemplifies, the other part of Niebuhr's vindication of democracy needs equal emphasis. Niebuhr argues that human capacity (*potential* if not, at any given time or place, actual practice) in some degree to sense what is fair, to understand right and wrong, to reason effectively, to exhibit compassion for others, and to act on behalf these qualities, is as much a part of human nature as the indelible tendencies (also in varying degree) toward greed, short-sightedness, and partiality for our own interests. In fact, the existence of both tendencies is what makes the problem of human government both complex and interesting, and teaching about it essential to civic education. Niebuhr's argument precisely follows that of James Madison: "If men were angels," he observed in the *Federalist*, "no government would be necessary." Yet, if the fundamental principle of some human capacity for reason and good judgement were impeached, then democracy would likely provide bad government – and a benevolent despot might even be better. "In framing a government...by men over men," Madison concluded, "auxiliary precautions" such as checks and balances and a large, pluralistic country were necessary, but a "dependence on the people [was still] the primary control on the government."[10]

It helps at this point to keep in mind that both Locke and Aristotle undergird this idea of democratic government. From Aristotle we learn, first, that human beings are "political animals", in that to govern and be governed are essential, fulfilling parts of their nature, and thus that to have government, to be part of a polity, is potentially rewarding and ennobling. Government is vitally important to the quality of life in any society, as a source of constructive guidance for the common life, and as an agent for such collective action as the polity might decide to undertake. Second, and following from this, Aristotle teaches us to judge government most essentially by the quality of the result – the characteristics of the society governed – rather than by the number who govern. That

- 155 -

is, since government is a crucial, positive part of society, then of course judgement of it has to rest on the degree to which it fulfills its obligations – to establish justice, promote the general welfare, and so on.

Locke adds the proposition that self-government, eventually government by all those governed, is the only just form. This eliminates the good forms of government by one and by a few validated by Aristotle, and thus narrows the critical need: to make government by the many result in good government. Once both the Aristotelian and the Lockean imperative are joined, the fundamental problems of democracy are in focus: how can those at the foundation of government – all the people – be nurtured so that they will be good rulers (essentially, possess the public spirit to attend to the common good), and how can the government be framed to ensure both efficient administration and fidelity to the people?

Such propositions create conditional democrats who endorse it only in so far as there are prospects that it might result in good government. This requires that government respect and protect the rights of the people (a Lockean dictum), but just as critically, that the people, as governors, take thought collectively to pursue the good of society as a whole (an Aristotelian dictum). This dual commitment is the continuing wager of any long experiment in democracy: that self-government can be good government.

The requirement to tie together the liberal arts, civic education, and good government stands out. Leaders need a thorough and sophisticated education in arts, letters, science, philosophy, and public right in order to fulfill the demanding tasks before them. They have much to do to enhance and promote "the good society." To properly choose and support such leaders, and to be able to judge them, and replace them if necessary, the people need to be properly educated for *their* public task. Implicitly, the more the principles of the liberal arts permeate in some fashion all levels of education, and the more larger portions of the people have access to liberal studies, the more cultivation there would be of public virtue. And only its widespread existence in a society, among all officers from citizens to senators and presidents, can result in the fulfillment of the human potential for an ennobled common life – that is, good democratic government.

Every bit of public-spiritedness nourished in a student or a worker or a leader provides a certain leaven in society that can yield small benefit in small ways – almost immediately. Every teacher knows such efficacy is occasionally possible any day in any classroom with some student, and any village can experience occasionally the useful influence of even one citizen or official qualifuied in this way. Within this understanding, teachers, practitioners, and students of civic education and the liberal arts stand at the very portals of good democratic government, with some degree of potential and efficacy at their command. The foundational need of any democratic society, as public philosophers from Aristotle to Jefferson and Vaclav Havel have explained (and practiced), is that if citizens seem "not enlightened enough...to exercise with wholesome discretion their part in self-government," the answer is not to take that part from them, but "to inform their discretion through education" – that's the task of liberal and civic education.

Endnotes

[1] Jefferson to Peter Carr, August 10, 1787; Merrill Peterson, (ed.), *The Portable Thomas Jefferson* (N.Y., 1975), pp. 425-427.

[2] Immanuel Kant, *On the Old Saw: That It May Be Right in Theory, but it Won't Work in Practice* (1793), (trans. E.B. Ashton, University of Pennsylvania Press, 1974), p. 54.

[3] William Perkins, "A Treatise of the Vocations or Callings of Men" (1626-1631), reprinted in E.S. Morgan, (ed.), *Puritan Political Ideas* (Indianapolis, 1965), pp. 39, 49-50.

[4] Claudia Dreifus, "The Passion of Suu Kyi," *New York Times Magazine,* January 7, 1996, p. 34.

[5] Jefferson "Autobiography," 1821, in Adrienne Koch and William Peden, (eds.), *The Life and Selected Writings of Thomas Jefferson* (Modern Library, 1944), p. 52; Jefferson to John Adams, Oct. 28, 1813, in Lester Cappon, (ed.), *The Adams-Jefferson Letters* (2 vols., Chapel Hill, N.C., 1959), II, pp. 387-391; Jefferson to W.C. Jarvis, Sept. 28, 1820, in Edward Dumbold, (ed.), *The Political Writings of Thomas Jefferson* (Indianapolis, 1955), p. 93.

[6] Mann, ninth and twelfth *Annual Reports*, 1845 and 1848; reprinted in S.A. Rippa, (ed.), *Educational Ideas in America* (N.Y., 1969), pp. 195-202.

[8] Joseph Tussman, *Obligation and the Body Politic* (N.Y., 1960).

[9] Reinhold Niebuhr, *The Children of Light and the Children of Darkness* (N.Y., 1944), xiii.

[10] Federalist Nos. 51 and 57; Clinton Rossiter, (ed.), *The Federalist Papers* (N.Y., 1962), pp. 322, 350-353.

- Chapter 9 -

Civic Education And The Concept Of Differentiated-Citizenship

Slavko Gaber

The words 'citizen' and 'citizenship' are powerful words. They speak of respect, of rights, of dignity.' (N. Fraser, L. Gordon, 1994, 90)

Introduction

It seems that two hundred years after people were proudly addressed as *citoyens*, the term has been gaining ground again since the fall of the Berlin Wall. Alain Touraine claims that "without the awareness of belonging to a political community (*collectivité*) in a certain nation ... there is, as a rule, no democracy... Democracy is founded on the commitment of the citizens to the state" (1994, 97). Together with the concept of representative democracy, "citizenship became a fashionable concept all over the political spectrum" (Dahrendorf 1994, 12) at the end of the 1980s. On the one hand it is true that the eighties saw a revived debate on citizenship and the quality of citizenship, but on the other hand, almost at the same time (partly in the eighties, partly in the nineties) the concept of citizenship became part of the self-conscious, rather puffed-up rhetoric which was especially appropriate for newly-formed states of East and Central Europe at the beginning of the nineties.

Civic education in various forms is often found in this context as one of the necessary satellites of the concept of citizenship and an important element of the enlightenment of the newly-formed nations, which have arisen from the ruins of socialism.

At the end of the 1980s and at the beginning of the 1990s, the knowledge of the fundamental rights, the freedom of speech, the rights of assembly and political organisation and similar rights was the "bread and butter" of the emergence of liberal democracies, including the democracy in Slovenia. The fight against the (in)famous *Article 133* which sanctioned the "verbal offence", gatherings in the *Revolution Square* in Ljubljana, writing drafts and proposals of the new constitution, the establishment of parapolitical parties, which were caught unawares in the middle of the struggle for power: all these represented a practical form of *civic education*. Without any international colloquiums we faced the most important lessons in civic education, persistently and deliberately, often seeking theoretical foundations for our actions. Such were the eighties, so began the nineties.

After the fall of the Berlin Wall, after Slovenia gained independence and after war broke out in the Balkans, we soon found ourselves in a totally different position. With the decrease in enthusiasm, the development of the real problems, and the establishment of new democratic structures, there also arose the need forr special attention to human rights, and the need for the 'Enlightened West' to show us, through various organisations, what fundamental human rights were all about. Various enlighteners came to Slovenia, very attractive publications of the Council of Europe were published, teachers were trained, and thousands of refugees led us to talk about tolerance and to support the"'all equal - all different" campaign, which was quite successful.

By sticking to the aforementioned conduct, both Slovenian and the foreign experts, the public, and the various civil entities and state institutions, showed a lack of social imagination; there was no deliberate consideration of the question of civic education. In an area like Slovenia, it *is* important to discuss civic education by discussing human rights and by highlighting the need for tolerance of people with different points of view; however, that was and it is not enough. Why?

Because we underestimated the civility formation background. During the so-called Slovenian Spring, the citizens not only came to understand but also to gain, by fighting, most of the civil and political rights, which were seriously underrated by the old regime, but which were not totally suppressed in the decade prior to its demise. It is possible and necessary to talk about civil and political rights to people who gathered almost a million signatures in support of the Albanians from the Kosovo region in 1989, who peacefully demonstrated for days and demanded that "the Four", open critics of the system, be released from military prison and that the people be given the right to political organisation and the use of their mother tongue (including in the military court). These same people had decided in favour of independence in a referendum, had repulsed the attack of the Federal Army and had taken care of tens of thousands of refugees. To now represent these rights to them as an astounding revelation is not particularly sensible.

An additional *problematic* element of propagating the aforementioned rights - because one can agree with Dahrendorf (1994) that the "integrity of the person, due process of law, freedom of speech and other rights of expression [represent the] hard core of fundamental and indispensable rights" (13) - is the fact that, in the last decade, the West fatally belittled the importance of the intertwined democratic and national drive.

Yugoslavia, in fear of disintegration, was erroneously betting on common citizenship and the centralism of the totalitarian regime. These ideas came from the strongest republic, which was trying to subdue the rest of the country by force. People were meeting and taking care of refugees in their homes, at their neighbours, in their towns and schools. The basic concern of liberal democracies, for fundamental human rights, was shown by the people. Daily news of ethnic cleansing, and of death and rape replaced the news of the intervention of liberal democracies who could have helped to end the suffering of people and simultaneously have stopped the escalation of nationalism motivated by these events. These and other facts of the eighties and nineties represent the background of the debate on civic education in the regions and countries around Slovenia.

On the other hand, if we keep on stressing only civil and political rights in the former socialist countries, we miss the real difficulties regarding the expansion of the concept of citizenship, which were mainly due to the pressure for social rights by the so-called workers' movements in Europe, and (whether we like it or not) to the work of differently oriented socialist and communist parties at the end of the nineteenth and in the first half of the twentieth centuries. The *ancien régime* in these regions underestimated the question of political rights which were often denied and withheld from us, especially with reference to the question of multiparty political organisation. However, we must not forget that in Slovenia the old regime had recognised the right to self-management or co-management in industry. Although it was rather insensitive to civil rights, the constitution gave women, for example, the right of abortion. With reference to social rights there was almost full-scale employment, a relatively high social security, and, in addition, a fair number of the so-called national rights. Furthermore, since the citizens actively practised citizenship at least twice, when they built an independent state, and when they went through the transition from socialism to liberal democracy, and even before that, when they were called upon to participate in active citizenship in the form of self-management, they were familiar with exaggerated appeals to the people regarding citizenship[1]. They had learnt scepticism, mainly because they had learnt from everyday-life experience that the old regime, which they considered not good enough, properly provided for social rights for the vast majority of the population. Since the unemployment rate at the turn of the decade was merely 1.3%, we cannot talk about the 'underclass' experience in Slovenia. The experience of today, when unemployment is at least five times greater even according to the International Labour Organisation standards, teaches them that, despite the fact that the rate is not so critical according to the EU standards, everything is not so black and white.

Civic Education and Citizenship

The question of civic education in former socialist countries is, of course, by definition the question of the awareness of the fundamental human rights from among civil and political rights. A discussion of human rights must be complemented by a discussion

- 162 -

of social rights. *If we avoid the issue of social rights, we call back to life the forces of the old regime.* Admittedly, Slovenia is not a good example for this, but we can find plenty of examples in some other former socialist countries. If what Nancy Fraser and Linda Gordon claim is true, namely that the "expression 'social citizenship' is almost never heard in public debate in the United States today" (1994, 91), and if we accept this, we also have to take into account that in the regions which experienced socialism, something like this is basically questionable. Even if it is true that the emergence of an underclass is "economically feasible and politically riskless" (Dahrendorf 1994, 15), the warning of the same author remains valid - that by not dealing with the question of the hard-core unemployed and the 'redundant', the system "betrays a readiness to suspend the basic values of citizenship - equal rights to participation for all." Dahrendorf goes on to say that if we allow five per cent to be denied access to our civic community, we should not be surprised if doubts about the validity of our values spread throughout the social fabric (*Ibid*, 15-16).

What conclusions can we draw on the basis of the experience described above? *Civic education must be conceptualised in such a way that it is for and about real people, their existence, and the problems they are dealing with; it must tell a story which is their story.*

The presentation of citizenship rights and duties which are not relevant to the actual problems of concrete populations and generations is doomed to failure, despite all the good intentions and high-quality publications on civic education. If we are to develop liberal democracies well in the former socialist countries, we must not put aside the so-called social rights and run away from discussing questions relating to the concept of citizenship rights and individual groups.

The list of solutions to the problems of dealing with crises in individual liberal democracies or parts of democratic countries seems to support the claim that we are looking at a process of the expansion and supplementation of citizenship rigths. Waldron justifiably emphasises, "There is talk today of a 'new generation' of human rights" (1993, 339). The greatest shifts can be observed in meeting the demands for the special treatment of the questions of representation, the rights of women and of different ethnic groups. The implementation of the right to self-determination is an issue in the former Soviet Union, and for example in the Baltic states and in other countries such as Yugoslavia. There are even requests for greater autonomy in such countries as the United Kingdom and Spain. There are also important demands for the implementation of special rights for women and ethnic rights.

After the implementation of the so-called first generation of citizenship rights (such as free speech, religious liberty, the right not to be tortured, the right for a fair trial (*Ibid*, 5)) and of the second-generation rights, chiefly socio-economic rights, we obviously face the demands for the implementation of third-generation rights.

Despite various open questions related to the discussion of the new generation of rights and their expansion in general, we can say that they typically have a "communal and nonindividualistic character" (*Ibid*) "Third-generation rights are the solidarity rights of communities .... They include minority language rights, the right to national self-determination, and the rights that people may have to diffuse goods such as peace ...." (*Ibid*, 5).

Similar to the preceding historically generated generations of rights, the emergence of third-generation rights[2] and the increasing number of claims for the expansion of citizenship rights to individual groups raises a logical question: will the "rise of group-based claims further erode the sense of shared civic purpose and solidarity?" (Kymlicka 1998, 168). In order to answer the question about the degree of the above-mentioned danger, we should take a closer look at the question concerning "group-based" claims and rights.

Kymlicka (his book *Multicultural Citizenship* will form the basis of our further discussion) highlights that some theorists of the liberal orientation, such as John Rawls, share the opinion of John Porter that the "organization of society on the basis of rights or claims that derive from group membership is sharply opposed to the concept of citizenship" (cf. *Ibid.*, 167). In our view, the author is justified in emphasising that the thesis on the concept of differentiated citizenship as being a contradiction in terms is overstated. "If differentiated citizenship is defined as the adoption of group specific, polyethnic representation, or self-government, then virtually every modern democracy recognizes some form of it" (*Ibid.*, 167-168). Furthermore, modern democracies do not recognise a form of differentiated citizenship by mistake. They recognise it because they are, one way or another, simply not in a position to avoid it. There are claims to the effect that group-differentiated citizenship ceases to be a device to cultivate a sense of community and a common sense of purpose. Ireland, former Yugoslavia, the Kosovo region, Belgium, Canada and many other countries or communities are not in a position to act in accordance with such a theoretical approach. In Macedonia, Kosovo, Northern Ireland, Bosnia and Herzegovina it is of course important and sensible to explain how the introduction of special rights for certain groups of people is contrary to the idea that citizenship is a "forum where people transcend their differences and think about [the] good of all citizens" (*Ibid.*, 168); however, beyond certain limits such an attitude is counter-productive. Macedonia has to face the fact that a third of its population is ethnically Albanian, especially in the area bordering Albania, and they want rights in the field of education - including higher education - and in some other fields. Ignoring the situation in Kosovo and denying the high degree of its autonomy in the socialist Yugoslavia led first to complete civil disobedience and finally to war. On the other hand, Canada (cf. Kymlicka 1996) as a federal state is better off since the introduction of "asymetrical federalism" which grants Quebec powers not given to other provinces" (*Ibid.*, 156). The same applies to the fact that in Slovenia, members of Italian and Hungarian ethnic minorities have special rights in the fields of education, culture and special representatives in the national parliament, which has *increased rather than diminished their sense of citizenship*. At first glance, it seems that the insistence on the so-called common citizenship - a good example is Yugoslavia - in relation to the newly-formed democracies represented the cover-up of the totalitarian rule and helped diminish the sense of citizenship.

On the basis of the reflection of changes in citizenship and citizenship rights, it seems right to support, at least in principle, the idea of the *combination* of *common citizenship* and *differentiated-citizenship* where the latter approach complements and is not necessarily the opposite of the former one. We could even say that the absence of theory and politics which considers differentiated-citizenship as a legitimate (but not unquestionable) part of theoretical and political confrontation with the reality of group-differentiated society, is the generator of escalated conflicts and loss of trust in the essential elements of common citizenship. Common citizenship is here defined as: (a) the first generation of citizenship rights (Waldron 1993), which can be described as "the civic element of citizenship" - composed of the rights necessary for individual freedom and institutions most directly associated with the rule of law and the system of courts - and (b) as "the political part of citizenship"- consisting of the right to participate in the exercise of political power (Barbalet 1988, 6).[3]

Taking into account the difficulties arising from the recognition and implementation of the concept of group-differentiated rights it is perhaps wise to point out the problems and the gradual process of the implementation of the first two generations or the first three elements of citizenship rights. Marshall explains the formation of the aforementioned elements of citizenship rights as a relatively complex process "of fusion and of separation. The fusion was geographical, the separation functional" (Marshall 1950, 12). The first important step in the introduction of citizenship rights of the first part or element, civil rights, dates from the twelfth century. The story of the development of the parliament and political rights is complicated. As far as social rights are concerned, they were at first locally rooted, "gradually dissolved", then subsumed into *Poor Law*, and later gradually implemented through the confrontation between liberal and socialist ideas. Although we should point out the liberal awareness of the fact that the implementation of civil liberties is not possible without "enjoying a fair degree of material security"(Waldron 1993, 5), there remains the correct deliberation about the inclusion of social rights (especially workers' rights) into the sphere of citizenship rights as an element radically cutting in between the revolutionary approach, which tries to eradicate bourgeois exploitation, and the democratic approach, which introduces social rights into the field of social equity and remains within the boundaries of representative democracy (cf. Touraine 1994, especially Chapter II).[4]

Differentiated Citizenship

The comprehension of citizenship is changing and requires careful deliberation about at least three other elements of the accommodation of group-rights. Kymlicka (1994, 1996) refers to three forms of group-differentiated citizenship. In discussing the case of a Canadian debate (1996) on citizenship rights, he highlights *special representation rights, polyethnic rights, and self-government rights*. We will examine each in turn.

The debate on *special representation rights*, which can be noticed in national minorities and ethnic groups as well (we will return to them later), is at least as old as the debate on representative democracy. As a matter of fact we could claim that the classic - Burke's - concept of representative democracy as citizenship representation emerged from the confrontation with delegating representatives of individual groups or classes of the population. What about the issue of representative democracy? Citizenship democracy is founded on the assumption of the representative *of the whole people*, a representative who as such is not tied to any class or individual party or group of voters. This assumption is clearly defined in the majority of modern constitutions. It is written in Article 82 of the Slovenian constitution. However, in reality there has been, for over two centuries, an inner tension between classic concepts of citizenship and classic representation. Political structures of contemporary states with: (a) bicameral structure of their parliaments, which often serve to represent individual groups and local entities (provinces), and (b) with the elements of different kinds of representation in lower chambers of parliaments (for example, the representation of minorities, setting gender quotas, etc.), point out that the inner tension between the general and particular or group representation is written into the structure of liberal democracies. The feeling that the "political process is 'unrepresentative', in the sense that it fails to reflect the diversity of the population" (Kymlicka 1996, 157) does not apply only to Canada - it can effortlessly be generalised to a vast majority of representative democracies. It does not relate just to the issue of "presence" (A. Phillips 1995 and 1996); ultimately, the rule highlights the desire of people for a delegate model of democracy.

The question of the introduction of group representation demands special treatment; therefore we will limit it to two remarks. Firstly: it is obvious that mere citizenship representation *does not suffice* in the reality of political systems. Many countries thus decide on local representation, and/or representation of individual groups (e.g. ethnic minorities or women). Thus we are not facing the question 'inclusion or not' - allowing the presence of groups' interests in decision-making in the system of parliamentary democracy or not - the real question is where (lower, upper chamber); how much power we give to group interests (presence only or ...); which groups represent an entity still appropriate for the presence/representation in parliaments. Secondly: (this remark relates to the question arising from a possible agreement with the first remark) how do we choose the present or the representatives of a particular group in representative bodies? There are obviously many questions regarding representation. Here it seems a good place to stress the need for various mechanisms of inclusion and to point out the fact that Hare and J. S. Mill developed the so-called single transferable vote system in the nineteenth century (around the turn of the eighteen-fifties) which offers solutions to a fair number of the above-mentioned questions and at the same time keeps citizenship and diffrentiated-citizenship alive.

The issues of *polyethnic, self-governance and self-determination* rights are quite another matter. Lehning illustrates his consideration of *polyethnic rights* with an example of 'state neutrality' in the field of education. Polyethnic society should encourage "education in shared political values, and the political virtues of toleration ..." (1998, 230) and diversity. Private schools should go a step further from shared values and should teach children, apart from the core or standard curriculum, for example "the specifics of their own Islamic culture, religion and language" (*Ibid.*, 231). However, the neutrality of the state does not suffice in these societies. "Minority groups within contemporary democracies sometimes claim that gaining formal equal democratic liberal citizenship is not enough as it does not capture their demand for the inclusion of their collective identities in the public sphere" (*Ibid.* 232). The desire of ethnic minorities in Canada for exemption from certain rules is described by Kymlicka (1998) as a proof "that members of minority groups want to participate within mainstream society" (170). Sikhs who wanted to join the Royal Canadian Mounted Police are such an exemption because of their religious requirement to wear a turban; they wanted to be exempted from the requirements regarding official uniform ceremonial headgear. A similar demand was expressed also by Jews. Many people consider such exemptions as a "sign of disrespect for 'national symbols'" (*Ibid.*); however, the author is right in pointing out that the demands of the members of the aforementioned religious communities in fact reflected their wish to become part of the wider society. In this respect it seems totally inappropriate to mark such wishes as "rights prompting 'ghettoization' or 'balkanization'" (*Ibid.*, 171). Contrary to the suppositions of the critics of polyethnic rights, these rights do not hinder immigrants in their social integration: the "experience to date suggests that first- and second-generation immigrants who remain proud of their heritage are also among the most patriotic citizens of their new country." (*Ibid.*) In their wish to integrate and accommodate they only desire to gain recognition of the value of their cultural heritage - in order not to subordinate the new culture to their own but to be able to survive with their culture in the new one. The incapability or unreadiness of the majority nation to grasp this integration as the acceptance of the new culture is, in Kymlicka's view, due to "a racist or xenophobic fear of these new immigrant groups" (*Ibid.*, 172). In principle, this case once again does not pose the question of whether an individual group can be integrated into society by being granted special rights or not. The questions arising from the acceptance of the need for this kind of rights are partly the same as those from the discussion of the issue of special representation rights: "What kind of minority groups should get those rights?" (Lehning 1998, 234) What is the basis for granting those rights - language, religion, ethnic membership? How big should such a group be in order to qualify for such rights? Who is the claimant for these rights? Who is eventually granting those rights? (*Ibid.*).

The questions regarding the rights of groups in differentiated citizenship do not stop here. Kymlicka (1998) thus highlights a new challenge issued by the demand for *self-determination and self-government rights*. If polyethnic rights and representation rights "can promote social integration and political unity, self-government rights pose more serious challenge to the integrative function of citizenship" (174). Since self-government presupposes the right to self-determination, it is not only the "most complete case of differentiated citizenship" (*Ibid.*, 175), but also a cause of serious worry for those who are in favour of the concept of common citizenship. The possible and the actual concern for the interests of one's own nation in a multinational state is thus regarded as something for which it "is not clear that ... would support solidarity and cohesiveness in liberal society." (Lehning 1998, 233)

It should not be denied that in discussing self-determination and self-government rights we are not dealing with the demand for the inclusion of one's own particularity into the whole; we are dealing with the permanent demand of individual units of the federation or even confederation for the right of self-determination and the formation of a separate political entity, which, if so decided, one day can no longer be part of the existent state. Yugoslavia is a typical example of such a state and for many a most welcome proof for the claim that "self-government rights ... seem to open the door for separation and secession and do not have an integrative function." (Lehning, 233)

Kymlicka regards self-government rights as "the most complete case of differentiated citizenship" (Kymlicka, 175). He emphasises that national entities with the above-mentioned kind of rights consider their subjectivity as the original one and the federal or confederate subjectivity as the derived one. There is only one step from this kind of approach to the wish "to ignore the demands of national minorities, [and] avoid any reference to such groups in the constitution." (*Ibid.*)

In line with common citizenship strategy for dealing with cultural pluralism, many multi-national or at least multi-ethnic states wish to circumvent the actual and mostly justified demands for self-government rights and replace them with the cultural-pluralism right. Kymlicka emphasises that the use of common citizenship strategy which believes that multi-national states can be organised without self-government strategy only "aggravates alienation among national minorities and increases the desire for secession" (176). Contrary to the Rawls's expectation that common citizenship promotes the political virtues of reasonableness and sense of fairness, a spirit of compromise and readiness to meet others halfway, "common citizenship may in fact threaten these virtues" (*Ibid.*, 176).

The case of Yugoslavia in the past and the case of Kosovo today show what can happen when the authorities, with the help from the world's powers, believe that the concept of common citizenship is the guardian of a possible democracy, while federalisation, confederalisation or even the emergence of new states are, by definition, instances of 'balkanisation' and 'tribalisation'. The case of Montenegro in the Balkans is new test of this point of view, especially with the fact remaining that changing national awareness is a very difficult task to perform, and on the other hand with the fact that "claims to self-government are here to stay, [and] we have no choice but to try to accommodate them." (*Ibid.*, 178)

Kymlicka is therefore right in claiming that this kind of "arrangement diminishes the likelihood of violent conflict." (*Ibid.*)

The approach described above is of course far from being unquestionable, but it is necessary and much more appropriate to deal with the reality of concrete democracies than the denial of the necessity and relevance of the recognition of the demands for group rights - in this case ethnic ones.

In my opinion it is crucial to recognise ethnic rights not only as negative (regardless of the race, ethnic membership, etc.) but also, in the framework of citizenship rights, as positive rights, as *provisions and entitlements*. They are not something to be afraid of like the return of the Real into the sphere of symbolic organisation of the modern western world - threats with Islam or tribalism, which is in opposition with liberal democracy. Co-existence of the national and democracy is obviously essential and necessary even today. Habermas emphasises that "citizenship was never conceptually tied to national identity" (1994, 23), but at the same time highlights the connection between republicanism and nationalism as well as the historical link between democracy and the nation-state. "The nation state provided both the infrastructure for rational administration and the legal frame for free individual and collective action" (*Ibid.*, 21); moreover, "the nation state laid the foundations for cultural and ethnic homogeneity on the basis of which it then proved possible to push ahead with the democratization .... The nation-state and democracy are the twins born of the French Revolution." (*Ibid.*, 22) Although the same author suggests that the modern concept of the nation-state, "loosening the semantic connections between national citizenship and national identity takes into account that the classic form of the nation-state is at present disintegrating"(*Ibid.*, 21), the fact remains that even in the process of formation of the European Union the "sort of nation-state we have seen to date would continue to exert a strong structural force"(*Ibid.* 29).

Like Habermas, Touraine (1994) also stresses the connection between democracy and the national and does not see any immanent opposition between them. "Modern democracy has been closely connected to the nation-state; social and industrial democracy have been defined by mediation of the nation-state in the field of economy. Moreover - the birth of democracy in the United States and in France was closely linked and identified with the emergence of the nation, its independence and freedom" (99). Touraine then suggests that it is also true that democracy has often been the victim of nationalism. In his opinion democracy is therefore "connected to a certain comprehension of the nation-state and is in conflict with another." (*Ibid.*) The comprehension of the nation-state connected to democracy is the one which founds politically articulate society "in itself - in the sovereignty of the people and not in God, tradition or race." (*Ibid.*, 100) Touraine is of course aware that every formation evokes tradition and nationalism. It seems that the axes drawn by the aforementioned modern theorists offer us an idea about certain contemporary realities which reaches beyond the reflection enabled by the concept of common citizenship. In our view, the events in Slovenia in the years prior to the declaration of independence show that the final decision of the people on the referendum for the formation of a sovereign state, who thus exercised the self-determination right written in the then constitution, was maturing through the violation of human rights in Slovenia as well as other federal republics. Circumscribing the right of assembly, freedom of speech, free organisation of political parties, restricting normal economic and cultural development - all this had a decisive impact on the resolution to take an independent path towards the formation of the nation-state, which gives special rights also to national minorities in the constitution itself (Article 64).

In other words: liberal democracy can hope for some more peace and boredom only if it is able to adopt the concept of differentiated citizenship and if individual groups will get their legitimate rights.

Bibliography

Barbalet, J. M., *Citizenship* (Milton Keynes: Open University Press, 1988)
Dahrendorf R. "The Changing Quality of Citizenship", in *The Condition of Citizenship*, Bart van Steenbergen (ed.), (London: Sage Publications, 1994)
Fraser, N. in Gordon, L. (1994), "Civil Citizenship against Social Citizenship", in *The Condition of Citizenship*, (ed. Bart van Steenbergen), London: Sage Publications.

Gutmann, A., "Introduction", in *Multiculturalism and "The Politics of Recognition"* (Princeton: Princeton University Press. 1992)

Habermas J. "Citizens and National Identity", in *The Condition of Citizenship*, Bart van Steenbergen (ed.) (London: Sage Publications 1994)

Kymlicka, W., "Multicultural Citizenship", in *The Citizenship Debates: A Reader*, G. Shafir (ed.) (Minneapolis, London: University of Minnesota Press1998)

Kymlicka, W. "The Forms of Group-Differentiated Citizenship in Canada", in *Democracy and Difference*, Seyla Benhabib(ed.) (Princeton: Princeton University Press.1996),

Lehning B. P., "Towards a Multicultural Civic Society: The Role of Social Capital and Democratic Citizenship", in *Government and Opposition*, Vol. 33, No 2, Spring 1998.

Marshal, T. H., *Citizenship and Social Class*, (Cambridge: Cambridge University Press, 1950)

Phillips, A., *The Politics of Presence* (Oxford: Oxford University Press, 1995)

Phillips, A., "Dealing with Difference: A politics of Ideas, or a Politics of Presence?", in *The Condition of Citizenship*, Bart van Steenbergen(ed.) (London: Sage Publications. 1996)

Rawls, J., *Political Liberalism* (New York: Columbia University Press. 1993),

Taylor, C., "The Politics of Recognition", in *The Politics of Recognition* (Princeton: Princeton University Press.1992)

Touraine, A., *Qu'est - ce que la Démocratie?* (Fayard,1994),

Waldron, J. , *Liberal Rights: Collected papers 1981-1991* (Cambridge: Cambridge University Press.1993),

Endnotes

---

[1] Dahrendorf justifiably emphasises the fact that the authorities call on citizens to participate in active citizenship when they want commitment. This is not bad in itself, it is even necessary, however, it is also nothing more than a *déja vu* deliverance.

[2] The term is borrowed from Waldron (1993). Our use does not correspond entirely to Waldron's - cf. Waldron 1993, Chapter 14.

³ Marshall (1950) talks about three parts or elements of citizenship, "I propose to divide citizenship into three parts. ... I shall call these three parts, or elements, civil, political and social" (10).

⁴ On the question of the accommodation of the so-called class conflict by means of the expansion of the concept of citizenship cf. also Barbalet 1988. Marshall is supposed not to have claimed "that class has been abolished by citizenship, but that citizenship 'has imposed modification on' class." According to Barbalet, Marshall "sees the development of citizenship and of the class system in terms of the interactions between them. Through their antagonistic relationship citizenship and class inequality each contribute to change in the other." (*Ibid.*, 10)

- Chapter 10 -

A More Perfect Union: Aristotle On Deliberation, Diversity, And Citizenship

Douglas F. Challenger

Introduction: The Impoverished Public Square

Standing at the beginning of that centuries-long journey toward self-government, Aristotle made the audacious claim that human beings are "political animals." In saying that he meant, among other things, to pay us a compliment. The fact that we are not likely to hear such a statement that way today is indicative of how far the contemporary meaning of politics is from that articulated by the great thinkers of ancient Greece.

Today, we are likely to hear Aristotle's words as an indictment in reference to various forms of corruption and self-interest that are all too evident in the actions of those we elect or appoint for us to do the work of government. Current condemnations of politics are also related, I believe, to the sense that politics, today, has been diminished by a lack of substantive rationality and normative discussion, which has emptied politics of any deep meaning for most ordinary people. Public discussion and decision making is constrained by norms that privilege utilitarian cost-benefit calculations and other kinds of instrumental and strategic modes of rationality that are largely the province of experts rather than the deliberative modes of reasoning of ordinary citizens that is guided by what people together consider valuable in addition to efficiency. Moreover, the privileging of instrumental and individualistic modes of rationality over substantive and communicative modes of reasoning tends to rule out people's deeper moral or religious convictions. These developments have helped to push ordinary citizens out of politics and to turn political decision making over to various political, economic, and professional elites that have increasingly shaped the society to their own interest and partial viewpoints.

This is happening not only at the nation-state level in democracies, but is increasingly the way the international public sphere is being shaped as well. In his famous 1918 address "Science as a Vocation," Max Weber poignantly noted these developments and saw their tragic meaning for the future. [1] Weber eloquently described the change in philosophical viewpoint that the modern world had ushered in even as he himself was ambivalent about the consequences that he foresaw in them.

The world that Max Weber described and helped further create stands in sharp contrast, however, to the one that we read about in the ancient texts of Aristotle. Almost a century after Max Weber's elegy of the classical world and its epistemology and politics, I wonder if both historical experience and a growing chorus of critics aren't together pointing toward a reconsideration of the political and social practices that have come to pass in modern times, in large part, because of these commitments to a diminished rationality and the practice of an elitist, power-oriented, and interest-based form of politics. Even as democracy gains a greater foothold around the world, and more and more nations are structuring their politics to fit this model, it has become increasingly clear that self-government does not necessarily lead to good government. This realization, I believe, points to the need to re-examine our theoretical and philosophical assumptions about modernist understandings of rationality and democratic participation, and the political practices that reflect them.

In saying that we are "political beings" and that we are "born for citizenship" Aristotle was making a point that has perhaps become unbelievable to most people today when they look at the way politics is currently conducted. Aristotle meant to suggest that political institutions (and our participation in them) are not arbitrary nor merely voluntary endeavors, but are rooted in the basic nature and necessities of human life. More strikingly than this, in light of the tremendous cynicism and political apathy we see today, he

- 177 -

argues, that human beings find their most complete actualization in their ties to the political community and through taking part in a well-governed state. Beyond the very legitimate pleasures of private life and encompassing its richly varied activities, he claims, is a field of human endeavor that holds inestimable possibility for human flourishing in the cooperative work of self-government.

But, this is hard to imagine today. Our theory and our practice have taught us not to look at political participation as a place of deep meaning and satisfaction, but rather to seek those things only in the separate sphere our private lives. Study after study in the United States continues to show a disconnection between the public and their elected and appointed representatives, and that in spite of all the peace and prosperity, people feel deeply alienated from, frustrated by, and generally displeased with government. This is unfortunate and ironic in a time when democracy has become such a dominant form of government around the world. To understand politics in such negative terms is regrettable, especially because, as a form of government, democracy extends the possibility of political participation, theoretically at least, to everyone through the "office" it bestows upon us as "citizens." For, in a democracy, the rulers are ultimately the people themselves. Although nowhere near matching our experience, this potential is recognized often in our rhetoric. An example of this was the lesson Jimmy Carter sought to share with the American people when he said, upon stepping down from the presidency, that he was leaving the second most important office in American society to return to the first most important one of "citizen." "Yeah, right", we say sarcastically. And we want to tell Mr. Carter that everything we know about the way politics works makes us draw the conclusion that citizens have very little input in political decision making--our participation, for the most part, boiling down to paying taxes, giving a little money to this or that special interest group, and occasionally voting.

Seeking to remedy this situation, many critics today are finding hope in a conception that puts the "office" of the citizen at the center of political life. This conception, around which many thinkers and practitioners have rallied as a remedy for democracy's varied ills, has recently come to be called deliberative democracy.[2] This theory advocates a return, in our thinking and practice, to the importance of citizenship and to the practice of more and better public deliberation. This renewal is essential, supporters argue, for the health and legitimacy of democratic government and political institutions. I think the development of a deliberative theory of politics also suggests a recognition of the losses we have experienced through our commitments to modernist epistemologies, conflict-of-interest theories of politics, and the political practices that have paralleled their hegemony. Interestingly enough, this turn to deliberative democracy and the emphasis that it puts on the role of citizens has a long tradition of proponents whose theoretical justifications for it cut across philosophical lines. This is also true today among its current defenders who range from communitarians to liberals to radical democrats.

In the new studies that are emerging on deliberative democracy, Aristotle's political philosophy has not been given the attention it deserves. My aim in the present article is to highlight the theme of public deliberation in Aristotle's writings and to show how deliberative politics can lead to a better society. Thinking of democracy as deliberative dialogue, as Aristotle does, underscores the need to have wider participation in political decision-making. It also shows the great potential that public reasoning holds for resolving the kinds of problems that often beset us in the political realm; namely, those issues that lend themselves to a variety of choices rooted in different value standpoints and definitions of the problem. Thus, a stronger commitment to the practice of deliberation, and its particular form of public moral reasoning, can create a new kind of public sphere. Through a more deliberative politics, a more genuine pluralism and more meaningful public sphere could be built that again invites substantive rationality and conceptions of the good life. And, at the same time, it would provide a way to manage the conflicts that arise from these different normative viewpoints. It may even create from diverse visions of the good life some common ground among them to serve as a more robust and dynamic set of collective ideals to guide public life.

The Wisdom of the Multitude

At the beginning of chapter 10, book 3 of his *Politics* Aristotle poses a problem that he goes on to answer in the very important succeeding pages of chapter 11. The answer he gives in chapter 11, which is supported by various other themes and passages in his writings, begins his discussion of public deliberation. The question he poses about political sovereignty at the beginning of chapter 10 is this: "A difficulty arises when we turn to consider what body of persons should be sovereign in the *polis*:--the people at large; the wealthy; the better sort of men; the man who is best of all; [or] the tyrant[?] But all of these alternatives appear to have unpleasant results."[3] In the rest of chapter 10 he reviews some of the undesirable consequences of the various alternative answers to this question. Then, at the beginning of chapter 11, Aristotle says the following in favor of the viewpoint that the people at large rather than the few best ought to rule the *polis*: "There is this to be said for the Many. Each of them by himself may not be of a good quality; but when they all come together it is possible that they may surpass--collectively and as a body, although not individually--the quality of the few best. Feasts to which many contribute may excel those provided at one man's expense. In the same way, when there are many [who contribute to the process of deliberation], each can bring his share of goodness and moral prudence; and when all meet together the people may thus become something in the nature of a single person, who--as he has many feet, many hands, and many senses--may also have many qualities of character and intelligence."[4]

The Aristotelian view that the Many possess a superior character and intelligence in comparison to the one best or the few best men, Jeremy Waldron calls, the doctrine of "the wisdom of the multitude."[5] This doctrine asserts that, compared with the alternatives, sovereignty is best invested in the people at large (the general body of citizens). "Although considered individual by individual," Waldron explains, "each of the people is inferior to the one best man, still considered as a body which is capable of collective deliberation, the people may make better, wiser, and abler decisions. For they have the benefit of each person's knowledge, experience, judgement, and insight--which they can synthesize into collective knowledge, experience, judgement, and insight--whereas the one best man can rely only on his own individual resources."[6]

A stronger version of this doctrine can be imagined. Following Aristotle's line of reasoning about the synthetic effects of the pooled resources of character and intelligence, a stronger claim could be made that the people as a whole are wiser rulers compared to all subsets of them. Even though a subset of the general body of citizens might benefit from pooling their accumulated wisdom, the multitude, Aristotle argues, would still have the advantage acting as a body because, being the larger of the two, it would still possess the greatest available resources from which to draw.

Both the stronger and the weaker versions of this doctrine are important for theories of deliberative democracy. The stronger version of this doctrine is interesting because of the light it sheds on the question of the relationship between representative and direct democracy. This has implications for the limits of representative democracy as well as the deficiencies of elite rule of all kinds-- bureaucratic, managerial, professional, expert, and economic--that foster a politics of guardianship. These issues were intriguing in ancient Athens where the political debates focused on the comparison between democracy and oligarchy, the rule of the many and the rule of the few, more than on the comparison between democracy and kingship. Still, today, as in Aristotle's Athens, the weaker version illuminates important aspects of the relationship between individuals and society that are central to understanding what happens in public deliberation.

This article will examine both versions of Aristotle's doctrine of the wisdom of the multitude in order to explain the workings of public deliberation and its potential for bringing into being a better quality of life in democratic societies. Focusing on the weaker version will show the essential components of deliberative dialogue, as Aristotle understands it, and the way that deliberation creates a "public." Examining the stronger version will bring out the unique role that the public at large can play in the work of self-government. The stronger version suggests the need for elected and appointed representatives to work with the people and not just for them through the operation of a deliberative public sphere.

Aristotle's belief in the wisdom of the multitude is what grounds his view of the centrality of the "office" of citizen and motivates the idea that political power is best placed in the hands of the people. He considers other alternatives including the idea that it is better that the laws rule and not people. He endorses the pre-eminence of the rule of law, yet, reminds us that laws are made and administered by human beings, and they reflect the social arrangements from which they spring. Thus, he steers our attention back to what is essential and primary about the issue of political sovereignty--strategies that will produce wise, intelligent, and good rulers.

Determining who should rule the *polis* is not Aristotle's only use for this principle, for this doctrine lies at the center of his overall conception of politics, and is applied throughout his political and social theory. The principle is applied in areas other than the executive function in politics and is useful in various branches of aesthetics, as well. Judicial and legislative functions, for example, are better when more people play a role in the work. And, interestingly, Aristotle thinks, the public should guide the determination of artistic quality, too. What's more, the capacity and efficiency of the civic body was apparently reflected broadly in Athenian society. It was their practice, for instance, to have the people at large pronounce on politics in the assembly, the courts, and the general council (a body chosen by lot from all classes of citizens over the age of 30), as well as to judge architectural plans and award prizes to theatre productions through general citizen-panels.[7] Not only this, but the public wisdom thesis is also used recurrently in his discussion of institutions:

It is not the individual member of the judicial court, or the council, or the assembly, who is vested with office: it is the court as a whole, the council as a whole, the popular assembly as a whole, which is vested; and each individual member--whether of the council, the assembly, or the court--is simply a part of the whole. It is therefore just and proper that the people, from which the assembly, the council, and the court are constituted, should be sovereign on issues more important than those assigned to the better sort of citizens. It may be added that the collective property of the members of all these bodies is greater than that of the persons who either as individuals or as members of small bodies hold the highest offices.[8]

The Creation of the Public through Deliberation

How, then, does Aristotle justify this widely applied doctrine? Recall that, in support of his doctrine, he offers a metaphor: as a "feast to which all the guests contribute is better than a banquet furnished by a single man, so a multitude is a better judge of many things than any individual."[9] The defence he gives for this thesis lies in the idea behind the metaphor, which is the view that variety makes a stronger and more vital foundation for social activity.

This makes sense applied to politics when we think of the job that legislators must do. They need to make decisions about issues that are multi-faceted and complex. They are helped in this work when they have maximum input about the various dimensions of a problem with which they are faced. Here is where the people at large, who pool their resources and act together on the widest possible acquaintance with the advantages and disadvantages, is clearly preferable to one person or a smaller number of them (however expert they may be on the issue) who work alone on solving the problem. Again, Aristotle thinks the variety of viewpoints and the accumulation of knowledge and experience that many people have in relation to any given issue is likely to be greater than the accumulated knowledge and experience of a lesser number.

But the basis for this superior capability of the many is not because it is an aggregation. That is, it does not come from a mechanical summing up of the resources that a greater number brings. Rather, it is due to a dynamic synthesis that takes place when people deliberate together. We must remember that, in expressing this doctrine, Aristotle is careful to make two very important qualifications. The many are superior to the few or to the one, Aristotle writes, only if they 1) are not "debased in character,"

- 183 -

and 2) work together as a group: Provided . . . that they are not debased in character. . . . Each individual may indeed, be a worse judge than the experts; but all, when they meet together, are either better than experts or at any rate are no worse. "[10]

The qualification, "when they meet together," is a qualification that recurs. It is in the quality of their interactions as a body, that makes a collection of individuals wiser and abler, and it is on this basis that they are better fit to rule and to produce a good quality of life for the society. Ernest Barker summarizes this point well in a footnote to Aristotle's text: "The people at large have the merit of a good collective judgement not as a static mass, but when they are dynamic--in other words when they assemble, and when the process of debate begins. It is thus not an unfair gloss to suggest that Aristotle by implication assumes that the dialectic of debate is the final foundation of the principle of popular government, so far as he accepts that principle. In other words democracy is based on discussion."[11] Thus, the capability of which the doctrine speaks lies ultimately in the epistemological advantage that comes from the activity of public deliberation.

But the advantage that the many have when acting deliberately is not only in matters of social utility. It is also, and most importantly, available in matters of ethics, value, and the nature of the good. Again, as with those problems that are of a strictly utilitarian type, the greater facility that the public has in dealing with problems that are ethical in nature comes about not as an aggregation, but by the dialectical and synthetic process of deliberative dialogue. The process, as Jeremy Waldron explains it, involves "bringing each citizen's ethical views and insights--such as they are--to bear on the views and insights of the others, so that they cast light on each other, providing a basis for reciprocal questioning and criticism, and enabling a position to emerge which is better than any of the inputs and much more than an aggregation or function of those inputs."[12]

Waldron goes on to show that the dialectic of deliberative dialogue is really the same process that Aristotle models as a philosophical method in his own writing on ethics. Aristotle's method suggests beginning by examining the current opinions and views that already exist instead of starting from some a priori principle or intellectual construction. The passage at the beginning of book 7 of the *Nichomachean Ethics* describes this methodology: "The proper procedure will be the one we have followed in our treatment of other subjects: we must present phenomena, [that is, the observed facts of moral life and the current beliefs about them,] and, after first stating the problems inherent in these, we must, if possible, demonstrate the validity of all the beliefs about these matters, and, if not, the validity of most of them or of the most authoritative. For if the difficulties are resolved and current beliefs are left intact, we shall have proved their validity sufficiently."[13]

The dialectical reasoning that deliberation employs, then, whether done individually or in public discussion with others, does not begin with the assumption that one point of view is right and all others are wrong. Rather, it begins with the supposition that in each generally-held perspective on an issue there lies some truth, as his remarks about the various views of happiness in book 1 illustrate: "Some of these views are expressed by many people and have come down from antiquity, some by a few men of high praise, and it is not reasonable to assume that both groups are altogether wrong: the presumption is rather that they are right in at least one or even in most respects."[14] The truth in each perspective, though, is hidden, to some extent, and can only be brought into view when held up to the light provided by the searching questions asked from the standpoint of the opposing views, i.e., the dialectical method.

The Kind of Public Deliberation Creates

Applied to questions of public policy and judicial or legislative matters, then, deliberative dialogue is the process whereby common ground is achieved among perspectives on an issue. The method of deliberation works to produce a synthesis that includes the best specific steps laid out by each approach as well as the underlying values of the varying perspectives. Such a result goes beyond that produced by a compromise, which boils down to bargaining and splitting of differences to achieve an agreement with which no one is very satisfied. Compromise is the aggregate result of debate that has not reached the level of deliberation. It occurs when competing perspectives, and those who hold them, will not empathetically entertain the opposing points of view on the issue. It also happens when a fake dialectic is employed as when a person "considers 'several views' but always on his own terms and in his own formulations," such as when elected and appointed officials seek the "input" of citizens to plans that they have already fashioned in large part.[15] But these methods never produce the kind of result that comes from genuine dialectic. The common ground developed by successful deliberation produces a better, more satisfying, and legitimate conclusion than debate that ends in compromise.

Again, the importance of variety cannot be underestimated. Deliberation is possible only when there is diversity of opinion and when the differences are brought sharply into focus. Diversity is the necessary condition of deliberation. But if this condition is to be turned into an opportunity for deliberative dialogue, the participants must examine their differences through a give-and-take process of mutual questioning and sharing of experience. If the participants are willing to engage and remain open to each other in this process, they stand the chance of seeing the problem from the point of view of the other's experience and learning from them something that they did not know before. At its best, the process will lead participants to a deeper understanding of their disagreements and the values upon which their perspectives are based. What's interesting is that rather than relying on people to be tolerant of others to have successful deliberation, experience has shown that the process itself actually helps to create tolerance in the participants.

Minimally, this learning leads to a greater respect of the other, even if participants remain unchanged in their views. This greater toleration is no small accomplishment, as the trust it engenders among the participants provides a basis of legitimacy for action that may come about subsequently. Although what deliberation strives for is much more than majority rule, the deliberative process can enrich such decision making mechanisms, as John Dewey's remarks in his essay 'The Public and Its Problems' indicate: "Majority rule, just as majority rule, is as foolish as its critics charge it with being. But it is never merely majority rule . . . The means by which a majority comes to be a majority is the important thing: antecedent debates, the modification of views to meet the opinions of minorities . . . The essential need, in other words, is the improvement of the methods and conditions of debate, discussion and persuasion."[16]

Ideally, however, deliberative dialogue, if sufficiently inclusive, structured, and sustained, can produce legislation and policies that address problems of the public in ways that integrate the various approaches to a problem into actions that are varied and complimentary. Such solutions to public problems cannot be created under the conditions of adversarial debate or where the goal of discussion is to seek a partisan victory. Deliberative dialogue seeks the greater common denominator of a win/win solution as much as possible, and not the lower common denominator solutions of win/lose or lose/lose policies that often come from compromise agreements and majority rule.

The common ground produced by successful deliberation, then, arises not by the unanimous repetition of shared views and sameness of viewpoint, as some communitarian writers would urge. If common ground is more than compromise, it is less than consensus, which aims to eliminate differences in an effort to produce like-mindedness.

The aim to achieve consensus often is based on the goal of establishing a comprehensive morality as a foundation for moral reasoning and political decision making. The traditional consensus-seeking strategy involves creating an impartial standpoint in what political philosophers Amy Gutmann and Dennis Thompson say amounts to "a single set of assumptions about the foundations of morality and understandings of human nature. In the face of disagreement, impartiality tells us to choose the morally correct view and demonstrate its correctness to our fellow citizens, who, if they are rational, should accept it."[17] A more modern strategy, which is today employed by communitarians, seeks a comprehensive morality within the partial perspective of a particular community. In neither the impartialist or communitarian case is there an effort to make one's own political and moral reasoning be mutually acceptable to others in the way that public deliberation requires.

Here again, the contrast between a consensus-oriented approach to political decision making and moral reasoning on the one hand, and an approach that seeks the less ambitious goal of common ground, which Aristotle's democratic theory advocates, is useful. In contrast to the ideal of impartialists, communitarians (and communists, for that matter), Aristotle would have the ideal state be founded on difference and diversity: "Not only is the *polis* composed of a number of men: it is also composed of different kinds of men, for similar cannot bring it into existence."[18] The difference and diversity of which Aristotle speaks implies a division of labor and a class structure, but is also meant with respect to knowledge and moral views. Contrary to the Platonic ideal of unity, Aristotle argues in favor of a plurality as the ideal foundation for social and political life. This plurality is a potential source of dialectic, openness, and energy in society, and is the foundation of a solidarity that may arise among its different and diverse members only through public deliberation and the reciprocity that it both creates and depends upon.

Toward a More Genuine and Constructive Pluralism

One of the major consequences of not embracing more and better deliberative politics is that we will have to live with less reciprocity and mutual respect in our collective lives. This should really give us pause. History, of course, is replete with examples of majorities who, in the name of some universal and impartial standpoint, have suppressed minorities with different views. This has been done through crusades, inquisitions, censorship, ostracism, and social discrimination. In modern times and recent days, we have seen the partial standpoint of particular groups used to justify their comprehensive views, special group-rights, and cultural superiority, and to fuel acts ranging from discrimination and hate crimes to ethnic cleansing and genocide. This was the outlook of the fascists earlier in this century and is the perspective of the religious traditionalists, ethnic nationalists, and the hate groups of today.

The intolerance bred within the chauvinistic frameworks of particularistic communities seems to be a specially virulent kind. Most modern liberal democracies, however, have managed to keep this type of development contained with the principle and practice of toleration. The principle of toleration keeps impartialists and other proponents of comprehensive doctrines from acting in such ways. The principle "requires majorities to let minorities express their views in public and practice them in private. Religious toleration is the paradigm."[19] But this paradigm, in its present form and practice, has led to a different kind of problem for the public sphere.

Modern liberalism, for a variety of reasons, has put forward the view that the state should be neutral not only on religious matters, but also on all views of the good life.[20] The justification for the neutral state relies on the Cartesian presumption that any reasoning falling short of absolute certainty and rigorous demonstration must be dismissed as irrational. The conclusion drawn is that on those problems that we cannot have such certainty, we must try to avoid as much as possible in public debate. The most extreme version of this view of the procedural state holds that, rather than trying to define the public good in substantive terms, the state should seek only to provide a neutral framework within which people can make their own choices about how they should lead their lives. A less extreme form of this position acknowledges the state's moral support in matters concerning justice and the right, but insists that it remain neutral among conceptions of the good. The practical intent of either version of this approach to organizing public life, it seems, was to play down moral conflict in society. But critics of this public philosophy claim that it leads to a situation where only liberal values are allowed to flourish in the public sphere.

In the context of the "neutral" procedural state of modern liberalism, religious toleration and the separation of church and state have taken on a new meaning and effect. The Establishment clause of the First Amendment, which for much of American history was understood as a protection of the religious world from a secular government, has, in recent times, come to be understood by some religious thinkers as administered principally as a protection of the secular from any religious influence. This is the view of Richard John Neuhaus who has argued that the net result of this inversion has led religious people to feel like the public sphere is not open to them anymore.[21] However, it is probably better to say that nowadays the "shoe is on the other foot," so to speak, because Christian perspectives no longer dominate the public sphere, as they have for much of the past. Still, Christians and other religious and spiritually-minded citizens find that in "the culture of disbelief," as legal and ethics philosopher Stephen Carter has termed it, which modern liberalism has produced, their sensibilities are trivialized, their rationality discredited, and their participation in public life significantly discouraged.[22]

So it would seem that the liberal principle of toleration, although immensely helpful to political life, does not go far enough. This is the case whether it is justified in the context of modern liberalism or in its earlier Lockean version, I believe.[23] And here again, a vigorous commitment to deliberative politics is what is really called for. As Gutmann and Thompson have said, the principle of toleration "provides no positive basis on which citizens can expect to resolve their moral disagreements in the future. Citizens go their separate ways, keeping their moral reasons to themselves, avoiding moral engagement. This may sometimes keep the peace (though often only temporarily, as the violent confrontations over abortion show). But mere toleration also locks into place the moral divisions in society and makes collective moral progress far more difficult. Deliberative democracy offers a more robust kind of citizenship...."[24]

The effect, then, of this more robust citizenship, which deliberative democracy both invites and creates, would be to open up the public sphere to a greater diversity. But the moral conflict and disagreement that lies within that diversity would be allowed to come out more openly in public life. In the light of that greater publicity, the moral disagreements and conflicts could be more honestly engaged, and toward more useful ends through the practice of public deliberation. Liberal democracy would, at long last, champion a genuine pluralism instead of the pseudo pluralism it now supports. And, what's more, the state would have a fuller use of its actual diversity.

Genuine deliberation, then, does not aim for consensus or complete agreement, but rather a solution upon which differences may remain. And yet, some mutual respect and appreciation for other points of view is produced, some economy of disagreement is gained, and a basis upon which some action can be taken together is achieved. This kind of social cooperation in political life is not mere complimentarity. Rather, it is a dialectical relationship whereby, as Waldron explains, "its members spark off each other's dissonant ethical views and practical interests and sharpen their moral and social awareness dialectically."[25]

Thus, deliberation, for Aristotle, is a form of interaction that moves people beyond self-interested perspectives and partisan conflict, not to consensus and unanimity, but to common ground for policies and actions, a part of which all may, more or less, find acceptable. The "public" that is created by this kind of dialectical deliberation is different from the "community" that derives from like-mindedness. Community of this kind, we should recognize, is not possible or even desirable today, and those who try to bring it about must do so through coercive measures and under authoritarian or totalitarian auspices. A "public," however, is different from a community of the like-minded. The former is rooted in a solidarity based on interdependence and difference, while the latter is grounded in unity and sameness. In more recent times, Emile Durkheim, synthesizing the social theories of Ferdinand Tönnies and Herbert Spencer, restated this idea in more recent times in his *Division of Labor in Society*, and, interestingly enough, gave us the clue that his social theory paralleled Aristotle's when he had inscribed on the title page of all the French editions of the work Aristotle's line: "A real unity, such as a *polis*, must be made up of elements which differ in kind."[26] Like Durkheim, Aristotle clearly favors the type of society that uses public deliberation to find its unity out of its continuing pluralism and diversity.

Education, Civic Character, and the Purpose of the State

Finally, and most importantly, more and better deliberation would help the public discover the opportunity and means for pursuing what Aristotle thought was the ultimate purpose of the state--"not mere life, but a good quality of life."[27] Creating the conditions for a good quality of life, he believed, required the goodness of its citizens and its rulers. The better part of goodness is summed up in the qualities that are required for public deliberation--mutual respect and accommodation, reciprocity, openness, and most of all, public-spiritedness. The good citizen, Aristotle believed, would have the same qualities that the good ruler would. The cardinal virtue of the good leader, Aristotle said, was the intention and willingness to make decisions that aimed to achieve what was best for the whole society rather than what was good for one's self-interest or the private interests of any group. The government has an interest and a role in helping to produce these kinds of leaders. In his discussion of the nature of the state, Aristotle says: "Any *polis* which is truly so called, and is not merely one in name, must devote itself to the end of encouraging goodness. Otherwise, a political association sinks into a mere alliance, which only differs in space from other forms of alliance where the members live at a distance from one another. Otherwise, too, law becomes a mere covenant--or (in the phrase of the Sophist Lycophron) 'a guarantor of men's rights against one another'--instead of being, as it should be, a rule of life such as will make the members of a *polis* good and just."[28]

So among other things, the encouraging of goodness is important because, without the skills and moral qualities that goodness includes, deliberation cannot be successful, the civic community remains unformed, and the public is unable to do its very important work. Much of that work may be summed up in the bringing about of justice, for this, Aristotle believes, is the crowning virtue of good civic character. It is a kind of complete virtue practiced in relation to our fellow human beings.[29] When it is present to a large extent in the relationships of people, then social harmony, or what Aristotle calls "concord," prevails, and the society or political association can be said to be functioning well.

Commentator Martin Ostwald suggests that the Greek word Aristotle uses for justice (*didaiosyne*) has wider connotations, including "righteousness" and "honesty." He notes, "It is, in short, the virtue which regulates all proper conduct within society, in the relations of individuals with one another, and to some extent even the proper attitude of an individual to himself." Its natural consequences are happiness and harmony within the self and among the members of the social and political community, i.e., the good functioning of the state.[30]

The practice of deliberation is one of the best "schools" for learning the habits of good civic character of which just action is the greater part. Fostering this kind of civic virtue should be part of the mission of public schools where young people can begin to learn the skills and perspective that genuine deliberation requires. Efforts to do the same with adults are also essential to fostering a stronger, more deliberative form of democracy. For while we are born for citizenship, we are not born knowing how to be citizens. This we must learn. Efforts along these lines could make a profound impact on the problems that beset democracies today.

Civic education in America, however, has tended to operate in ways that support "politics as usual" rather than to promote a more deliberative democracy. The politics-as-usual form of civic education operates with an interest-oriented model of citizenship and a conception of the political as mostly what governments and politicians do. Citizens, from this point of view, are quite properly at the margins. The effects of this perspective on the education that young people get about citizenship is clear. In both their schooling and socialization, citizens are taught that they have a minimal role in democratic government. But, more importantly, when they are taught about participation, they are trained not to look at the public as a whole or to engage others in a mutual search for the common interest. Instead, they are instructed to define precisely their particular interests and goals, to organize with others of like mind, to see those with opposing viewpoints as enemies, and to engage their political opponents in adversarial debate and contest in an effort to achieve a partisan victory.[31]

What is missing from this form of political education is what would be the essential characteristics of a deliberative politics in which people talk and think together in ways that enable them to act together. Interestingly enough, young people are beginning to see what is wrong with the way we do things now. In one recent study of college students, for example, the participants complained that they are put off by the tone and tenor of what they see in their classrooms as much as what they observe in the broader political culture.[32] What they said was missing in both, David Mathews reports, was "a diversity of perspectives, a habit of listening, and a careful weighing of trade-offs. They could even identify what they would need in order to practice a different kind of politics--the discipline to keep an open mind, the willingness to stand in someone else's shoes, the capacity to change, and the ability to make decisions with others."[33]

Gaining these deliberative skills and this public-spirited perspective requires a different way of educating for citizenship. To foster such characteristics, it will be necessary to do more than teach the liberal arts, or supplement the curriculum with more common or diverse readings, or add community service to the list of requirements. A deliberative kind of politics needs citizens with more than knowledge and expertise or the willingness to help others in apolitical forms of community service. Instead, what is needed is the opportunity for students to engage in deliberative dialogue in an active and hands-on way. My own experience with this type of political education has shown me that it is best grounded first in practice and then supplemented by reflection. As one who has had much more experience in developing ways to teach and promote the skills and theory of deliberative democracy, Kettering Foundation president David Mathews has said, education for citizenship of this type is learned in a way that is not unlike that of the performing arts.[34]

The form of reasoning that this kind of political education involves will also be different from the kind used for scientific work. After having tried for more than a century to find scientific techniques and bases for confronting problems of social policy, we must now accept our failure, and turn again to a form of reasoning that Aristotle called "moral," and which is similar to what theorists of deliberative politics are advocating today. The problems of the public cannot be addressed by the limited rationality of science.[35] Max Weber knew that scientific rationality could not address the problems of politics, which were ultimately rooted in contrasting value standpoints and fundamentally different definitions of the problem. Yet he erred in the conclusion that he drew from this observation, which cast politics into the realm of the irrational and

- 194 -

saw political leadership as essentially the harnessing and manipulating of those irrational elements. We must recover what Weber would not concede--that there is a form of reasoning that, although not as conclusive as the technical rationality of the scientific method, is essential for addressing public problems.

This form of rationality we might call public reasoning is based on interrogating shared human experience and recognizes that the thinking we do together in deliberation produces a "public" knowledge that is not available to us when we are acting alone.[36] The wisdom of the multitude is the result, Aristotle says, of thinking and reasoning together as a public. It is a form of reasoning that must again find expression in our pedagogy and in our politics if we are to make significant improvements to democracy.

Conclusion

The deliberative model of democracy is clearly a bolder step toward embracing the difference and diversity that exists in most modern-day societies. Public deliberation provides the best way to overcome and cope with the conflicts of interest and moral disagreements that such diversity inevitably creates. Deliberative democracy also aims at a wiser and more inclusive politics through more and better involvement. Advocating deliberative democracy is not just a matter of living up to the ideals of self-government and opening the door to those who have been shut out of politics; it is also about pursuing a path that maximizes the input that is possible in our societies.

The increased participation of deliberative democracy results in better and fairer solutions to public problems because the policies and solutions generated by it are formed with the benefit of a wider range of viewpoints on the issue at hand. What's more, the approach of public deliberation asks more of us as people and holds out more hope for overcoming those qualities that are impoverishing our political culture. In other words, beyond its usefulness in creating policies of greater social utility and justice, deliberative democracy can be transformative. Through discussion people of varying kinds of difference, interest, and outlook--ethnic, cultural, economic, gender, and religious--begin to see beyond their private or group interests and find interests they have in common. They begin to develop informed judgments on issues, to share responsibility and power in addressing them, and to find a basis of common ownership in the outcomes of public action. These things provide the foundation of common purpose needed for both citizen and government action.

Many analysts have shown that the conditions and intentions that foster deliberative dialogue are not a strong part of contemporary American political theory or practice. Studies of both political institutions and of the public more generally show a lack of familiarity with deliberative politics. Instead, special interest groups dominate the landscape, partisan elites fight to control political outcomes, and significant portions of the public are shut out of the decision making process. The result is leadership that bends to elite interest, and policies and laws that die by a thousand cuts in partisan gridlock and compromise.

The problem in America is two-fold. First, deliberative dialogue is not understood or practiced in our political culture generally--neither by officeholders or citizens--and, second, there is a disconnection between government and the people. Because politicians tend to see themselves as the guardians of the public, they are not inclined to genuinely seek the participation of the people. Both these factors, in Aristotle's view, rob us of "the wisdom of the multitude," as well as the benefits of a stronger unity to balance our diversity. Our society is the worse for it.

As John Dewey and countless others have been saying for over 70 years, what has been missing most in American society is the opportunity for both elected officials and ordinary citizens to form themselves into a "public" and to go through the disciplined process of coming to public judgment. And what makes a people a public is deliberation, as reformer David Mathews, in his book *Politics for People*, puts it: "Without deliberation, people remain just a collection of individuals, not a public. They become a public through the connecting process of deliberation. By deliberation, I do not mean just "talking about" problems. To deliberate means to weigh carefully both the consequences of various options for action and the views of others. It is what we require of juries. Without the discipline of serious deliberation, it is impossible for a body of people to articulate what they believe to be in the best interest of all--in the 'public interest'."[37]

Surely, the common interest is not served to the degree that our democracy practices a diminished form of public deliberation. To remedy that situation, we will be best served by attending to "the improvement of the methods and conditions of debate, discussion and persuasion. That is the problem of the public" John Dewey said in 1927.[38] The problem that faced democrats at the beginning of the twentieth century is even more so the challenge we face at the beginning of the twenty-first.

Bibliography

Aristotle. *Politics*, ed. and trans. Ernest Barker, Oxford: Oxford University Press, 1946.
Nicomachean Ethics, ed. Martin Ostwald, Indianapolis: Bobbs-Merrill, 1962.
Barber, Benjamin R. *Strong Democracy*, Berkeley: University of California Press, 1984.
Bessette, Joseph. *The Mild Voice of Reason: Deliberative Democracy and American National Government*, Chicago: University of Chicago Press, 1994.
Bohman, James. *Public Deliberation: Pluralism, Complexity, and Democracy*, Cambridge, Mass: The MIT Press, 1996
Boyte, Harry C., and Sara M. Evans, *Free Spaces: The Sources of Democratic Change in America*, New York: Harper and Row, 1986.
Carter, Stephen L. *The Culture of Disbelief: How American Law and Politics Trivialize Religious Devotion*, New York: Doubleday, 1993.
Challenger, Douglas F. Durkheim *Through the Lens of Aristotle*, Lanham, MD: Rowman and Littlefield Publishers, 1994.
"The Positive Potential in Public Life: Citizenship and Civic Education," *Kettering Review*, Spring, 1998
Cohen, Joshua. "Deliberation and Democratic Legitimacy," in *The Good Polity*, ed. A. Hamlin and P. Pettit, Boston: Blackwell, 1989.

Dewey, John. *The Public and Its Problems* (1927), Chicago: Swallow Press, 1954.

Durkheim, Emile. *The Division of Labor in Society* (1893), New York: The Free Press, 1933.

Fishkin, James. *Democracy and Deliberation: New Directions for Democratic Reform*, New Haven: Yale University Press, 1991.

Gutmann, Amy, and Dennis Thompson. "Moral Conflict and Political Consensus," *Ethics*, 101 (October, 1990): 65-69.

Democracy and Disagreement, Cambridge, Mass: Harvard University Press, 1996

Habermas, Jurgen. *Between Facts and Norms: Contributions to a Discourse Theory of Law and Democracy*, Cambridge, Mass: The MIT Press, 1996.

"Reconciliation through the Public Use of Reason: Remarks on John Rawls' Political Liberalism," *Journal of Philosophy* (1995) 52: 109-131.

The Harwood Group. *College Students Talk Politics*, Dayton, OH: Kettering Foundation, 1993.

Kelman, Steven. *Making Public Policy: A Hopeful View of American Government*, New York: Basic Books, 1987.

Ketcham, Ralph. *Individualism and Public Life*, New York: Basil Blackwell, 1987

Mathews, David. *Politics for People: Finding a Responsible Public Voice*, Chicago: Illinois University Press, 1992.

"Character for What? Higher Education and Public Life," *Educational Record*, (Spring/Fall), 1997.

"Creating More Public Space in Higher Education," Washington, D. C.: *The Council on Public Policy Education*, 1998.

Neuhaus, Richard John. *The Naked Public Square: Religion and Democracy in America*, Grand Rapids, MI: William B. Eerdmans, 1984.

Nino, Carlos Santiago. *The Constitution of Deliberative Democracy*, New Haven: Yale University Press, 1996.

Rawls, John. *Political Liberalism*, New York: Columbia University Press, 1993.

Reich, Robert B., ed. *The Power of Public Ideas*, Cambridge, Mass: Ballinger Publishing, 1988.

Sandel, Michael J. "The Political Theory of the Procedural Republic," *The Power of Public Ideas*, 1988, pp. 109-121.

Rittel, Horst W. J., and Melvin M. Webber, "Dilemmas in a General Theory of Planning," *Policy Sciences*, 4 (1973), pp. 155-169.

Weber, Max. "Science as a Vocation," in From Max Weber: *Essays in Sociology*, trans. and ed. H. H. Gerth and C. W. Mills, New York: Oxford University Press, 1958.

Waldron, Jeremy. "The Wisdom of the Multitude: Some Reflections on Book 3, Chapter 11 of Aristotle's *Politics*," *Political Theory* (November, 1995), 23:4, pp. 563-584.

Wallwork, Ernest. Durkheim: *Morality and Milieu*, Cambridge, MA: Harvard University Press, 1972.

Endnotes

---

[1] Max Weber, "Science as a Vocation," in From Max Weber: *Essays in Sociology*, trans. and ed. H. H. Gerth and C. W. Mills, New York: Oxford University Press, 1958, pp. 129-156.

2 Amy Gutmann and Dennis Thompson, *Democracy and Disagreement*, Cambridge, Mass: Harvard University Press, 1996; James Bohman, *Public Deliberation: Pluralism, Complexity, and Democracy*, Cambridge, Mass: The MIT Press, 1996; Carlos Santiago Nino, *The Constitution of Deliberative Democracy*, New Haven: Yale University Press, 1996. The two main works that guide the contemporary theory of deliberative democracy are that of Jurgen Habermas, *Between Facts and Norms: Contributions to a Discourse Theory of Law and Democracy*, Cambridge, Mass: The MIT Press, 1996, "Reconciliation through the Public Use of Reason: Remarks on John Rawls' Political Liberalism," *Journal of Philosophy* (1995) 52: 109-131, and that of John Rawls, *Political Liberalism*, New York: Columbia University Press, 1993. See also Joshua Cohen, "Deliberation and Democratic Legitimacy," in *The Good Polity*, ed. A. Hamlin and P. Pettit, Boston: Blackwell, 1989. For more specific institutional proposals see James Fishkin, *Democracy and Deliberation: New Directions for Democratic Reform*, New Haven: Yale University Press, 1991; for a more historical treatment and a case study see Joseph Bessette, *The Mild Voice of Reason: Deliberative Democracy and American National Government*, Chicago: University of Chicago Press, 1994. This new school of thought began to emerge in the 1980s in works like Benjamin R. Barber, *Strong Democracy*, Berkeley: University of California Press, 1984, Harry C. Boyte and Sara M. Evans, *Free Spaces: The Sources of Democratic Change in America*, New York: Harper and Row, 1986, Steven

Kelman, *Making Public Policy: A Hopeful View of American Government*, New York: Basic Books, 1987, and Robert B. Reich, ed., *The Power of Public Ideas*, Cambridge, Mass: Ballinger Publishing, 1988. During the 1980s and up to the present the Kettering Foundation of Dayton, Ohio under the leadership of David Mathews began to study deliberative dialogue and, through its affiliation with the National Issues Forums Network, began to promote its practice through citizen forums on issues of public policy. See David Mathews, *Politics for People: Finding a Responsible Public Voice*, Chicago: Illinois University Press, 1992.

3 Aristotle, *Politics*, ed. and trans. Ernest Barker, Oxford: Oxford University Press, 1946, 121-22:
book 3, chap. 10, 1281a11.

4 *Ibid.*, 123: book 3, chap. 11, 1281a43-b9.

5 I wish to acknowledge my indebtedness to Jeremy Waldron's, "The Wisdom of the Multitude: Some Reflections on Book 3, Chapter 11 of Aristotle's *Politics*," *Political Theory* (November, 1995), 23:4, pp. 563-584, not only as to this particular point, but for ideas involved in my entire discussion even when it reaches conclusions diverging from his.

6 Waldron, p. 564.

7 Aristotle, *Politics*, 127-28: book 3, chap. 11, 1281b10-1282b13. See also Barker's footnote 1 and Y to this section of Aristotle's text. Here it is important also to acknowledge that Aristotle's democratic argument did not include women, slaves, and other property-less persons, which reflected the customs and practices of ancient Greece.

8 *Ibid.*, 127: 1282a34-41.

9 Quoted by Waldron, p. 567. Aristotle, *Politics*, (Jowett/Barnes trans.), ed. Stephen Everson, Cambridge: University Press, 1988, 76: book 3, chap. 15, 1286a29.

10 Aristotle, *Politics*, 126: book 3, chap. 11, 1282a14.

11 See Barker's footnote 1 to Aristotle's text, p. 126.

12 Waldron, p. 569-70.

13 Aristotle, *Nicomachean Ethics*, ed. Martin Ostwald, Indianapolis: Bobbs-Merrill, 1962, 175: book 7, chap. 1, 1145b1.

14 *Ibid.*, 20: book 1, chap. 8, 1098b.

15 Waldron, p. 571.

16 John Dewey, *The Public and Its Problems* (1927), Chicago: Swallow Press, 1954, pp. 207-8.

17 Gutmann and Thompson, Democracy and Disagreement, p. 59.

18 Aristotle, *Politics*, 41: book 2, chap. 2, 1261a18-25.

19 Gutmann and Thompson, *Democracy and Disagreement*, p. 61.

20 Michael J. Sandel, "The Political Theory of the Procedural Republic," *The Power of Public Ideas*, 1988, pp. 109-121.

21 See Richard John Neuhaus, *The Naked Public Square: Religion and Democracy in America*, Grand Rapids, MI: William B. Eerdmans, 1984.
22 See Stephen L. Carter, *The Culture of Disbelief: How American Law and Politics Trivialize Religious Devotion*, New York: Doubleday, 1993.
23 For a criticism of the modern liberal argument for religious toleration and a defense of the stronger Lochean argument for religious toleration, see Amy Gutmann and Dennis Thompson, "Moral Conflict and Political Consensus," *Ethics*, 101 (October, 1990): 65-69.
24 Gutmann and Thompson, *Democracy and Disagreement*, p. 62-3.
25 Waldron, p. 578.
26 Emile Durkheim, *The Division of Labor in Society* (1893), New York: The Free Press, 1933. For a study of linkages between the ideas of Aristotle and Durkheim, see Douglas F. Challenger, *Durkheim Through the Lens of Aristotle*, Lanham, MD: Rowman and Littlefield Publishers, 1994. For a discussion of the synthesis that Durkheim created from the theories of Tonnies and Spencer, see Ernest Wallwork, *Durkheim: Morality and Milieu*, Harvard University Press, 1972, pp. 77-78. The claim that this quotation of Aristotle's appeared on the title pages of all French editions of Durkheim's text is made by George Simpson in his preface to his 1933 English translation of *The Division of Labor in Society*, viii.
27 Aristotle, *Politics*, 118: book 3, chap. 9, 1280a28.
29 Aristotle, *Ethics*, 114: 1129b26-30.
30 Ostwald, (trans.), Aristotle, *Ethics*, p. 111, n.1.
31 For a discussion of contrasting notions of citizenship and their implications for civic education, see Ralph Ketcham, *Individualism and Public Life*, New York: Basil Blackwell, 1987, pp. 144-151 and Douglas F. Challenger's comparative essay on these ideas and practices in America and Slovenia in "The Positive Potential in Public Life: Citizenship and Civic Education," *Kettering Review*, Spring, 1998, pp. 50-58.
32 The Harwood Group, *College Students Talk Politics*, Dayton, OH: Kettering Foundation, 1993.
33 David Mathews, "Creating More Public Space in Higher Education," Washington, D. C.: *The Council on Public Policy Education*, 1998, p. 2.
34 David Mathews, "Character for What? Higher Education and Public Life," *Educational Record*, (Spring/Fall), 1997, p. 16.
35 For an insightful analysis of the limitations of the scientific bases for confronting problems of social policy and a discussion of the characteristics of the kinds of problems science can and cannot deal with, see Horst W. J. Rittel and Melvin M. Webber, "Dilemmas in a General Theory of Planning," *Policy Sciences*, 4 (1973), pp. 155-169.
36 Mathews, "Character for What? Higher Education and Public Life," *Educational Record*, pp. 13-14.
37 Mathews, *Politics for People*, p. 111.

38 John Dewey, *The Public and Its Problems*, p. 208.

- Chapter 11 -

Civic Education, Values and the Experience of a Breakdown of an Illusion

Janez Krek, Mojca K. Šebart

This article has two parts, the boundaries of which are set by two different conceptualisations of the relationship between civic education and values in the state school system.

In the first part, we will examine the current public debates regarding civic education to reveal how it is strongly influenced by public and political expectations and beliefs which are established through mechanisms of political power. The concept of civic education is therefore a discursive phenomenon. We interpret discourse as a *social bond* or a means of identification where we may recognise ourselves.

In the second part, we will attempt to provide an answer to the question of establishing civic education in the aftermath of the breakdown of the illusion, that is, at the end of Grand Stories and after the "break" in former socialist or communist countries which came after the introduction of liberal parliamentary democracy and the market economy. How is civic education as a subject regarded by teachers? What should be the contents of civic education if the subject is regarded by students as being without worth and alien to them? Should the contents reflect the wishes of the students?

Civic Education as the Result of a Discursive Subject

In Slovenia there are, and there were historically, two divergent concepts of the position of civic education in the state schools.

1. According to the first concept, which at the moment is based in law (the subject is soon to be called "Civic education and ethics"), the contents of civic education are learned or taught

through different subjects of the curriculum but they are also conveyed through a specific subject which is *compulsory* for *all* students. It educates for values that reflect a consensus of fundamental values and value systems and must, just like all other subjects in state schools, meet the criteria of *non-ideology* or *neutrality* according to which indoctrination may not be the objective of educational process. Is it naïve to ask if it is possible for a school to educate *for* values and without indoctrination?

In a brief search for an answer to the question, let us examine the decisions and reasoning which the *European Court of Human Rights* applied in several of the disputes involving educational issues. Beside Articles 8 and 9 of the *European Convention of Human Rights* the provision of primary importance in the sphere of education is Article 2 of the *First Protocol to the Convention,* which provides that: "No person shall be denied the right to education. In the exercise of any functions which it assumes in relation to education and to teaching, the State shall respect the right of parents to ensure such education and teaching in conformity with their own religious and philosophical convictions."

Article 2 requires the State to respect actively parental convictions within the state schools and this requitrement poses the question of what is the meaning and scope of the "respect" clause. *The European Commission* took the view that the essence of the second sentence of the *Protocol* was "'the safeguarding of pluralism and tolerance in public education and the prohibition of indoctrination', and it stressed that parents' philosophical convictions had to be *respected,* not necessarily *reflected* in the state school system"[1]. *The European Court* repeatedly said: "The primary concern of Article 2 is to protect the children of certain parents from compulsory religious or philosophical instruction which is not directed at providing information but which is concerned with indoctrinating children with unacceptable beliefs, convictions or ideologies."[2] It went on to say that on the other hand, Article 2 "neither expressly nor implicitly grants a general right of exemption from all subjects where religious and philosophical convictions may be involved."[3] Therefore, we may ask: what can be

- 204 -

considered as the "positive" meaning of the "respect" clause? In several of their rulings, the *Commission* and the *Court* took the standpoint that "the State in fulfilling the functions assumed by it in regard to education and teaching must take care that information or knowledge included in the curriculum is conveyed in an objective, critical and pluralistic manner. The State is forbidden to pursue an aim of indoctrination that might be considered as not respecting parents' religious and philosophical convictions. That is the limit that must not be exceeded"[4]. In its decisions the *European Commission* and the *Court of Human Rights* with respect to the right of parents "to ensure such education and teaching in conformity with their own religious and philosophical convictions" thus established the fundamental principle[5] of *objective, critical* and *pluralistic* teaching and education.

This reasoning applies to state schools and to teaching in general. It means that all of school education is required to follow the above principle. The above cited court's interpretations of the right are valid for the state school including all educational activity in it. They are not limited to a particular content or subject. Therefore, the interpretations are valid also for civic education, including civic education through any subject.

According to this interpretation, the clause *in conformity* in Article 2 therefore does not mean that the parents' demand and the school education have to agree. In order to respect the right of parents, there exists an educational principle which is established and accepted: a certain *discord* in outcome or as a consequence is to be expected as an inevitable element of any education and teaching that respects the criteria of objective, critical and pluralistic teaching and education.

2. Now let us move to *the second concept of civic education* which has two variants (which we will call variant A and variant B). According to this concept, the contents of civic education should be put into effect in the variant A as a *compulsory* subject for *all* students (in state schools) based on a specific value system[6]; or in the variant B as an subject which is an alternative to (optional) religious instruction classes. Today no one is arguing for variant A.

The foremost and probably most insistent advocate of the variant B in Slovenia is now the Roman Catholic Church. As the alternative to religious instruction, the subject of civic education is perceived as "lay ethics".[7]

After the change of political system at the beginning of the nineties, the variant B of this concept was first put forward during the debates which took place in about 1993-4 between the Church and the Government concerning the concept of religious education as a separate subject in the curriculum of state schools. The question was whether to teach about religions or to give Catholic religious instruction. The Church would like to see (its) religious instruction incorporated into the state schools curriculum and under its control. For illustration let us add the wording of *Slovene Episcopal Conference* which in its comment and annotations to the school legislation in 1995 proposed: "The religious instruction is a compulsory-optional subject in all classes of compulsory [primary and secondary] school. The alternative to that lessons is ethics, ecology, civic education [literally "homeland" education] ...."[8]

We should add that in the nineties the concrete *demand* for denominational religious instruction has been more often than not (self-)represented as something particular, limited to only one subject. It was not a demand aimed at education as a whole. (We believe this was also or precisely due to the balance of power in the political sphere.)[9] For this reason, the distinction *in form* between obligational *or* optional in regard to civic education has to be examined first. Why does *civic education* in the variant B of the second concept become an optional subject and alternative to religious instruction?

Freedom of choice is not only a notion related to the right to have freedom of thought, conscience and religion but also a method of educational practice. To have an option is a practical solution which secures also the right of children to be educated in conformity with religious and philosophical convictions of their parents. According to the *European Court of Human Rights*, it is "the only appropriate method for denominational education in one religion. Compulsory education in one religion without the possibility of exemption would violate Article 2."[10] What has to be taken into account is that the ethical and jurisprudential principle of freedom of choice incorporated in the *Convention* and in Article 2 has already been the "answer" which is in the case of denominational instruction in one religion consistent with the fact that such instruction is fundamentally conceived with *the aim* to educate *for* a specific religion. According to its own understanding and comprehension, that kind of education and teaching does not want merely to transmit information concerning the religion and its primary aim is not mastering the knowledge about it. It seems that the proposed concept of civic education as an optional and laical subject is indeed related to the fact that the optional or exemption form is now in our society necessarily applied in the case of denominational religious instruction because of its specifically understood and directed educational aim. That is the reason why from the perspective of the variant B it seems plausible that the necessity of a form of choice in regard to the 'first subject', which is of course religious instruction, brings with it also the logic of option in regard to civic education and the other side of religious instruction - the necessity of civic education conceived as laical ethics.

In other words, the notion of freedom of choice (a consequence of freedom of thought, consciousness and religion) gained the position of a universally accepted ethical principle in a long history (in many instances cruel and bloody) of how to resolve and "loosen" the antagonistic conflict of human subjectivity at the core of which the problem is precisely that in a certain respect there is no such a thing as freedom of choice. Only from the point when *the subjectivity* has already become an universally asserted principle and basis for the form of option, can we *now* find ourselves in a position from which *a priori* of believing, the initiation into certain belief or religion, is comprehended as a question of freedom of consciousness. From that position, which was gained with difficulty, and which arose from our own cultural context, a method of educational practice based on the rights of the individual has to follow as a result. From the standpoint of the variant B of the second concept of civic education, whose aim is the initiation into belief or faith, it now may seem that civic education also (because it is considered an addition to the denominational religious instruction and therefore perceived as laical ethics) *has to be* the object of choice - because teaching and education comprehended in this way turned out to be the *a priori* object of choice in our culture.

3. Now, we may ask whether there can be any legitimate concept of civic education compulsory *for all* students which *would* convey the values and norms of a society but would *not* break the norm of non-indoctrination. In answering the question. we will first make a detour via history of discussions that took place in Slovenia about eighty years ago after World War I in 1920s.

The discussions on education which started in the wake of the transition from socialism and the emergence of a new state[11] often resemble ideological confrontations that took place in Slovenia between the two World Wars, when two political parties fought for dominance.[12] Today their positions would be represented by the Slovene People's Party or SPP,[13] and the Liberal Democracy of Slovenia or LDS, which together form the governing coalition. Each articulated its views through the confrontation of a traditionalist-rural and a liberal-bourgeois discourse. Even though the contemporary ideological set-up, as we believe, cannot be simply applied to the past, a look back into history will nevertheless provide a more generalised view on the issue of religious instruction in state schools and the difference between the two concepts in general. Through that discussion, it is possible to illustrate how the division between the two concepts itself is always a particular issue - be it the contemporary issue of *religious instruction* or the idea of *homeland education* or the now obsolete idea of *self-management with fundamentals of Marxism* or the disputes and struggles in history to which we now move - and strongly influenced by what we call the structure of subjectivity.

We will try to support that argument by using the book *Attempts at a School Reform (Poizkusi reforme šolstva* by M. Bergant) which offers a flashback into the period of the implementation of civic education and religious instruction in schools after 1918. At that time, there were public debates which related to the problems of today discussed above; they reflected not only different educational concepts of state school, but also the forces involved and the balance of power according to which circumstantial demands were formed and articulated, and, finally, solutions were reached. As Bergant pointed out, the constitutional article concerning schools, adopted on 8 March 1921, defined educational guidelines for state schools: "All schools should provide moral education and develop civic consciousness in the spirit of national unity and religious community. ... Religious instruction is provided on the wish of parents or guardians, and divided according to creeds."[14] This article dealt a severe blow to the Slovenian Peoples Party (SPP) and the Catholic Church, since it showed the political desire to separate church and state. As the author said, "... the definition of the educational aim in the sense of civic and national education, and especially the provision of optional religious instruction in schools, indicates and indirectly defines this [separation]."[15] The SPP and the Church considered religious-moral education to be a question of "... the entire approach to teaching all school subjects." This was the reason why the Church was not satisfied with control over religious instruction alone; it wanted control over education as a whole. The political rise of the SPP in 1923 once again pushed the demand that religious-moral education be introduced in Slovenian schools to the forefront. The immediate consequence of this rise was that the ruling regime, the state school authorities, and the Slovenian liberal circles soon began to compromise with the Churches about educational issues. Namely, despite the differently stated constitutional provision, they started to recognise religious instruction alongside "national education". "The provisions of the constitutional article concerning schools which indicated the separation of school and church and school education in the laical-ethical sense were not carried out in practice..."[16] Bergant reported. However, despite the fact that state forums, with their yielding attitude towards church education issues, gave up laical-moral education in favour of the religious one, the clerical side was still not content. It built its influence on the "... religious feelings of the Slovenian rural population, [and, consequently]

- 209 -

represented the struggle for religious schools and the rights of the Church to educate as a struggle for the principle of the parents' right to their children. ... It proclaimed that the issue could be settled in principle only if the following question was resolved: was the child the property of the state (society) or of parents? ... In defining the spirit in which children should be brought up, it put the rights of parents before the rights of the state ... therefore, the SPP appealed to parents to fight for the so-called 'self-determination of parents', which should be seen as the decisive factor in defining the school's educational guidelines. ... The state may require ethical education; however, it was the parents as the proprietors of the child who should demarcate, by way of public campaigns, what the ethical education should be like."[17]

The "self-determination of parents with regard to their children's education" slogan was used by the SPP in parliamentary and constitutional debates; however, the party failed in its endeavours to change the constitutional article concerning schools. It drew up a new, contemporary Catholic educational programme, which was again founded on parents' self-determination. The complete or maximum programme demanded the introduction of an obligatory, co-educational religious school. The minimum educational programme, with which the party was conforming to the unfavourable balance of power in the ideological and political sphere, suggested that "... for Catholics, special denominational schools be introduced, which could teach the youth in the spirit of all the demands of religious-moral education. ... Alongside these schools and in accordance with the constitution, free atheistic schools should be allowed as well...."[18]

It is highly interesting that the struggle regarding the educational aim of Slovenian schools was also connected to the national issue. It should be pointed out that "... the SPP defended the Slovenian nationality with very particular arguments, which enabled it to inseparably tie education and the raising of the Slovenian national consciousness to religious-moral education of the youth. ... The starting-point of this theory was the view that what was the truly national was ... for example, religion, traditional costumes, deeply rooted customs, and the tradition of the people, and the only true service to the nation was to protect the old and sacred tradition from immoral influences of the modern world. Linking nationality and the protection of tradition to religion as the most precious part of it in their opinion, led to a unique ... characterisation of nationality, namely, that the essential attribute of a nation was its religion."[19] From this perspective, it is understandable that the first book on civic education in Slovenia was written by a teacher of theology, J. Jeraj,[20] who was also a follower of the SPP and, consequently, an advocate of the Church's school education. It is therefore no wonder that his book tried to combine the tasks of civic education with all the characteristics of Catholic religious-moral education.

Despite their clear intent, the SPP and the Catholic Church implemented religious-moral education only to the extent or status of a "helper" in civic education and did not secure the "principal aim" of implementing religious school education and instruction,[21] as had existed in Austria-Hungary before the process of the separation of church and state began. That probably answers the question why the political angle of the issue at that time was the reverse of the present. The question then was not whether to integrate or how to integrate religious instruction into state schools, as is now the case, but what any limiting of religious education to a mere *school subject* of religious instruction would mean in general. Nevertheless, the fact is that, irrespective of the above mentioned indulgence of state educational authorities, the Church at that time lost a great part of its former control and in spite of compromises the state educational authorities were careful, at least formally, to keep the educational system in the hands of the state.

Additionally, to show how troubling the question of what the limiting of religious education to a mere *school subject* would mean *in general* for the clerical side, let us consider two other ideas from 1919 - a time which was probably just as much a turning point for Slovenia as the nineties. Aleš Ušenicnik, one of the leading Catholic philosophers of the time in Slovenia, demanded that the Church should control education as a whole since that is the only way to guarantee that the educational aim is truly respected in teaching of all subjects or that the teaching is not in contradiction with religious doctrines. He expressed the controversial nature of the new curriculum with the following words: "The curriculum does contain religious lessons as a subject, but the question is not about the subject, but about the spirit, educational principles, and educational means and in this regard, the curriculum completely precludes any influence that religious communities might have in education."[22] A particular conceptual apparatus with the terminology from the educational field that is used in reflections on educational institutions (e. g. curriculum, educational principles, educational means) could lead us away from the universality of the problem. Probably an even clearer manifestation of the spirit as the object that constitutes the discourse and in consequence reveals the education field as a discursive phenomenon is provided by daily newspapers. Their criticism is less academic. Our point is that a specific subjective demand for a *social bond* establishes itself through the demands concerning education. The educational field becomes the place of establishing the specific desire for unity. Let us read the following criticism: "Now some liberal-thinking teachers are saying: it is not that we are against lessons on Christianity in schools. Why not continue with lessons on Christianity, as long as other lessons and education are free of religious ideas and tendencies. Is not such a school a Christian school? No, it is not. To start with, these teachers will keep lessons on Christianity in school just because they are afraid to remove them yet... Therefore a school, which knows nothing about religion – except for those teaching Christianity – is simply not Christian. If a Jew should teach in a school like this and make disparaging comments about Christ and the Catholic Church in a history lesson – would such a school be Christian? (...) What meaning would religious classes have then if the teacher was allowed to despise what the teacher of religion has sown with such effort?"[23]

In the balance of power in Slovenia today, the ideological sphere is quilted with solutions similar to those in the reform plan of the liberal part of the teaching body in the beginning of the twenties.

The plan rejected 'religious-moral education' as the principal aim of education and demanded instead the introduction of "national education" and education for humanity. It defined the "educational aim" in the sense of unified national and laical-ethical education. With regard to religious education, it suggested a compromise and a rather contradictory standpoint: religious instruction remained a school subject, with an addition, however, that "... the Church should have no influence over the educational work in school anymore. Furthermore, the plan made it perfectly clear that the teachers in state schools should under no circumstances be forced to participate, in any manner whatsoever, in religious instruction, ecclesiastical exercises, or any other pieties of the school youth."[24]

If we compare the past with the present, the actual demands of the Roman Catholic Church have deeper meaning. Today, at first glance the issue is reversed. The Roman Catholic Church is demanding that religion as a school subject, nothing else, be introduced into state schools - under the auspices of the Catholic Church. A letter which Slovene bishops addressed to their congregations at the beginning of September 1998 was explicitly placed in the context of defending the necessity of such a subject, but the arguments that were used surprisingly echo the words which were said so many years ago, but which were not aimed at one subject but at state schools in general - at the spirit, which has to be inscribed in the educational principles and in teaching. The bishops wrote: "[The subject] should be under the jurisdiction of the Church. Only in this way will we be able to avoid the danger where children hear one thing about faith and the Church from their parents and from the Church, and another thing in school". Or: "Do not allow any ideology to kill in your children the values which you hold sacred, which made your predecessors into an honest, diligent, sturdy and proud nation. Dear parents, do not allow the memory of Christianity to be erased from the hearts of your children."[25] After the walk through the past, it is of no surprise if together with the demands for teaching religion or a subject, there are also voices in our contemporary society which do not conceal that their aim is a school as a totality. The truth of the spirit seems to be the whole -

and that spirit of truth is discernible from the *Statement of Clergymen of the Maribor Deanery*, which expresses quite openly that the instruction in state school should be founded on the Christian system of values. That is to say, the religious dimension is supposed to be the most potent bonding power in human beings which unites into a harmonious whole even such opposites as death, suffering, forgiveness, creativity, and, last but not least, the will to live. Therefore, it is the duty of the state to develop this fundamental dimension in every citizen, within the boundaries of its competencies.[26] In other words, the state that does not develop this "fundamental religious dimension" in its citizens does not really take care of personal development of children as a whole. Such a standpoint imposes on us the supposition that those individuals who are not educated in school in accordance with such perspectives are handicapped developmentally.

Of course, discourse of exclusion is not typical only of the current leadership of the Roman-Catholic hierarchy which happens to be the most important traditional religious group in Slovenia by far. It can be imagined in contexts quite different from religious or educational ones. Needless to say, the possibility of a discursive subject to shift is such that the issue discussed (either of civic education or education in general) cannot be confined to the field of education alone. This faculty of our subjectivity enables the discourse on one occasion to directly seize the political sphere, on the second one to shift into the school field, and, on the third one to shift somewhere else. What is at stake here is the *manner of argumentation* that ensures support to the structure of subjectivity, not the content of whatever is said. The specificity of the phenomenon and its influence on the conceptualisation of education that we are trying to delineate here, therefore, cannot be grasped as a specific matter of the educational field – rather, it seems that the discursive subject in its constitution *creates* specificity of *a more universally* structured object which in this particular case appropriates the issue of education. The subjectivity can in the same manner take hold of the question of nationality, or race, or gender and sexualty, or other such values ...

- 214 -

4. At this point we should go to the theory of subjectivity for the detailed explanation of the division between the two concepts. [27] However, as our primary interest here lies with the question of civic education, we will only make some remarks which follow from the previous discussion.

First, the demand for unity as the deeper meaning of the cited words bears some resemblance to the issue of the "preservation of one's identity", and these can be seen as a legitimate desire to ensure the survival of a certain identity through "endless future generations"[28], which is a legitimate demand that has to be seriously judged and deserves opportunity for assessment, if not fulfilment and realisation.

The trouble is that whatever the answer in a concrete situation (for instance if the state would introduce "homeland education" in the curriculum of state schools) there still remains the question why the reason for the persuasiveness of the above mentioned utterances is *not bound* to their contents. It is possible either that identity is really in danger or that there is no real threat. The fact is that the utterances alone are convincing and powerful because they bring forward a kind of *self-sufficiency* that does not need any real threat to have the power of persuasiveness. Regardless of the concrete contents of utterances which could be radically different, the mode of argumentation alone could establish the identification of a listener (reader) with the specific subject, the subject of *enunciation*. If this is the key goal of the utterance, it is achieved each time by the act of speaking, by the announcement, regardless and irrespective of the context, of its reality.

In other words, the power of utterance is not the consequence of knowledge and judging, rather it emerges from the ability of a particular individual to identify with something that is specific but on the other hand absolutely uniform in enunciation. Precisely that specificity and uniformity would of course need a further theoretical explanation. However, on account of a goal being reached *in advance*, so to speak, it is possible to doubt seriously whether the expectations expressed through such a discursive subject *could* be fulfilled at all.

Namely, if the mode of argumentation, of which we have given some examples, is an inherent part of the *concept of education* which is at a certain moment in reality represented by the demand for e.g. denominational religious education in one religion, but which could emerge as a reason, as indeed has happened throughout history, for the demands that aim at the whole in regard to the field of education and also to entirely different spheres of life, it is pertinent to conclude that between the *subjective demand* concerning education and the reality of the introduction of a particular subject there is no such tie where one could say that the demand could ever be fulfilled by the introduction of a certain subject, for example.

However, we don't want to suggest that the demand is not 'objective' and that it therefore should not be fulfilled. Our point is simply that even if it is fulfilled in relaity, the subjective demand as such would still exist, only the subject would switch the demand to another content area.

Secondly, there is a real discrepancy between the two concepts. The demand for non-indoctrination in state schools, which is met by maintaining the criteria of *objective, critical* and *pluralistic* education and teaching will bring with it knowledge as a norm. It will bring with it also the necessity of confronting possible contradictory reasoning because, in order to meet the criteria, a critical and pluralist nature of the answers is required especially for ethical questions. These questions imply a need for reflection, and they cause a child to be faced with ethical dilemmas. The world is more open; the answers are no longer self-evident. To put it differently, a child may be exposed to moral distress in state schools precisely because of the respect for the above mentioned criteria of non-indoctrination.

On the other hand, the second concept quilts the demand for unity which overdetermines this view of education and teaching. That "unity" as the "quilting point"[29] of such a discourse could be traced in several utterances: "What meaning would religious classes have then if the teacher was allowed to despise what the teacher of religion has sown with such effort?" Or: "Only in this way will we be able to avoid the danger where children hear one thing about faith and the Church from their parents and from the Church, and another thing in school." In these the meaning of enunciation is the demand for *unbrokenness* or *wholeness* or *unity* - in this instance in the field of education. The second concept therefore poses the opposite demand - the demand for hypothetical unity viewed as the unity of parents and school, or even the unity of church, parents and school, the demand for instruction that tells the child the same as his parentstell him, and so on. For the perspective of such a subjective demand which enforces unity modernity, with its universally acknowledged principle of freedom of choice, remains its *reverse side* and possibly the unintended consequence. Therefore, the application of method of option in teaching and education which allows at least initial freedom in such a perspective can also be viewed as a forced choice.

Of course, the difference between the two concepts may also be observed through the difference in defining the role of the teacher. The role of the teacher as the person about whose way of educating we want to be sure is seen in at least two incompatible ways. Since the teacher teaches on behalf of someone, this question is constantly intertwined with the question of (legal) constraint. One of the reasons for establishing private schools is also the possibility of deciding who will teach in them. As a rule, the concept of denominational religious instruction includes the demand that the religious community has the right to decide on the suitability of a teacher for teaching. However, the state does not work in any other way; through authority delegated to the heads of schools or enacted in laws, it is the state which, in the last instance, has the right to decide *who* will teach in state schools. This is the question of legal constraints and sovereignty over the decision on who teaches. But often the *certainty* regarding education establishes the belief in the teacher's *declaration for* values, religion, or world view, which, in turn, becomes the judgement criterion for the ability to teach *a priori*.[30] However, a reverse question can be posed: how can the society or the individual be certain regarding the constitution of the ethical in the state schools, if the judgement criterion for the ability to teach are teacher's formal qualifications for education, not his or her belief?

To conclude, it is important to recognise that the antagonism between the first and the second concept of (civic) education and consequences could be perhaps most succinctly described by the following words: the *split of the subject* (for example, moral distress to which the student could be exposed) in the first concept is in the second concept replaced by the necessity of the *division of reality* (the division into two different alternative and optional subjects, or looking from a wider perspective, into the reality of division between public and private schools).

Third, we assume that the gap between the 'pre-modern' subject of the utterances quoted previously which expresses itself as the demand for unity and the modern subject of non-indoctrination that accepts the split of the subject even at the cost of moral distress, cannot be removed *in principle*.

The sometimes revived subject of 'pre-modern' discourse, which in one way or another claims unity and an unmediated relationship between *the self* and *the other* is an inherent element of subjectivity or consciousness. In education and teaching, we have to deal with the desire of people to impose certain behaviour on others. Furthermore, as teachers and parents we have to impart values to our students and children and in doing that we are by definition in the position of a 'conscious self' with the belief that education and teaching could take place without the effects of our and students' unconsciousness. Nevertheless, we are all subjects of unconsciousness and therefore in education, especially education for values, one can never be quite confident about the effects of "the working of the unconscious for itself" and consequently, about the result of educational process. In regard to our aim and intent the result of education may be quite unexpected. On the other hand, human beings are subjects of language and through its use unavoidably exposed to the social net and its values from the very beginning. The difference between the two concepts can be seen as two different answers to the same perplexing question. The first concept of civic education recognises that our own personal values

- 218 -

are not the consequence of a process of absolute autonomy because the field of values is constituted also *for us* through the processes of our unconsciousness and those of others and through the use of language - which carries values of The Other. At the base of the second concept of civic education is the desire that this double edged sword - the autonomy of the unconscious and the autonomy of language regarded as representation of the Uncontrollable Other - would be *excluded* and consequently put under control.

The described axis of subjectivity, although it is *by definition* "an unexpressed, hidden supposition, which frames the occurrence of the subjectivity and Self",[31] can not be simply excluded since it is an inherent element of subjectivity. However, we often attempt either to escape it or to use it - even by means of force and fear. Nevertheless, the 'modern' subject was established precisely by recognising that this is a futile attempt as far as it tries to solve this problem forcefully, and to bring to an end something of which the individual and human society can never be relieved. The objective of the second concept, which splits the reality of civic education into 'two realities' (of two subjects, or of 'allowed' and 'excluded' symbolic reality), instead of splitting a subject within civic education itself, is an inevitably failed attempt to avoid interference with the symbolic and with the unconscious which is precisely the drive of human subjectivity. The reason why civic education can and should be *education for all* which we derive from this interpretation lies in the recognition that the occurrence of what the second concept attempts to avoid has already taken place and that in the long run no division of reality can prevent or exclude the interference with the 'otherness' of the other's values and the level of unpredictedness of ours and others' intimate values governed by the silent working of the unconscious.

This brings us to a short comment on the question of the modern individual and individualism. When discussing the term *dignity* in *The Politics of Recognition*, Charles Taylor says that for Kant "what commanded respect in us was our status as rational agents, capable of directing our lives through principles"[32]. In relation to *equality in dignity*, i.e. in respect and recognition of the other, whom we respect because he or she is capable of living according to principles, Kant's notion of principle means both the ability to have *a reflective attitude* towards values and at the same time the capacity of an individual to adhere to his or her own values *unconditionally* - these two make an individual who can act beyond interest.

The notion of the unconscious, a part of the modern notion of dignity, gives the term of *universal human potential as a capacity that all humans share* a different undertone. This term implies the ability to reflect about values and for the conscious Self this reflection is unmediated. But the modern subject recognises that the "shifts of consciousness are driven and regulated on our behalf"[33] by the unconscious and at the same time by the Other of *language*. It means not only that the pre-modern subject is trapped in his or her predicament but also that the modern subject of individuality and autonomy is anything but a subject which is simply liberated. Both reasons for autonomy *as a capacity that all humans share* constitute a real force, but it is the force that chases and haunts the subject.

Fourth, at first glance the first concept of civic education as *education for all* - which is based on a consensus about values that could be considered as common values for all - seems to be totalitarian. Namely, its starting point is "The Whole" in the sense that it includes all children and because at its very beginning it is compulsory for all children, it does not allow any free choice, any exemption. Contrarily, the variant B of the second concept initially allows freedom of choice and therefore it might be seen as libertarian (but not the first variant: it involves obligation for all and its aim is a particular belief, e.g. in self-managing socialism - as such, the concept initially meets all conditions for ideology). But if we take into consideration the aims of education of both concepts respectively, the opposition between the two concepts - with absence of choice in the first one and the freedom of choice in the second one - is overturned: according to the first concept, in realising its goals the process of education as a whole has to satisfy the criteria of *objective*, *critical* and *pluralistic* teaching and education. *The aim* of education is freedom of choice, the subject capable of it, the autonomy of the human being. The need for consensus about at least a minimal set of values in the first concept reveals its supposition that at the level of values - values as the things most important for each individual or society - it is impossible to grasp *the whole*. From this perspective, there is no such thing as "All" in regard to values common to each and every individual. Nevertheless, the aim of that concept should be interpreted as *the forced choice*, because the education and teaching will in its actual performance educate for values but will require knowledge, reasoning and judging, will therefore put the student in "a split" in regard to reality and in principle it will consent to the inevitability of moral distress. Contrarily, the aim of civic education conceived according to the second concept (either according to variant A or B) would merely be education for belief. The aim of education and teaching of the second concept is *excluded choice*: after the consummation of the initial freedom of choice, the education as a process is directed towards the absence of choice; the aim is the subject of belief, and the concept supports the view that teaching gives "All" in regard to values.

Permissiveness, the Hegemony of Particular Values and the Breakdown of the Illusion

The notion of *universal human potential* leads us to the second discursive reference important for the concept of civic education in modern times. In post-modern times civic education as education for values is defined also by the subject of discourse which can be succinctly described by the terms "culture of narcissism" (Lasch), permissiveness and progressive education.

This is quite an influential orientation in the teaching profession, and not just in this profession, in Slovenia. What does permissive education say about the issue of values? Let us summarise here the work of one expert, J. Svetina, who says that it is not enough to implant or attempt to implant in children and adults generally-recognised values or rules and standards of the society they live in. As he says, a step further must be taken: one's own

- 221 -

personal values, maxims and principles which are the guiding light of one's life need to be uncovered in each individual. It is not enough only to nurture conventional morals if we want to achieve an admirable moral culture in society; what also needs to be done is to promote the development of people's ethical autonomy. The ideal that needs to be pursued is a fuller and more genuine human being. School can only contribute towards the attainment of this ideal if it deliberately removes from its practice everything which smothers personal development in children. Thus, it will enable developmental forces to achieve in children what official pedagogy or standard pedagogical theory set as their objective. The present-day Slovenian school, however, with its inadequate methods, for example "... by forcing children and the youth to study, which in itself causes them to rebel against learning itself, and all the subjects they are forced to learn very frequently smothers the joy for learning."[34] A typically ideological picture is at work here, according to which the human is good, hard-working and creative in his or her natural core, and this natural core is the only hope for humans' successful control of social misery some day.[35] In other words, in education we are now dealing with the belief that the individual's conformity to society is not paid for by irrational, compulsive, uncontrolled renunciation.[36]

The obvious difference between the traditionalist-rural and permissive ideologies is the difference in the value placed on individuality. In the first, often everything takes place at the level of the institutionalised other. State schools are seen as "whole" institutions, which is why on the one hand, the teacher, who is the person that actually carries out the teaching and education, is often overlooked, while on the other hand, the Church believes its right to choose the proper teachers is the guarantee that lessons on Christianity will be correctly taught.

Through the eyes of the other perspective we are, on the contrary, entirely on the level of the individual. However, that does not mean the individuality of the teacher or parents but the individuality of the child or pupil. The only mission that remains for the teacher is to enable fulfilment of the *universal human potential* of each student. Education should only foster and release the child's inner growth potential and reveal his or her own personal values, maxims, principles, norms and ideals.[37]

As the criticism of progressive education is very well known,[38] allow us to repeat only a few points: at the end of the day the result of permissiveness was a radically non-autonomous individual, able only to establish a mirror-like, imaginary relationship to the other, completely dependent and in permanent anxiety, and in relation to others unable to reflect the desire, e.g. the desire of his or her own child. The outcome of the permissiveness of parents and teachers, who with the best intentions do not provide resistance against the desires of the child, is a lack of capacity for individuality in the child.

Now we have to ask the question what are the beliefs of the youth in Slovenia regarding the political sphere and civic life in general. In the first half of the nineties, the research on youth (carried out in 1993) indicated considerable changes of value preferences in comparison to the results of research carried out in the middle of the previous decade: "In comparison with the year 1985, 1993 saw a marked decrease in the importance of all problems connected with either the personal emancipation of young people or their political influence."[39]

How is this lesson related to civic education? Let us consider the recent history of the subject which in the curriculum of Slovenian schools should play the role of education for citizenship. For those acquainted with the evolution of the subject of "Ethics and Society" after the transition to the new regime, they will learn nothing new and will not be surprised to hear that the reasons for uncertainty and the tentative steps about the ways of teaching this subject and its contents in general are to be found in the teachers and the experts who *themselves* are victims of an illusion of individuality through the discourse of permissiveness. The illusion of the *universal human potential* brings with it the fantasy that the universal human potential and the inner interest of the children themselves will inevitably provide the contents which would be thought of as civics. In the last few years the subject survived as "hours" where the themes are defined by the students - about problems relating to the youth - and where students' discussion is the only method of teaching. Even now, after the curriculum reform, a quite important portion of available hours of the *syllabus* of civic education is assigned to the themes which proved to be "popular" and "interesting for students".

At the same time, research has shown that the Slovenian youth does not ascribe great importance to the political with the exception of national identity: "National identity and the consequences derived from it are actually the only themes - conditionally speaking - of political identity, of the political consciousness of this younger generation."[40] Only 7.6 percent of the younger generation think that their problem is a lack of political influence. As a result of that attitude towards the political field and with the help of the permissive approach in teaching the subject ("Ethics and Society"), which conforms to the value preferences of pupils, civic education lost most of the elements that help to develop citizens' knowledge and skills for entering and participating in the political life in general. As a consequence, there still exists a quite considerable difference between the content of civic education in the Slovenian syllabus and some recent drafts of curricula that are prepared for teaching civics in United States, for example. In Slovenia much less attention is still paid to knowledge that enables understanding of the institutions of democracy and also less room is left for grasping some notions that are essential for entering into the democratic political life. It is more than questionable whether civic education *in schools* provides the necessary standards required for all *in the reality* of democratic political life.

What has been called the permissive approach can be seen partly as the result of a different philosophy of education which tends to abandon 'the coercion of the youth to learn' and develop the student's activity on the basis of autonomous motivation instead of external constraint. Even if one agrees with this assertion, one cannot ignore the fact that the ability of children to speak for themselves, to express their autonomous motivation, is mediated by the social network, which means that the motivation and autonomy are established only through the pressure or coercion in the process of education. Therefore one is advised not to reject the old wisdom of a classic theorist of education J. F. Herbart, who says, "... there is a well-known educational rule that the teacher should strive to arouse interest of the students in what he or she teaches. However, the rule is usually given and understood in the sense that learning is the aim and the interest is the means to achieve it." He inverts this relationship: "Learning is temporary, the interest has to endure the entire life."[41]

Nevertheless, the following questions should be posed: Why has the new philosophy of education caused – if we overstate – the devaluing or disintegration of content, particularly in civic education? Why has it put it in a position which is much weaker than the strong positions of the contents of core subjects? And what has happened to the content of civic education in other subjects? In what kind of a cleft stick does the education for citizenship find itself?

A possible explanation could be the permissive concept was linked with the experience of the breakdown of the illusion, which could have a special effect on those who were in any way connected to the subject back in the seventies and the eighties. The subject "Ethics and Society" emerged from the subject "Socio-moral Education" (on the upper-secondary school level it was "Self-management and the Basics of Marxism") which was conceived as civic education compulsory for all and educational aim of which was supposed to be teaching the belief in "the self-management socialist system". Encouraged by social events and the rise of the freedom of discussion in the eighties, this concept began to break down in schools and among teachers, and it finally broke down with the emergence of the democratic political system in the new state. The subject, with its aim of inculcation of belief, was increasingly understood as indoctrination even by teachers themselves. For nearly a decade (in the nineties), civic education in Slovenia seemed to carry with itself the experience of the breakdown of the illusion regarding its own aim. However, it was because of the hidden and unarticulated *preservation* of the form *of the aim*, i.e. the aim of inculcation of belief, and not because of some unfavourable external circumstances that it *did not dare* to establish its contents. The problem is (was) not in that the experience of the breakdown of the illusion was too radical, but rather that it created a new subject: the subject of the breakdown of the illusion, which withdrew from the consequences of its own experience. Therefore, civic education remained in the interregnum: it did not want to be indoctrination, but on the other hand it did not manage to become equal to the other subjects on the level of knowledge and in the mediation of values. It is due to the specificity of the aim that the subject was established and comprehended as an exception among subjects and the exceptionality was maintained at least at the conceptual level. Nevertheless, why should a subject like civic education have a radically different aim from the rest of the subjects? A possible guilty conscience of teachers and the discontent about civic education can endure as long as the education of this subject is interpreted through the *demand* for the education of the illusion, merely as the inculcation of belief. However, civic education cannot be reduced – and it is not sensible to reduce it – to a concreteness of aims and contents in one subject; furthermore, in the contemporary democratic society, whose common and minimal ethical fundamental is the notion of human rights, indoctrination is not a permissible aim of education. Finally, how are we to understand the instruction of civic education in the rest of the subjects? Insofar as the above-mentioned scheme (see note 27) can structure *and connect* the elements of subjectivity, which are opposite on the level of consciousness, it follows that by persevering in pure opposition of aims, we have posed the wrong question. The first step towards self-assurance in the concept and instruction of civic education is therefore *the breakdown of the illusion* that the excluded choice (the aim of inculcation of belief) *can* be the privileged and exclusive aim of civic education. It may seem contradictory, but *even* civic education must bear the burden of *the forced choice*, both as a subject and instruction. This would mean, for example, that we teach *even about the homeland* in accordance with the criteria of objectivity, criticalness, and pluralism and that we do not persevere in the illusion that by avoiding the knowledge about the ethical fundamentals of democracy as a political system, we can circumvent the predicaments of subjectivity. Every form of education and instruction is *excluded choice* in its very first step – the question is only if it wants to, and how it can, reflect this through the set (operational) aims and in the concreteness of education.

In short: the aim of education for civic values and for citizenship should not be merely the intentional education of a patriot. As the Slovenian history of the breakdown of the illusion shows, the education will in that way by definition fail to achieve its aims. If civic education will aim at more carefully elaborated knowledge-based and self confident education and teaching for entering a democratic political life it will be able to claim the merits of patriotism, which is much less confined to the imaginary concreteness, and at the same time be better qualified to endure the demands of the ethical and to facilitate decisions regarding contemporary social and political life.

Endnotes

[1] P. Meredith, *Government, Schooling and the Law*, p. 27. Cf. Z. Kodelja, *Laična šola: Pro et contra* (Ljubljana: Mladinska knjiga, 1995), p. 23.

[2] *Digest of Strasbourg Case-Law relating to the European Convention on Human Rights*, Vol. 5, (Koeln, Berlin, Bonn, München: Carl Heymanns Veerlag KG, 1985), p. 805.

[3] *Ibid.*

[4] *Digest of Strasbourg Case-Law relating to the European Convention on Human Rights*, Vol. 5, (Koeln, Berlin, Bonn, München: Carl Heymanns Veerlag KG, 1985), p. 805. Cf. Zdenko Kodelja, *Laična šola: pro et contra*, p. 24.

[5] P. Meredith, *Government, Schooling and the Law*, p. 28.

[6] Z. Kodelja points out that, in the Slovenian area, both the Church and the Party demanded from schools that a certain world view should permeate them; in the first case, it should be Catholicism, in the second one, the "diamatic" Marxism, i. e. the most totalitarian spiritual form of communism. Historically speaking, the demands were met in such a manner that, on the one side, all subjects were 'quilted' either by the religious spirit or the Marxist one (cf. Kodelja 1995, p. 114). Apart from that, the school field was also defined by subjects like Self-management with Marxism, Civic Education (conceptually, a

more appropriate name would be "Homeland Education" [or *Heimaterziehung*]) – with Christian values forming its basis, where the nation and homeland had rights which were above the rights of individual.

[7] In order to understand the context from which the idea of alternativeness originates, it should be added that the concept was re-established in Slovenia at the beginning of the discussions between the Church and the Government in 1993. The discussions were about the dilemma whether to convey the knowledge about religions (as a special subject) or to have Catholic religious instruction which should be - such were wishes of the Church - incorporated in the curriculum of state school and, at the same time, under the auspices of the Church. To put it literally, in their original proposal from 1993, the Church representatives suggested 'religious-ethical instruction' and 'ethics or civic education' as an alternative (cf. Commission on Education at the Slovenian Episcopal Conference, *The Proposal of Issues to Be Discussed with the Ministry of Education and Sport*, 1993).

[8] Cf. R. Podberšič, *The Proposals* of *Slovene Episcopal Conference*, 15. 2. 1995, p. 5

[9] In the time of reaching the agreement on school legislation, the National Assembly (within the Primary School Act) passed the solution that "Ethics and Society" was a compulsory subject and the non-denominational subject "Religions and Ethics" an optional subject in the social sciences and humanities' complex which the school was obliged to offer. Furthermore, the agreement on the modifications of the Act signed by the coalition partners (the LDS, SPP, and DeSUS) in January 1998 did not make any drastic changes to the solutions set before. After a clearly expressed wish of the SPP that the subject "Ethics and Society" be named "Homeland Education" and its content changed accordingly, the agreement was reached on the subject to be named "Civic Education". Likewise, the proposal that the school should offer denominational religious instruction and "laical ethics" as its alternative, which the Church has been demanding more and more loudly, was not accepted in the agreement.

[10] *Digest of Strasbourg Case-Law relating to the European Convention on Human Rights*, Vol. 5, (Koeln, Berlin, Bonn, München: Carl Heymanns Veerlag KG, 1985), p. 801.

[11] The Republic of Slovenia as a part of former Yugoslavia declared independence on 25th June 1991.

[12] Before W.W.I, the territory of present day Slovenia was part of Austro-Hungarian Empire and after W.W.I, it was one of the constituent parts of Yugoslavia which was in the time between the two World Wars a parliamentary democracy with a monarch.

[13] In the original: Slovenska ljudska stranka (SLS).

[14] M. Bergant, *Poizkusi refome šolstva* [Attempts at School Reform] (Ljubljana: DZS, 1958), p. 85.

[15] *Ibid.*

[16] *Ibid.*, p. 100.

[17] *Ibid.*, p. 103.

[18] *Ibid.*, p. 104.

[19] *Ibid.*, p. 105.

[20] J. Jeraj, *Drzavljanska vzgoja* [Civic Education] (Maribor 1926).

[21] Cf. Bergant 1958, pp. 108-112.

[22] Bergant 1958, p. 84.

[23] *Ibid.*, pp. 84-85.

[24] Načrt preustrojitve šolstva in narodne vzgoje [The plan of the reform of school and national education] 1919, p. 83

[25] *Kakršna bo šola takšna bo prihodnja podoba slovenskega naroda.* [Pastoral letter at the start of 1998/99 school year], *Družina*, No. 37, September 20 1998.

[26] Cf. Milharčič Hladnik and Kovač Šebart, *Delo*, 16 October 1993.

[27] Variations of differently illustrated antagonism - which in the political field persists as a dilemma between acknowledging certain universal rights on one side and acknowledging particular identities on the other side - could be treated with a schematic outline, which is in the interpretation of a Freudian psychoanalysis by Jacques Lacan known as "scheme L", with which he (mostly in 50's) tried to depict the elementary structure of consciousness. Of course, Lacan has made a number of different theoretical interpretations of that structure. The "scheme L" we suggest here is not the only one which could be used for the purpose. Cf. Jacques Lacan, *Écrits* (Paris: Seuil, 1966), p. 53 or p. 548

[28] Cf. C. Taylor, *The politics of recognition* (Princeton: Princeton University Press, 1992), pp. 40-41.

[29] We are referring to the concept J. Lacan called *le point de capiton* ("quilting point", literally "upholstery button in his seminar *Les Psychoses*"). Cf. J. Lacan, *Le Séminaire, livre III: Les Psychoses* (Paris: Éditions de Seuil, 1981), pp. 281-306. For the concept of "quilting point", see S. Zizek, *For they know not what they do: Enjoyment as a political factor* (London, New York: Verso, 1991).

[30] Such demands were made in Slovenia in the nineties with relation to denominational *and* non-denominational religious instruction. We also have experience from our "Yugoslav" past, when the demand for "self-management Socialist education..." implied the demand for the teacher's *declaration*, etc.

[31] M. Dolar, *Heglova Fenomenologija duha 1* (Ljubljana: Analecta, 1990), p. 98

[32] C. Taylor, *The Politics of Recognition* (Princeton: Princeton University Press, 1992), p. 41.

[33] Dolar 1990, p. 98.

[34]J. Svetina: *Slovenska šola za novo tisočletje* (Radovljica: Didakta 1990), p. 32.

[35]Cf. S. Žižek: "Wilhelm Reich ali protislovja 'freudo-marksizma'", V: W. Reich: *Sexpol*, Knjižnica revolucionarne teorije (KRT: Ljubljana 1983), p. 11.

[36]In this sense it is owing to C. Lasch that we can see how the cult of authenticity, spontaneity, liberating from compulsion is nothing else than a phenomenon of pre-Oedipal dependence and that this dependence can be overcome merely by identifying oneself with a decentred, foreign, ego-external instance of symbolic law (cf. Žižek, S.: *Jezik, ideologija, Slovenci* (Delavska enotnost: Ljubljana 1987), p. 136).

[37]Cf. Svetina 1990, str. 26 -27.

[38]C. Lasch, *The Culture of Narcissism* (London: Abacus, 1980); *The Minimal Self* (New York: Norton, 1984).

[39]V. Miheljak, "Mladina vrača pogled", M. Ule and V. Miheljak, eds., *Pri(e)hodnost mladine* (Ljubljana: DZS, 1995) pp. 121.

[40]*Ibid.*, pp.175.

[41]J. F. Herbart, *Johan Friedrich Herbarts Pädagogische Schriften (mit Einleitungen, Anmerkungen und Registern sowie reichem bisher ungedruckten Material aus Herbarts Nachlass).* Hrsg. Von O. Willmann und Th. Fritzsch. Dritte Ausgabe, 3. Band, Verlag von A.W. Zickfeldt, Osterwieck/harz und Leipzig 1919, p. 111.

- Chapter 12 -

Nationalism And Democratic Citizenship

Rudolf M. Rizman

Both concepts in the title, nationalism and democratic citizenship, are moot concepts in the sociological literature. We could emphasize their multiple questionableness: their different meanings and roles in various empirical contexts, in history, and in particular theoretical discourses. One of the essential tasks of social sciences is, in this regard, to make a connection between concepts or theories on one side and each empirical situation on the other. Without such a necessary step, the concepts would hang in the air. At the same time the scholars would not only lose the possibility of understanding the *logos* of empirical events, but also the possibility to influence them in the best possible way.

If at the end of the 1970s only a few social scientists were still interested in the topic of citizenship; we could add that at the beginning of the 1990s this topic was among the most discussed in the social sciences (Kymlicka and Norman in Beiner 1995:283). There are two kinds of reasons for the increased interest: they are theoretical and political. Amongst the theoretical reasons the one I should mention is that the concept of citizenship connects the requirement for both justice and membership within the community. Amongst political reasons for increased interest I should mention four: the growing apathy of the voters in Western democracies; the dependency of these citizens on everything which has been offered to them during the last few decades by their prosperous countries; a large influx of immigrants to Western Europe; and not least the rise of the nationalistic movements in the Eastern and Central Europe during the crisis of communism and after its fall. The problem of citizenship was promoted in the 1990s by two additional important factors both of which greatly involved healthy and stable democratic society. These two factors are justice and identity. Justice is first of all related to the following question: Do the established social institutions and structures consider justice at all when we look at the treatment of the citizens in different kinds of mutual transactions? Considering identity, we can say that the previously mentioned institutions and structures should not keep citizens from professing and developing their plural identities be they national, regional, cultural, ethnic or confessional. All of them, if they do not, of course, violate some normal or tolerant frameworks, help to construct a common social good. This is also true when there is a kind of a competitive spirit between them.

The understanding of citizenship – as we can see – was never limited to the legal or formal status of persons or their full membership in a particular political community. Citizenship also contained a dimension of cultural identity along with the political. The early or classical theory of citizenship did not pay much attention to the cultural dimension of citizenship. For T.H. Marshall (1965), one of its most visible representatives, this kind of approach was entirely a matter of course. He divided the evolution of citizenship, seen as something that assures individuals a just and equal status in society, into the following sequences or categories of rights: civil rights, political rights, and social rights, of which the first became naturalised in the 18th, the second in the 19th, and the third in the 20th century. Bigger or smaller assurances of these generations of rights, which do not require from citizens their active participation in the management of social matters, simply overlook that the membership in society is much more a complex sociological relationship than is presupposed by the classical concept of a citizenship. The critics of the classical concept of citizenship have already called our attention to some of its fundamental deficiencies. First of all they have pointed out that the passive acceptance of citizenship should be replaced by an active role which would include civic responsibilities and civic virtues. The second criticism they have developed is closer to the broader understanding of citizenship, which I use in this article, that is advocating that kind of a concept of a citizenship which would also include cultural pluralism which is at the disposal of modern societies.

Many groups, mainly ethnic, cultural, racial, as well as others, complain that although their basic elementary civil rights are formally provided, they feel excluded or underprivileged whenever they look at their membership in a particular group or cultural community within a society or country. Among the critics the "cultural pluralists" are most salient as they stand for the concept of "differential citizenship" (Kymlicka and Norman in Beiner 1995:301). The rights which they include in such an extended definition of citizenship would be special rights for endangered groups, multicultural rights for immigrant and religious communities, and the right to autonomy for national minorities. Only under these conditions would the citizens' responsibility towards their country extend beyond their responsibility to their particular community. It is much easier, of course, to write this down than to actualise it in real life. The problem is compounded if we think of different and controversial sociological discourses about this question. Let us, just as an example, mention three political situations: the liberal-individualistic, the republican and the communitarian (van Steenbergen 1994:2).

However, before we can pose the question about citizenship, the particular society has to be clear about the boundaries of such a pluralist polity. In a classical political theory this problem was widely discussed (Bauböck 1994:204). Let me recall that Carl Schmitt's comprehension of politics is almost fully subordinated to the differentiation between a friend and an enemy, while Thomas Hobbes looked at the mutual relationships between different countries exclusively through the prism of a latent state of war. Today's countries still hold the right to decide for themselves whom they are prepared to accept into their social community and grant complete legal civil rights. The policies of inclusion and exclusion are great daily themes of political discourse, which are again and again put forth whenever there are more intensive waves of immigration or more extensive influxes of refugees who, because of internal conflicts or for some other reason are leaving their countries.

The problem of definition is even more acute for young and recently independent countries which are only beginning to mark their political and territorial boundaries. Joseph Schumpeter has based his general theory of democracy on the fundamental assertion that it has to be left to the populus to define itself. Nevertheless we could say that in the recent times these types of rigid definitions – at least in some older and well established countries – have lost their sharpness. The trends in Western Europe indicate a tolerance of dual citizenship, something which has until recently (see for instance Raymond Aron) not been acceptable. Regardless of this fact, it would nevertheless be premature to entertain hopes that the time of a universal understanding of citizenship is close. Such an understanding would, several authors remind us, by transcending the differences between different groups, actually be unjust, because it would offend those groups which were during previous historical progress oppressed or excluded.

In the following section I will try to discuss in more detail the relationship between nationalism and democratic citizenship, which for many social theoreticians goes by unnoticed. Nationalism as a political doctrine enables development without hindrance of democratic consciousness in a particular politically defined area (Brendan O'Leary in Hall 1998:79). Nationalism is - in our understanding - the political discourse of a nation, which is spatially defined with internationally recognised borders. The life of political élites and political institutions unwind within the framework of the borders with development of the nation. Therefore, it is not surprising that previously mentioned political agencies often proclaim themselves as the guardians of national interests and of the nation. They point their fingers at those internal real or imagined external enemies in such a way to extend the life of their own political hegemony. Such a subjective perspective, however, would not in itself be sufficient for the survival of the nation. The achievements of the struggles of the nationalistic ideologies would be insignificant if they did not include in their programme the conquest of the state itself as the principal tool which enables the nation to protect its vital interests and secure development in a way which is as unrestrained as possible. There are, for example, many such cases within modern history, among which the most noticeable are: the French after the year 1789, the Germans and the Italians in the nineteenth century, and, of course, the Americans.

It seems that no other ideology has instrumentalized history as much as nationalism (Smith 1998:168). It is easy to find several proofs for such a claim. In the history text-books of most nations, used for learning starting in the primary school, we can see the efforts of historians to find the roots or ethnic sources of their hardly-formed nations at least in the Middle Ages if not in antiquity. In these cases, more deliberately than accidentally, one forgets those salient processes which influenced the modern formation of the nations, such as the advances in technology, the development in communication, the internationalization or globalization of the economy, and the demographic changes, and so on. We are conditionally going to call the first instance cited above "historical"; we can use it to explain the long-term process of political revolution that lead to the formation of modern nations which could not suddenly emerge without leaving some preceding traces in the history. In the second instance, which in the literature of this field is known as "modernistic", there is a willingness of a modern nation to connect its own destiny with other accompanying social phenomena, including a modern form of democracy which in our case re-establishes the bridge with democratic citizenship.

Therefore, to have common political principles is not sufficient for the existence of some kind of political community. It is important that its members share the feeling of belonging to the same community and be prepared to continue to live in it (Kymlicka 1997:18). Consciousness about the common identity which is put forward by the nationalistic discourse strengthens among the members of the political community the confidence and solidarity which lead the citizens to adopt democratic decisions and responsibilities. National identity, as we commonly call it, refers to a common history and a common language or to the feeling of belonging to a particular historically formed society shared by the citizens. They speak their common language and have behind them their common history. In such a way the citizens use and create their social and political institutions. This does not mean, however, that their narrower ethnic (subnational: regional, for instance, or any other) identity, religious allegiance or their understanding of social good, are identical.

Kymlicka rightly emphasises that the question of language, which is taught in schools, is too much neglected in liberal theory. In such a connection, one rightly feels that there is abundant talk about the language of politics, and very little, if any at all, about the politics of language. There are simplified understandings, which frequently appear in circulation, that the common national identity requires teaching in just one, that is, in a common language. The examples are not rare, however, where a common language is forced upon people and therefore does not contribute towards an environment in which the citizens would develop or feel there was justice and equal rights in what is understood under their national identity. We have to take into account, of course, that we are faced with different situations. In some cases, for instance, immigrants are prepared, without any resistance, to accept the language of their new society. However, this is not always the case. In the case of larger multi-ethnic or multinational states we can generalise that they are most stable when they are organised as political units composed of different smaller 'nations'. Each of these nations controls within its own territory linguistic rights and the possibility of self-determination. In this sense a democratic civic education has to have at least the following two fundamental functions: on the one hand it has to promote national identity of all constitutive national groups (this concerns mainly their common language and history), on the other hand it has to solidify some sort of transnational common identity, which connects different national groups in a common country. This, of course, is not a simple task as we can quickly learn from modern history. Yugoslavia and Czechoslovakia are in this view defeated, while in the case of Belgium and Canada it is not possible to foretell with some kind of confidence what awaits them in the future.

Recently, referring mainly of those who are affectionate towards the paradigm of postmodern citizenship, the theorists of citizenship are concerned with the problem of how to anchor the concept of citizenship to the society and not mainly to the state, which has been the case until now (Donati 1995:300). The shifting from state citizenship to social citizenship requires new thinking which shows the positive inclusion of identity as one of the main components of nationalism. It regains a new role: it does not support the glorification of a nation-state any more, but has to be understood as a complex social formation in which there is enough space for a larger number and levels of identities which among themselves are not in permanent conflict. In such a way the citizenship loses its former self-evident role of being a controlling mechanism for checking people's relationship towards the country in which they live. This means that this label includes also all those who do not, for instance, agree with a particular political system. In a slightly more refined theoretical language of sociology we could say that methodological holism has left or at least is slowly leaving its place to methodological individualism which affirms individual and group identities and is not inclined towards them being simply drowned in social solidarity.

From what has just been said it is obvious that the nation-state is not the centre of the political universe anymore, though I do not maintain, as some do, that the life of a nation-state is expiring. Nevertheless, we have to realise that the achieved complexity or differentiation of modern society requires a certain amount of decentralizing of institutions of nation-states (Keane in Sukumar 1995:198). If this did not happen, the nation-state would in the final consequence block itself or would be an impediment to everything that was positive and actually progressive and which was developed by the nation-state during last few decades. In this context sociologists often talk about postnational circumstances. By this they do not think mainly of a purely and qualitatively new social situation which has occurred but of the fact that the nation-state will not be the only and the privileged actor on the stage of history anymore, but will have to tolerate by its side new historical actors. Although they will not necessarily be loyal to the old concept of the nation-state, it will have to share the existent political arena with them.

In addition to the decentralisation of a nation-state Keane proposed another four important conditions for the formation of a democratic citizenship in modern times. From the ideology of nationalism they remove that sharpness which was used to make or cause wars and to subordinate the lives of individuals to the dictates of the state with no chance to appeal. The second condition is related to the required international respect of the existent juridical norms associated with the protection of national identity. No nation-state can spread its sovereignty so far that it could escape international (supra-national) control or sanctions in a case of threatening the lives of any one of constituent national identities in the multinational society.

The suggestions of the Badinter Commision for the resolution of the Yugoslav crisis were in principle, in this regard, assuring international control and the right to preserve or to protect the national identity. The international recognition of Slovenia, Croatia and Macedonia was conditional upon their recognition of civil and political freedom for the members of national minorities. Another condition was each countries' obligations to contribute towards development of a pluralistic mosaic of national identities within their own civil society. The countries could do this indirectly, that is, in such a way that they secured the space for the self-organisation of the civil society and within it for activity of both the inherited national identities and those which were chosen by individuals by their own will. In such a way it is possible to hinder the state and political parties from hyperpoliticizing or even manipulating the national identity following their short term interests. The last condition of the above mentioned Commision was the hardest to be fulfilled. Instead of the political arena of the nation-state being left exclusively to the wilfulness of the nationalistic ideology, consideration had to given to international

- 238 -

civil society, which would ensure a much wider frame for action and connection of the citizens who belong to many different nationalities. Especially during the times of crisis (natural catastrophe, economic break-down, political crisis) the established international networks of civil society help in the maintenance of unity or solidarity, which would otherwise be based upon aggressive nationalism or the accumulated hostile feelings between the members of the different national groups.

Those social scientists who, in their analysis of democracy and citizenship, simply leave out the problem of national identity are not rare. Kean's argument (in Hall 1995:186), which underlines the importance of being conscious of the national identity as the context for both previously mentioned social concepts, democracy and citizenship, is apt. Regardless of the fact that national identity is an ideal characteristic construct and as such is not physically quantifiable, people feel it as something which connects them with language, common territory, historical memory, ecosystem, common habits and customs. National identity in such a sense is of a recent origin and gives to the citizens the impression of some specific purpose. A particular community then serves this purpose, and provides it with that level of confidence and dignity; therefore, the great majority of people on this planet feel that their society is their 'home'. If it happens that someone is taking away their national identity, they find themselves in an unbearable or even hostile situation, which in its extreme version pushes people so far that they emigrate. Life in fear does not give even the slightest assurance about the possibility that democracy could begin to live. At the end it does not surprise anyone if we can furthermore add the language of democratic freedom to the constituents of national identity. Adam Michnik often discussed such a situation in Poland in the middle of the eighties.

From the perspective of liberal theory, which proceeds from the principle of the moral equality of individual persons and open borders, it is hard to become reconciled to the fact that the previously mentioned principle ends at moral equality, which is supposed to be available only for citizens (Kymlicka 1995:125).

However, the liberal theory has in this regard blunted the rigidity of its doctrine, because it would otherwise apply, that liberalism is actually indifferent towards personal cultural membership, that is, towards his or her national identity. It is nice to hear, of course, that the borders should be opened. This would increase mobility and opportunities which would arise for individuals. On the other hand, liberalism cannot be indifferent to the requirements that people's membership in different cultural communities has to be protected at the same time. This requires some limitations for immigration, if we want to remain true to the liberal principle that people belong to particular societal cultures, that is, to social contexts where they realise and on the whole recognise their needs. If the opposite was the case the liberal thinking should renounce its position, that the existence of states has whatever meaning or rational foundation at all.

This path is one of the most reliable ways for the realisation of nationalistic demands within democratic principles. Although many liberal thinkers discuss the right for self-determination of nations as negative or pronounce it as illusory, it is nevertheless necessary to establish that it can be, within some reasonable boundaries, treated as a response to the combination of nationalism and democratic theory (Bauböck 1993:9). If society was robbed of its common cultural or national identity, it would remain only as a union of atomised individuals. This does not mean the acceptance, however, of every kind of pluralism or every kind of culture, if these do not allow, as Albert Hirschman argued, both options: 'exit' and 'voice'. From a consistent liberal perspective it is possible to support only such a constitutional and legal framework in which its citizens can be loyal towards different cultures, where none of them has a monopolistic position over all others. We will be easily assured about the real democracy of such a constitutionally legal frame if we look at the situation in which small national communities or cultural groups find themselves in opposition to the major national community.

In Europe we are able to observe different historically conditioned constructs of citizenship and nationality (Mitchell and

Russel 1995:19). The first construct depicts the ethnic model of citizenship, which defines the nation as an ethnic phenomenon which is deeply anchored in culture and language. This model does not enable minorities to obtain citizenship; at best they can only count on limited legal and social rights. Although there have been some important changes recently, Germany was the closest to such a model. The second, the so called civic model, is characteristic of France, which grants citizenship to all its inhabitants, regardless of their ethnic origin, who identify themselves or actively participate in national culture.

In effect we have an alternative multicultural model of citizenship or a nationl; this one is of recent origin, which provides a social framework for maintenance and preservation of cultural and ethnic differences. In immigrant countries of this kind, such as Australia and Canada, cultural pluralism is one of the fundamental and self-evident components of the process of nation-building. In other words, this means that though different ethnic groups were incorporated in a nation, they retained cultural particularities at the same time. In Europe we are acquainted with only one multicultural model, that is in Sweden, which operated its policy of multiculturalism 'from above'; however, it has been confronted, especially in recent times, with severe criticism and serious problems.

Nevertheless, the situation in today's democratic world, even in the most developed parts, is far from the proclaimed democratic ideals. Besides confronting deeply anchored racist perspectives which resist the integration of ethnic minorities into the mainstream society, we have to deal with assimilatory pressures, which bring civil rights into confrontation with cultural conformity. It is encouraging that the violation of collective rights in relation to identity and the related issue of citizenship have met with a greater general attention by the public and in the media. Many more people, as well as official institutions, have been engaged in their defence than in the past. We have to be slightly more precise in regard to this issue. Supporting unity or collective identities is a basic part of new democratic culture, and this is connected to the more complex understanding of citizenship in which there is enough space for multiple identity and even, as some would argue, for a global citizenship. This need to provide for a broader definition of citizenship is necessary to provide a sustainable a balance in society and for the democratic recognition of communities as well as protecting the basic unit of democracy, the individual.

Discourse about global or just European citizenship is not the same as our authentic understanding of democratic citizenship (Oommen 1997:224). Therefore, for example, we could speak of citizenship in relation to the European Union only if the Union was in reality a multinational federal state. It is even more deceptive to speak of global citizenship as long as there is no global state. At this moment, we are unable to know if one is going to exist. When nation-states have in recent times transferred part of their sovereignty to interstate, suprastate and other international (regional) organisations, we have been confronted, in this sense, with the urgent task of redefining our previous understanding of (national) sovereignty. However, the largest and central feature concerning sovereignty is still in the competence of nation-states. In situations when nation-states are confronted with severe economical and internal political flaws, their national élite, regardless of its political colour, resorts to national power. The consequence of this is the revitalisation of national sovereignty and the minimisation of its further erosion. It is understandable that this kind of political process informs every constitution and understanding of democratic citizenship.

Although it is possible from some other theoretical or ideological point of view to contradict this kind of understanding of democratic citizenship, we could not reproach a person for being burdened with *a priori* nationalism. In such a case, we can, for example, first of all lean on one of the most esteemed liberal thinkers, John Rawls, who argued that a well-ordered society coincides with a "self-contained national community" (Scheffler in McKim and McMahan 1997:195). The modern liberal viewpoint speaks, in this sense, about citizens in a democratic society who have culturally defined responsibilities towards other citizens;

especially important among these responsibilities is the transmission by them to the forthcoming generations.

Liberal theorist Yael Tamir (*Ibid.*) did not overlook that the previously mentioned point of view contains a tension between explicit voluntarism and implicit nationalism or, in other words, the often overlooked fact that nationalism ascribes to unity a particular moral and political meaning, which in the voluntaristic point of view simply is not there. In these explanations of two distinguished liberal theorists one can see important contributions for setting up a theoretical paradigm – which is only beginning to show on the horizon and is therefore, in its major features, not yet worked out. Thus, it will be possible in a much more complex and exact way to explain one day the nature of the relations between democratic citizenship and nationalism.

This does not mean, of course, that we walk in gloom. We already know that the legitimacy and the focus of mobilisation are based on the principle of nationality and on the ideology of nationalism (Smith 1995:154). Even more: although some states have renounced their sovereignty or some national communities have decided to join a particular federation, we cannot, in a democratic process, ignore or do away with the fact that the nation and nationalism will for a long time remain the main point of support and endeavour for asserting the people's will – the people's sovereignty. From here to a paradigm of democratic citizenship there is only one further small step.

Bibliography:

Bauböck, Rainer. "Integration in a Pluralistic Society". Unpublished MS. 1993.

Bauböck, Rainer. *Transnational Citizenship. Membership and Rights in International Migration.* Avebury: Edward Elgar. 1994

Beiner, Ronald (ed.) *Theorizing Citizenship.* Albany: State University of New York Press. 1995

Dahl, Robert A. *Democracy and Its Critics.* New Haven: Yale University Press. 1989

Donati, Pierpalo. "Identity and Solidarity in the Complex of Citizenship: The Relational Approach". *International Sociology* 10(3):299-314. 1995

Guibernau, Montserrrat. *Nationalisms – The Nation-State and Nationalism in the Twentieth Century.* Cambridge: Polity Press. 1996

McCrone, David. *The Sociology of Nationalism – Tomorrow's Ancestors.* London: Routledge. 1998

Hall, John (ed.) *The State of the Nation. Ernest Gellner and the Theory of Nationalism.* Cambridge: Cambridge University Press. 1998

Hutchinson, John and Anthony Smith (eds.). *Nationalism.* Oxford: Oxford University Press. 1994

Hutchinson, John and Anthony Smith (eds.) *Ethnicity.* Oxford: Oxford University Press. 1996

Kymlicka, Will. *Multicultural Citizenship – A Liberal Theory of Minority Rights.* Oxford: Clarendon Press. 1995

Kymlicka, Will. "Education for Citizenship". Vienna: Political Science Series, No.40. 1997

McKim, Robert and Jeff McMahan (eds.) *The Morality of Nationalism.* Oxford: Oxford University Press. 1997

Marshall, T.H.. *Class, Citizenship and Social Development.* New York: Anchor. 1965

Mitchell, Mark and Dave Russell. "Nationalism, National Identity and Citizenship in the New Europe". Paper presented at the European Sociological Conference, Budapest. 1995

Oommen, T.K.. *Citizenship, Nationality and Ethnicity.* Cambridge: Polity Press. 1997

Periwal, Sukumar (ed.) *Nations of Nationalism.* Budapest: Central European University Press. 1995

Smith, Anthony. *Nations and Nationalism in a Global Era.* Cambridge: Polity Press. 1995

Smith, Anthony. *Nationalism and Modernism – A Critical Survey of Recent Theories of Nations and Nationalism.* London: Routledge. 1998

Van Steenbergen, Bart (ed.) *The Condition of Citizenship.* London: Sage Publications. 1994

- Chapter 13 -

Multiculturalism As Citizenship; Multiculturalism As Education

Keith A McLeod

State policy with reference to citizenship cannot be viewed outside of the complex historical background of national-states, empires, plural states and concepts of government, including liberal democratic politics.[1] The operation and the images of plural states, especially polyglot empires, have been seen as less than stellar. In the first portion of this paper I will discuss, to a limited extent, the nature of the plural state in the post-modern world. In the second part I will examine the characteristics of multicultural education as it has developed in Canada. As will become clear, in Canada, there has not been a one way process of policy leading to implementation, rather there has been a continuous interaction between the reality of pluralism and the policy. This interaction has often involved education.

I must also add one further characteristic of this paper. I am not writing and speaking, to prove and justify each thought and generalization or the analysis and commentary. The substantiation of my observations will be included in some cases or in part; however, the essential thrust of this discourse is rather to exemplify various ideas and actions. The justification can be found in other writing and research I have done or which colleagues have published.[2] What I will address is the appropriateness of multiculturalism as a basis of citizenship today and then I will examine multicultural education as it was developed in Canada.

Part I Multiculturalism As Citizenship

It is commonplace for people to say "We are living in a new world". While many people have used this expression to indicate that the cultural context of their life has changed, it is important for me to state that using that phraseology to assess the present is certainly appropriate. The transformation of culture from the industrial to the post-industrial or post-modern world is transforming life. While not all social units in the world are entering post-modernism, all are affected by it. As one colleague argues, the change underway to post-modernism is probably as profound or more profound than the shift from hunting/gathering to agrarian culture or the shift from that to industrial/modern life. (When we speak in such broad terms it is important that we recognize the various stages that societies and parts of societies are at in the world. We must also then temper our cultural 'superiority' not with simplistic cultural relativism but with international cultural understandings.)

This is not an exposition of post-modernism. I only wish to use my understanding of post-modernism to establish a context and a few key points. Among the points I would like to make is the idea that we are experiencing a change in the role of work in societies – its prevalence, control, and effects. Such volumes as *The End of Work* symbolize the process of change and the impact on life of the change.[3] Globalization is bringing a host of changes in production and distribution, in corporate structure and power, expectations and values, and even of symbolic depiction and understanding. The speed of change is rapid, the robotization of work is creating redundancies, and unemployment and underemployment are such, that the rate of youth unemployment in industrial and post-industrial societies is enormous. If anything, life is returning closer to the pre-industrial norm where youth was a time of apprenticeship and for many a much slower induction into the society including 'work' or occupation. At the same time that induction is slower, the participants in the process, youth, must acquire greater skills than formerly, especially the skills to deal with change, an apparently major criterion of post-modernism. As one Minister of Education in Canada said several years ago, "We must educate ourselves not just to deal with the effects of change, but to deal with change itself." So another feature of post-modernism we can surmise is that "life is change," life is open-ended.

You can already see the relationship of post-modern thought to education (or perhaps the reverse). Schooling itself has become more open-ended. Students used to be taught or told a generation or two ago that they were to graduate into a field or occupation; they now graduate into further studies. Students used to be taught in mathematics what equaled what; they are now equally taught about the unequal. Children were taught so that when they become adults they could make decisions and participate; they are now being taught to make decisions and participate. Children were taught what was right and wrong; they now learn to assess and analyze.

So what do the open-endedness and speed of change in post-industrialism life and the parallel changes in education have to do with citizenship?

In the pre-industrial world people moved about – they migrated and immigrated to better agricultural lands; in the industrial modern world they moved – migrated to industrial centers and immigrated to modernism. In the post-modern world, with the speed of transportation and communication, people not only move rapidly but they are living in the 'global village' to use Marshall McLuhan's old cliché. However, contrary to the old village, the new one is post-modern.

The nation-state, with the much written-about nationalities, nationalism, cultural uniformity, and assimilation has been developed, argued about, lived for and died for, now for several centuries. But was it ever a reality? Some say, "Unfortunately, yes". The history of Western Europe, Asia, Africa, Eastern Europe, the world --- have all been affected by the idea of the nation-state. The disrepute of "polyglot empires" can be found in most school texts. The oversimplification of mixed societies to fit the 'national' ideals is historically quite clear; the belief in and the use of state education to try to produce homogeneity or teach that "we are" a people and a culture has been well documented. The policies of governments to reduce diversity to 'minorities' or even worse (my value judgement) to segregate or ghettoize or even expel or exterminate them is well-known and documented world wide. Let us stop and reflect, is it not transparent that diversity is a common feature of societies and political units or countries?[4]

My argument is straight-forward. We must explore and provide for the reality of diversity globally, or should I say, earthly or planetary as well as in our various countries. There has been some analysis of plural states, multicultural states, or polyglot states; however, even a quick analysis of the literature regarding plural states will reveal that the continued noticeably uncomfortable use of the words 'nation-states' to describe countries that are characterized by diversity is commonplace in the literature on states and nation-states.

The effect of these 'shoulds', 'oughts' and myths in didactic national education of citizens, especially of the young who are being socialized, creates false impressions and premises, incorrect knowledge, false reasoning, conflicting values, and attachments to false symbols. I would argue that these effects should be evident in our recent history. Or to reverse it – the 'teaching' of nation-state, nationalistic history and schooling has had a very negative effect upon human and group relations. Even mathematics and science have been taught in many states as doctrines, I would argue.

That multiculturalism or diversity should be a primary reality we recognize about societies and about the world is to see and understand a major social characteristic or reality. Moreover, I am not talking about a single interpretation of diversity. That would be a contradiction of the essence of diversity. Multiculturalism is the recognition that a country or society is diverse; it does not posit a homogeneous national culture. I might add that multiculturalism relates directly with what I view to be a positive feature of post-modernism: the 'open-ended' nature of post-modernism...and today's education, in which the primary characteristic is change itself. We are always becoming.[5]

The commitment to see diversity as a primary feature of societies, countries or life does not mean rootlessness, amorality, cultural relativism, social disruption or continuous conflict. There are symbols, values, structures and institutions, including patterns of behaviours, by which we can live or through which we can live. Institutions, structures or patterns of behaviours which focus upon sharing, collaboration, co-operation, mediation and resolution or negotiating differences and reconciling conflict, that focus upon living together, understanding one another, supporting others, and respecting each others human rights are obvious. We see here the commitment to values associated not with simple personal or social exclusiveness or cultural superiority but with humanness and human commitment and cohesion including through tolerance, mutual respect and human rights. We are dealing with symbols, doctrines and principles and behaviour norms that demonstrate or idealize our commitments to humanity – socially and individually. Multiculturalism, or simply stated, the belief in the normalcy and acceptance of diversity, therefore, is, in my mind and my world, the keystone of citizenship. Or, to reverse the thought, citizenship must be characterized by tolerance, human rights, mutual respect, and a commitment to humanity.

Part II: Multiculturalism as Education

If I may be permitted to interpret the second focus of this paper 'multiculturalism as education', the question is how multiculturalism can be reflected or should be reflected in education, including particularly in schooling – state schooling, the vehicle of critical modern and post-modern socialization.

A key to understanding state schooling is that it is more than parental socialization of their children, although it is that in part; it is the induction of children, and adults, into citizenship (and patriotism, not nationalism). State schooling must provide students with the knowledge, skills and values or dispositions by which to lead a reflective, moral, and liberal democratic life – individually and collectively. What state schooling is not and must not be is the promotion of nationalism and unquestioned commitment to loyalty and the preservation of the state. It must also not be the inculcation of a commitment to inequity or inequities, and limiting ideologies and doctrines – to symbols, values, and structures that are inhuman or inhumane. There must be provision for learning liberal and democratic ideas and practices including tolerance and human rights.

In order to examine the relationships between multiculturalism and education let us the take a look at what can deciphered from the Canadian experience with multicultural education over the past generation or thirty years.

Phases of Multiculturalism and Multicultural Education

Multiculturalism and multicultural education have gone through several phases in various parts of the country since the announcement of the policy in the Canadian House of Commons on October 8, 1971. In the century or so prior to 1971, since even before Confederation in 1867, parts of what is now Canada had attempted to come to terms with ethnic diversity, especially in relation to religion and language. In the 1840s, both English and French were official languages in the legislature of the United Canadas. In the 1840s, various provisions were made for 'separate' or 'denominational' state supported schools in places like Upper and Lower Canada, New Brunswick and Nova Scotia. In the late 19th and early 20th century in the Western Prairie Provinces, various 'concessions' were made to separate schools and to the diversity of languages there. The diversity in Canada increased after World War II when immigration from Europe was revived. The multi-racial picture of Canada was enhanced by the arrival in the 60s of people who added their communities of blacks to those who had come from the US via the Underground Railroad (1850s) and post US Civil War immigration. From the 1960s, when immigration policy began to be deracialized, Canada experienced a significant increase in the number of Asian and SE Asian people from India, Pakistan, the Philippines, Japan, Hong Kong, Sri Lanka and Vietnam. Canada became increasingly diverse, multicultural, that is multi-ethnic and multi-racial. It also became more multi-religious and linguistically diverse. This was the reality before the 1971 enunciation of the policy .

The policy of multiculturalism recognized the reality. The policy set out three or four basic principles. The policy announced that diversity, or the belief in a plural society or state was being endorsed; that people, if they desired, might retain their cultural heritage; but that people should share their cultures and live creatively together. In particular, the policy said that all immigrants to Canada would have access to learning English or French; this matched the policy statement which said that multiculturalism should be seen within a bilingual context. In other words English and French were to be the link languages of Canada. The policy has been further detailed since that time but the essence was there.[6] Let me now turn to the phases through which multiculturalism has gone in Canada, particularly with reference to education.[7]

Phase I Cultural Reinforcement & Immigrant Adjustment

Two phenomena characterized the first period of multicultural development. Within the various groups there was a new-found feeling of participation and liberation. Years of cultural retention at their own expense, primarily demonstrated for and practised only within their own institutions, including the legendary 'church basements', were brought out into the mainstream of public life, often now supported or even 'celebrated' at public events or even public expense. (Among those critics who scoffed at what was dismissed as 'song and dance multiculturalism' were, on the one hand, those who were against endorsing diversity and, on the other, those who thought it a superficial recognition of diversity. In fact, these cultural activities were experiential, a thought which was lost on some; moreover, they were community based and ethnic driven.) Many cultural groups, led by larger 'older' immigrants groups such as the Ukrainians, Germans, Poles, and Mennonites, pushed for recognition and full participation.

The second thread of this phase was the integration of immigrants. Settlement programs and second language instruction (ESL) grew and flourished. (As a teacher educator I can also tell you that it was difficult to get students to concentrate on learning anything beyond immigrant adjustment/ESL programs.)

It is important that we note that alone, the features of multiculturalism in phase one, did not represent a balanced policy.

- 251 -

Phase II Group Relations

In the late 1970s there was increasing awareness that there was an aspect of diversity that had not been sufficiently addressed – group relations. The increased emphasis on diverse groups and diversity, in part, produced the awareness that power relations and priorities in Canada were shifting. Cities were increasingly cosmopolitan; ethnicity was increasingly 'different' as new groups became more evident; languages were increasingly less private; multi-racialism was changing the image of communities, and Aboriginal Peoples were demanding their Aboriginal Rights.[8] Some persons from traditionally dominant groups were feeling the change and attempting to maintain their power and control although often they did not express it in these terms. Rather, multiculturalism was attacked as divisive, epithets such as Paki and Wop were thrown; the right to public institutions and access were contested. Consequently, the thrust to support and implement multiculturalism led to increasing organization and support for intergroup relations. It was during this period that professions such as teaching, nursing and medicine and social work were increasingly sensitized to diversity. The Canadian Council for Multicultural and Intercultural Education was organized (1979-1981) and the Canadian Council for Multicultural Health first developed (1984-86); there were many efforts to improve group relations and to adjust Canadian and community institutions. Advisory Councils to governments were developed at the Federal level as well as by several provinces.[9] Cultural retention programs which had been especially sought by groups were now balanced by those which focused on group relations; however, visible minorities pointed out that there should be greater attention to racism.

Phase III Anti-Racism and Equity Phase

A third emphasis that developed with reference to diversity and multiculturalism focused upon anti-racism and equity. It became a feature of large urban centers that were more multi-racial – such as Toronto, Vancouver, and Montreal. The thrust, emanating from multiple sources and stimuli, had several streams. One variation was very akin to multiculturalism; the belief that the multicultural movement had not addressed racism sufficiently and that racism must be countered. As the other end of the anti-racism spectrum were those who considered multiculturalism as a 'cultural' approach to diversity that had little or nothing to do with 'race'; within this school of thought there seemed to be little awareness that when many spoke of culture and multicultural issues this included people's physical characteristics and the addressing of racism.[10]

The second issue to emerge in this phase was the issue of equity – whether people were being treated fairly or equitably, whether there was equal access, and whether, if equity was to be achieved, there had to be quotas, preferences, incentives, targets – or some form of affirmative action.

Governments as well as private companies were enjoined to examine their work forces, to establish equity programs, and to hire a work force who reflected the community or society and which promoted persons of 'minority' background. Education to promote equity through schooling and through the education of adults and the community were, for example, two foci of attention. There were also attempts in Ontario government hiring to introduce preferential hiring to redress historical inequities; this was quashed when the 'ad' became public. Canadians who prided themselves on their 'sense of fairness' rejected this 'introduction' of unfairness. A result, however, was increased access because school authorities, private companies, and governments did employ increased numbers of 'minorities'. Greater attention was paid to racism and equity. But there was a reaction. [11]

Phase IV Multiculturalism as Citizenship & Human Rights

As to the most recent times, I can only but assess that the concept and policy of multiculturalism is becoming an everyday assumption of Canadian life – an integral part of our concept of Canadian liberal democratic citizenship. In that both citizenship and multiculturalism are process-oriented rather than product-focused, they are congruent. Similarly, as post-modernism and education are process-oriented, they also are congruent with multiculturalism as citizenship. I would argue that tolerance and human rights have increased in practice and importance and become a central basis for both multiculturalism and citizenship. Post-modern life features personal participation and globalism or internationalism, and to me it is equally important to focus on tolerance, human rights, and inclusiveness in this age of rapid transportation and communication. The international implications are crucial because liberal democratic citizenship is now beyond one's country; tolerance and human rights are world-wide. Perhaps human rights and inclusiveness are appropriate countervailing forces to globalization. Cultural change goes on. For some, what is involved is being an international person (or society) rather than an ethnic person within a country. What has been evolving is a new definition or a transformation of the 'nation and national societies'. I might add here, that I can only speculate whether we will see the development of the extensive adoption of 'non-racialism'. The International Human Rights Declaration, whose 50th anniversary is currently being marked, and other international rights codes and conventions as well as standards of international tolerance, sharing and living are increasingly being heralded even if contested. (However, nothing is inevitable or necessarily forever.). It is important to note that what is espoused is an equal citizenship, in which affirmative action is voluntary not mandatory or set with quotas. (These provoked a reaction.)

Multiculturalism, therefore, can be viewed as a cultural basis for citizenship and for education. But it is not any one of the above phases; it is all of them. Depending upon the community, the needs of people, and the needs in a province, region or in the country, the emphasis may be different. Nevertheless, human rights and tolerance or mutual respect, essentials of living in and with diversity, must be present.

Let me now turn directly to some of the main features of multicultural education as it was developed and discussed in Canada. What is there that people can consider for adaptation or even adoption? Let me sample what has been recommended, researched, advocated, and implemented in multicultural education in the past 25 years.

1. Policy

There has been much said about multicultural education policy development. There was a push through the 1970s and 80s and even the early 1990s for provincial governments to adopt multicultural education policies.[12] Most did – 9 of the 10 provinces. Similarly, there has been a thrust, and in one instance, Ontario, for a short while, a requirement, that all Boards of Education or local school authorities develop policies which would guide and enhance the implementation of what was variously described as multicultural, race relations, intercultural, ethnocultural, inclusive, anti-racist or equity education. In one very real sense, these overt statements of educational commitment to diversity some said were 'political' and unnecessary; however, they were a feature of the expectations and commitment of the 1980s; in another sense they were the affirmation of the changed direction of cultural and socio-political commitment. They were commitments to providing an education based upon tolerance and human rights.

What did these multi-racial, anti-racist and ethnocultural equity education policies include? To make a generalization, they usually included a 'mission' declaration, (a commitment by the local school board, as a community board), as well as sections on administration, curriculum, community, teachers/teaching, student leadership or participation, language and possibly immigrant adjustment.[13] In a few instances implementation plans or goals were set out. However, rarely were there references to one key area – educational or learning and teaching strategies or teaching techniques. (What I have called "Establishing a Positive Environment").[14]

A couple of phenomena associated with these policy statements should be noted. The development of the policies or guidelines was usually delegated to a Board employee who was often the designated Multicultural, Equity, Anti-Racist or Intercultural Education Coordinator for that Board. The policy was also usually developed by a committee composed of Board personnel, community persons, and a couple of the 'trustees'. They consulted with a variety of persons and then submitted the 'policy' to the Board for discussion, consultation and ratification. The discourse and discussions became a major education process in the community and among the employees.

2. Administration

Aside from often stating the Board's commitment or mission and outlining the need for Board personnel to stimulate, supervise, provide, and oversee multicultural education, the Reports commissioned by Boards also advocated that the educational administrative hierarchy should be committed to implementation – that the Director, consultants, Superintendents, and the local school Principals or Heads, should be leaders in developing an education based upon human rights and tolerance and one that was culturally appropriate to the students, the community, and society. There were suggestions that schools and teachers take account of the various religious holidays when assigning work or devising programs; there were also suggestions that the linguistic capabilities of parents be considered when information was sent to parents. There were ideas set forth regarding the provision of specific courses such as English as a Second Language. There were also suggestions regarding how to multiculturalize the curriculum and to organize in-service education.[15]

In the early years of multicultural development these reports were very important in establishing the guidelines and outlining for educators 'what' constituted education for diversity.

3. Teachers

Having done years of in-service education of teachers as well as educating pre-service teachers I am acutely aware of teachers' needs. Exhorting teachers to pay attention to 'minority' needs or to teach in a multicultural manner, to be inclusive, anti-racist or non-racial is of little help to teachers who already feel threatened, bewildered or helpless. What countless teachers have asked for are the skills and knowledge by which they can carry out the public wish to respect tolerance and diversity, enhance human rights, and understand cultural particularities- to socialize children for diversity.[16]

First of all, in working with teachers one must remember the great personal and cultural variations of the students with whom they work. Moreover, the 'who' they teach may change dramatically from year to year. Therefore, what is needed by most teachers is not a 'recipe' to follow, but skills to use. Skills by which to analyze culture, cultural behaviour, cultural change, the influences of language, immigration and migration, religious affiliation, gender relations and on one can go just in relation to the cultural background of the students. However there are education related questions. How is learning and education regarded, valued, and institutionalized in the family culture? How is education symbolized, valued and structured or built into the familial culture? The community culture? Or seen from the immigrant experience? What is its relationship to social class? Last, but not least, what should the curriculum include and how should it be organized?

But there are other aspects to 'the teacher'. The teacher in a classroom represents certain cultural factors. Some of the obvious are ethnicity, race, language, gender, class, and knowledge, skills, and attitudes. Countless research studies have shown that not only what the teacher 'says' affects learning but 'who' the teacher is. The school setting is a planned setting and it is incumbent upon the providers of education to see that the teachers represent in general the variety or diversity in the community; students should not be at unnecessary consistent disadvantage. It is affirming through our own actions that we believe in and practice tolerance and human rights. Awareness of this educational factor is one that must affect long term personnel policies. It is also one that 'threatens' teachers, especially student teachers in pre-service programs.

However, there is nothing which guarantees that any teacher will automatically have the professional dispositions to deliver multicultural schooling. The growth of multicultural, intercultural, cross cultural or anti-racist courses guarantees nothing either but they do provide the opportunities for teachers or potential teachers to develop knowledge skills, and dispositions.

4. Curriculum

An interesting aspect of curriculum or the school program is that the discussions of it usually do not include, or include little, regarding teaching strategies; therefore, my comments about curriculum will, as the literature usually does, be restricted to 'content'. Sometimes there is a clear distinction made between multicultural curriculum and an anti-racist one; usually there is not, and in fact in Ontario what was listed as the 'characteristics of an anti-racist and ethnocultural equity curriculum' was what had been traditionally advocated under the multicultural rubric. Though more focused upon racism, it was basically the same package with another name.

Multicultural curricula usually include the following: tolerance; language retention and development; second language instruction; ethno-cultural content; countering prejudice, discrimination, and racism; conflict resolution and mediation; human rights; and such things as media education, communication and student participation activities. The emphasis each is given at various age/grade levels, with what particular slant is usually dependent upon the teacher, the classroom, and the community needs. The curriculum is also dependent upon how experienced everyone is – their cumulative background in previous 'education'.

Curriculum materials development or suggestions have been a favourite endeavour of Ministries of Education. I can cite a few, for instance "Black Studies, Native Studies, Human Rights in the Curriculum, Multiculturalism in Action and Anti-Racism and Ethnocultural Equity".[17]

There have also been guidelines set out in some provinces for authors and publishers; the most elaborate I can cite is "Race, Religion and Culture In Ontario School Materials – Suggestions for Authors and Publishers" (1980). These guidelines in one very real sense were the response to critiques of texts, textbook selection, the depiction and description of people (omission and commission), the needs of writers and publishers, and the frustrations of various people in communities.

Teaching Strategies

What has not been dealt with extensively in multicultural implementation, at least until the 1990s, were suggestions regarding how people come to change their attitudes or learn; how teachers could teach and present multicultural content and develop multicultural skills and positive dispositions. Although Gordon Allport's classic volume first addressed strategies, little had been explored in the Canadian context.[18] In short, we know that conditioning (operant conditioning), contact theory, and principle testing are three strategies that are more likely to produce positive effects and positive human relations. A study of these also concluded that it was the personal factor, which they had in common, that was the most likely effective factor. To these three strategies and their characteristics we can add others found from practice and other research on effective education. We know that experiential learning is an effective means of affecting knowledge and changing students' values and attitudes. We also know the following: that children with positive self-esteem are more likely to learn and more likely to develop positive and tolerant attitudes; that children learn positive attitudes from contacts that are enjoyable and satisfying; and that where there is constant reinforcement there will be greater chance of success. This reinforcement may be by teachers who are consistently exemplary. We also know that children of various differences will in groups learn to relate to one another if they are equal in status and have a common goal or task. There have also been studies which demonstrate the positive effect of exploring the similarities among people rather than concentrating on the differences. However, it has also been shown that we can help students to live together by developing their skills to cope with differences (e.g. critical thinking, tolerance, values clarification, respecting the rights of others, and mediation and conflict resolution). Lastly, in this outline of ideas I must add that we should develop a total school approach and do this with not only student involvement which helps commitment, but with parental and community involvement.

There have been countless studies in Canada regarding language teaching. To conclude this brief analysis I would only add that the research shows the better the students know their mother tongue, the more likely they will learn L2.[19]

Students, Parents and Communities

Most of the Reports promoting policies and implementation suggest that student councils and student activities be positive vehicles for promoting human and group relations. Among the most outstanding programs which involves the students in leadership in the school and community was STOP (Students and Teachers Opposed to Prejudice) in Red Deer, Alberta, but there are many others. Similarly, securing support and involvement from parents supports and promotes reinforcement. Similarly, community support or even student analysis of the attitudes and communities, help them to understand relations-tolerance and human rights, and the ethnoracial context of their community, country or the world.

Among the international or community aspects of multiculturalism that students can learn from are the International Charters of Rights of the United Nations. They may also study experientially such issues as the Holocaust, genocide, and other instances of inhumanity; when teaching these topics, teachers must be aware of the level of students' development, critical thinking, and moral reasoning.[20]

Conclusion

Whether there is explicit state/provincial policy or not speaking to multicultural education in the Canadian provinces there is a 'national' or federal level state policy on multiculturalism. I would argue that even if there weren't, the state educational system(s) should still be working toward positive human and group relations. Why? – because diversity exists in the reality of the community and the world and we need to live together. I would argue that liberalism, human rights and democratic commitment involve the freedom 'to be'. This means choice, and therefore the choice to retain and develop one's cultural background within the context of Canadian citizenship. The pluralism or diversity in a society can be incorporated into the structure of a state school system. Parallel systems or even institutions, whether in education or health, are not necessary or even seen as desirable. The 'public' may in fact view parallel systems as costly, inefficient, and divisive.

Some may even go on to say they indicate that there is insufficient attention being given to 'living together'. However, let me add one last time, there can be no single interpretation of living with diversity within a liberal-democratic context..

In the societies in which we live there is diversity, to a greater or lesser extent, and the cultural particularities we hold are held with a variety of 'strengths'. I would argue that in a free society, the three kinds of socio-cultural attachment are in fact all going on. There are people who are acculturating totally or nearly totally to another group, usually the dominant. There are persons who are creating a new amalgam or their own 'melting pot', and there are people who are retaining their cultural heritage. What the state policy of multiculturalism does is endorse the freedom 'to be'—tolerance and human rights.

The adoption of multiculturalism in Canada has resulted increasingly in a country in which multiculturalism has become an integral feature of liberal democratic citizenship– where citizenship implies a commitment to the reality of diversity. In order to fulfill the freedom 'to be', for young Canadians, an education, a schooling, which helps socialize them into society or through which they can learn the citizenship of being Canadian, is an expectation of their freedom and their human rights. Stated another way, being Canadian means learning to live with each other and being committed to tolerance or respecting 'the other' citizen. It is obviously also a good basis for international living.[21]

Endnotes

[1] I am indebted to my fellow presenters at the Conference for their ideas and analysis. At the risk of citing one presenter, I am particularly indebted to Prof. Sabrina Ramet for her analysis of liberalism, democracy, tolerance, and cultural relativism

[2] For studies by Canadian colleagues, see for example, the research presented in the reports of the three year National Study which I had the privilege of being National Director:
Report #1 *Multicultural Education: The State of the Art National Study*, ed., Keith A. McLeod.

Report #2 *Multicultural Education: The State of the Art*, ed., Keith A. McLeod.

Report #3 *L'Education multiculturelle: etat de la question—Ecole et societe*, ed., Zita De Koninck

Report #4 *Multicultural Education: The State of the Art-The Challenges and the Future*. ed., Keith A. McLeod. All the above are published by the Canadian Association of Second Language Teachers, 176 Gloucester St., Suite 310, Ottawa, Canada, K2p 0A6.

See also such books as that edited by Jean Leonard Elliott, *Two Nations, Many Cultures—Ethnic Groups in Canada*, 1979, Prentice Hall, Toronto, and Evelyn Kallen, *Ethnicity and Human Rights in Canada*, (2nd ed.), 1995, Oxford University Press, Toronto

I should add here that I am grateful to colleagues with whom I have worked such as Vandra Masemann, Roberta Russell, Mavis Burke, Kogila Moodley, Walter Temelini, Inez Elliston, and Ralph Masi and many people in the community and in the fields of education and health

[3] Jeremy Rifkin, *The End of Work, The Decline of the Global Labour Force and the Dawn of the Post-Market Era*. New York: G.P. Putnam's Sons. 1995. See also Robert Theobald, *Reworking Success: New Communities at the Millennium*. Gabriola Island, BC: New Society Publisher ,1997.

[4] For a discussion of nationalism see Heribert Adams, 'The Politics of Identity: Nationalism, Patriotism, and Multiculturalism', in the *Journal of Ethno-Development*, Vol. 1, #2, 1992, Michigan Heritage Studies Center. The General Editor of the Journal is Otto Feinstein, Wayne State University, Detroit. The issue also has studies of multiculturalism in Canada in relation to racism, health care, equity, languages education, media, and voluntarism.

[5] If an existing generation or society establishes the normalcy of diversity and respect for human rights it enhances the likelihood, I think, that the future generations of that society will do so.

[6] See, for example the article by the Hon. Gerry Weiner in the *Journal of Ethno-Development*, Vol. 1, #2, 1992 for the history of the policy.

[7] Keith A. McLeod and Eva Krugly-Smolska, *Multicultural Education: A Place To Start - A Guideline For Classroom, Schools And Communities*, 1979,Canadian Association of Second Language Teachers, 176 Gloucester St., Ste. 110, Ottawa, Canada, K2P 0A6. This was published as a follow-up to the National study. See end-note #2

[8] In this paper I am not placing an emphasis on any group; however, it important to note that the original people in Canada have been increasingly insistent that their Aboriginal Rights be recognized. But, one can say, there is a long way to go. Land claims are only now starting to be settled. Native People in Canada have played a small role in multiculturalism, *per se*; they have

preferred to speak out and speak of Aboriginal Rights. However, they do usually see themselves as part of the diversity in this plural society.

[9] I spent four years as a member of the Ontario Advisory Council On Multiculturalism And Citizenship. There have also been advisory committees or mayor's committee in various municipalities, especially large cities. Many provinces such as Saskatchewan, Alberta and Quebec have had such councils or committees. The councils were useful vehicles by which governments could tap minority views, and people could encourage adjustment or change in policy or structure

[10] See comments in the 1987 Ontario government document *The Development of a Policy on Race and Ethnocultural Equity*. The report condemns 'multicultural education' through a series of negative over-generalizations. See also *Canada; Access to Education in a Multicultural Society*, 1988.

[11] Perhaps I should add that the concept of 'equity' has, in a much more pragmatic non-governmental or non didactic form, enhanced Canadian belief in 'fairness'; however, there is still a long way to go in implementing equity in daily life,---in hiring and promotion, and in access to services. Ask, for example, the Native People in Canada.
Reports form this period should be noted: Canada, House of Commons, 1984, *Equality Now! The Report of the Special Committee in Canadian Society.* And R. Robinson et al, *Access to Trades and Professions in Ontario*, Ontario Cabinet Committee on Race Relations, 1987

[12] For the early development of the policy in Ontario see Keith A McLeod 'Multiculturalism in Ontario' published in bicentennial conference proceedings, *Two Hundred Years: Learning to Live Together*, 1985, Toronto, Government of Ontario, In the same publication you will find an article by Canon Purcell, ' The Development of Human Rights and Race Relations in Ontario".

[13] There were policies set out by a large number of Ontario Boards of Education. Here are a few of their reports or policy statements: *Toronto Board of Education, Final Report of the Work Group on Multicultural Programs, 1976; Final Report of Sub-Committee on Race Relations; Towards a Comprehensive Language Policy* (Final Report of the Work Group on Third Language Instruction). The Board of Education for the City of North York Race and Ethnic Relations and Procedures, [1981]; *The Metropolitan Separate School Board, Race and Ethnic Relations and Multicultural Policy, Guidelines and Procedures*, 1984. See also the policies of Scarborough, East York and Etobicoke .

[14] *Putting it All Together - Ethnic and Race Relations: Establishing a Positive Learning Environment*. Video. Available from Information Commons, Media Center, U of T, 130 St. George St, Toronto, M5S 3H1

[15] The development of in-service education of teachers was crucial for the implementation of education. While in pre-service you could provide students with the opportunity to learn general principles and strategies and techniques in-service gave teachers the opportunity to discuss approaches, curriculum and strategies, student needs and to apply them. Among the most systematic in-service programs which I witnessed was that of Dr. Inez Elliston of the Scarborough Board of Education. See also the *Report of the Intervisitation Program for Trustees and Administrators, Multiculturalism and Education*, 1984, OISE.

[16] Vandra Masemann, *Multicultural Policy in Teachers' and Trustees' Organizations*, Multicultural Directorate, 1984. Several Teachers Federations put anti-discriminatory clauses in their Codes of Ethics.

[17] These I have listed came from the Ontario Ministry of Education. Probably the most extensive 'support documents' for teachers came from the Ontario Ministry of Education when Dr. Mavis Burke of the Ministry, encouraged change,. See also Jack Kehoe, *Multicultural Canada: Considerations for Schools, Teachers, and Curriculum*. Public Issues in Canada Project, University of British Columbia, 1984.

[18] Gordon Allport , *The Nature of Prejudice*, New York: Anchor Books, 1954, ,. A classic that examines prejudice from a psychological perspective. For an earlier discussion regarding teaching strategies, see my article 'Multiculturalism and Multicultural Education in Canada: Human Rights and Human Rights Education'. It is published in two books: Kogila Moodley. ed., *Beyond Multicultural Education.*, 1992, Detselig Enterprises Ltd., Calgary; and in Hugh Starkey, ed. *The Challenge of Human Rights Education,* 1991, Cassell, London

[19] See article by Marcel Danesi and others in Marcel Danesi, Keith McLeod and Sonia Morris, eds., *Heritage Languages and Education- The Canadian Experience*. Oakville: Mosaic Press, 1993. See also
Jim Cummins, *Heritage Language Education - A Literature Review,* Ontario Ministry of Education, 1983.
Walter Temelini, 'The Humanities and Multicultural Education', in K.A. McLeod ,ed., *Multicultural Education; a Partnership* Canadian Council for Multicultural and Intercultural Education, 1987.

[20] Community involvement and support can take many forms- from school councils, to community resources people, and community reports and articles. In Ontario and elsewhere in Canada, while schools and educators were developing multicultural, anti-racist, ethnocultural, equity education there were other strategies and programs being done, for example, in relation to policing, health, libraries, and community behaviour. See for example the work of the League of Human Rights, B'nai Brith. See also *Report of Proceedings of the*

Symposium on Policing In Multicultural/Multiracial Urban Communities, published by Multiculturalism Canada and Canadian Association of Chiefs of Police; and Dorothy Davies *et al*, *Multicultural Library Services: A Partnership in Responsibility*. 1981, Ontario Public Libraries Review. A community oriented book, edited by M.I. Alladin and N. Spilios, *Enhancing Social; Harmony and Economic Development in a Pluralist Canada*, 1993, Canadian Multicultural Foundation, Edmonton. Regarding the development of children in relationship to prejudice there is a highly acclaimed study regarding early childhood by Francis Aboud, *Children and Prejudice*. Oxford and New York: Basil Blackwell, 1998.

[21] There are several web sites listed in *A Place To Start*. Another website in relation to Canada is that of Statistics Canada www.statcan.ca

- Chapter 14 -

Theoretical Approaches To Multicultural Education From A British Perspective

Geri Smyth

Introduction

The purpose of this paper is to consider the role of education in strengthening citizenship in democracies. One of the challenges which democracies face is the changing demographies due to worldwide political changes and increased economic mobility. The population of a democracy may consist of many ethnic groups, and education needs to address the needs of all these groups.

This paper discusses the ways in which the British education system has responded to the needs of an ethnically diverse population. For many years the term "multicultural education" has been in use in educational circles throughout Britain and many other parts of the world. What does the term mean? What are the aims of multicultural education? What are the dilemmas that are associated with the terminology? What are the resources, both human and physical, required to achieve Multicultural Education? This paper considers these questions in relation to the development of the terminology from a British perspective. The main focus in terms of official curriculum guidance will be on Scotland.

Nieto (1992) has suggested that teachers tend to internalize and perpetuate negative societal attitudes toward ethnic groups. It is vital that teachers themselves are educated for teaching in a multiracial society. Nieto has argued that a teacher cannot be a multicultural teacher unless they see themselves as a multicultural person, able to see reality from a variety of perspectives.

A Brief History of Responses to Multicultural Education in Britain

Britain has a history of acknowledging in a range of ways the need for education to respond to the changing ethnic makeup of the population. Educational policy began to respond to the presence of black children in schools in the late 1950s to early 1960s when the children of migrants from the Caribbean and South Asia who had been encouraged to come to Britain to solve the labour shortages in low status jobs started to attend British schools. The history of this policy has been well documented elsewhere (Mullard; Rose et al.; Rex and Tomlinson). It is clear from an examination of the responses that black pupils have been seen as a problem by the educational policy makers: linguistically, administratively and politically. Initial, assimilationist responses focused on absorbing black pupils into the majority population as soon as possible, in order to neutralize the influences of their home culture and language. This monoculturalist response was highlighted in the 1964 report of the Commonwealth Immigrants Advisory Council: "a national system of education cannot be expected to perpetuate the different values of immigrant groups." [1]

From the late 1960s, the notion of cultural superiority was replaced, in rhetoric at least, by the liberal concept of cultural tolerance as exemplified by Roy Jenkins, then Labour Home Secretary, who urged: "not a flattening process of assimilation but equal opportunity, accompanied by cultural diversity, in mutual tolerance."

The Department of Education and Science made it quite clear however that although the terminology might have changed, the aims were the same: "to safeguard against any lowering of standards due to the presence of large numbers of non-English speaking children which might adversely affect the progress of other children." (DES, 1971)

After thirty years, the assimilationist stance appears to continue to be the basis of the thinking and attitudes of many teachers, who insist, for what they believe to be the best of intentions that they make no distinctions between black and white pupils. The Rampton Report, which resulted from a British Government Committee of Enquiry into the Education of Children of West Indian Origin, referred to this as a colour blind approach which in fact ignores important differences among them which may give rise to particular educational needs (DES, 1981p.13). Such thinking also seems to inform some teacher's attitudes to children's first languages. Frequent assumptions are made that in order for children to learn anything at school they need to be fluent in the language of education (English in the context under discussion). This totally denies the value of the child's own language as a learning medium.

From the early 1970s, the official response became one of cultural pluralism, as stated in the Green Paper published by the British Government *Education in Schools*: "Our society is a multicultural, multiracial one, and the curriculum should reflect a sympathetic understanding of the different cultures and races that now make up our society. We also live in a complex, interdependent world, and many of our problems in Britain require international solutions. The curriculum should therefore reflect our need to know about and understand other countries." (DES, 1977*)*. It is from this multiculturalist stance that many of the education authorities in Britain have drawn their position and policy.

Multicultural Education in the Scottish Education System

The need for a 'multicultural curriculum' is specifically argued for in the Scottish Office Education Department (SOED) curricular guidelines for *English Language* (p.59), *Environmental Studies* (p. 96), *Religious and Moral Education* (p.52) and *Expressive Arts* (p.81). Thus four of the five compulsory curricular areas in Scottish education for five to fourteen year old children (only Mathematics being excluded) require schools and teachers to consider multiculturalism when they are devising a curriculum. However, none of these documents explain what is meant by a multicultural curriculum.

The Scottish Office Education and Industry Department (SOEID) published *Guidelines on Teacher Training* (1993) which incorporate a list of competencies deemed necessary in newly qualified teachers. One of these competencies is that newly qualified teachers should be able to demonstrate that they can take cultural differences into account. Most of the existing thirty-two local education authorities in Scotland have policy statements on Multicultural Anti-Racist Education (MCARE) which are translated into schools' mission statements and published in schools' handbooks. Thus, for example, although the Multicultural Education policy document (SRC, 1986) of Strathclyde Regional Council (SRC), the then biggest education authority in Scotland) did not appear until nine years after the DES Green Paper, the tone of it is very similar: "...the United Kingdom is a multicultural and multiracial society existing within an interdependent world. From this it follows that the education system must serve the particular needs of such a society and equip young people for life within it." (SRC, 1986, pp. 4-5) This similarity to the Green Paper (DES, 1977) suggests that the document had been influenced by developments and policies outside Strathclyde, but that Strathclyde had not in fact concerned itself with the critiques of existing policies in the intervening nine years or had dismissed these criticisms as irrelevant to its situation.

What Is Multicultural Education?

A simple definition of multicultural education, as suggested from a study of the above documents, would be an education for and/or about many cultures in response to the changing demography of the world. For this definition to be of any use, there is a need to define the concept of culture. This is itself a difficult task for culture is not a static and finite body of content but a complex and dynamic formation of identity that results from a combination of environmental, linguistic, hereditary, gender, religious and other influences.

The term "multicultural education" can be applied at both a descriptive and a normative level, describing educational issues and problems related to a multicultural society or considering policies and strategies for the education of children in a multicultural society.

- 269 -

It is at the normative level of policies and strategies that two competing ideologies have influenced multicultural education in Britain; these will be examined in this paper.

Strathclyde Regional Council, in arguing for the development of a multicultural curriculum stated: " The promotion of wider knowledge and understanding of different cultures and of respect for the values of each, and the accurate location of the pupil's immediate environment within a national and international context can contribute to the elimination of the ignorance, prejudice and fear from which racist attitudes grow --- many individual schools have embraced some aspect of multiculturalism. There is a growing awareness of the need to take account of the cultural diversity of the West of Scotland when planning the curriculum. These efforts have frequently been directed towards such matters as the celebration of a variety of ethnic minority festivals or the development of topics concerned with religious or cultural differences. Much good practice has already been developed." (SRC, 1986, pp. 8-9)

Farrukh Dhondy finds that this emphasis on and concern with culture and cultural differences is absurd: "For the first time in a hundred years the state has concerned itself with the culture of the people who pass through schools. ---If the state, the educational authorities and inspectors of schools are serious about what they say, it will mean that teachers will have to examine what working class values and cultures are, and begin to feed into the curriculum the primary fact of working class life - the struggle against the ownership of wealth and distribution of wealth in a capitalist society If I, as a teacher, want to represent black culture, black values, histories, assumptions, lifestyles of the people 1 am paid to school, I am determined to start from the fact that young blacks fight the police, they refuse dirty jobs; their forms of culture gathering always bring them into conflict with the rulers of this society..." (Dhondy, 1981 : 267-268).

The criticisms of such approaches to multicultural education were encapsulated in the Institute of Race Relations' statement to the Rampton Committee, established in 1978. The Institute's statement alleged that the multicultural model prescribed reforms which tinker with educational techniques and methods and leave unaltered the racist fabric of the educational system.[2]

The SRC document recognized the existence of racism. However it suggested that, "The most significant single long term approach towards tackling the problems of racism lies in the development of a multicultural curriculum" (SRC, 1986, p.7). The Minority Ethnic Teachers' Association pointed out in their comments on the policy statement: "tackling racism through the development of a multicultural education is misguided and ill - informed." (META, 1986). The singular lack of success of such a development in eliminating racism is well documented in the literature, and the majority of the Local Education Authorities in England are moving away from multiculturalism towards an anti-racist education.

Distinctive educational responses were being made in Britain to the needs of a multi-ethnic school population. Brandt (1986) represents the relationship between multicultural and anti - racist education on a continuum:

Perspectives on the relationship between multiculturalism (x) and anti-racism (y)
1<------------2----------------3----------------4--------------->5
x   x>y   x:y   y>x   y

The left end of the continuum represents the exclusively multicultural approach to educational practice. Brandt points out that there is a strong 'progressive' argument which makes the case for the need to value 'other people's culture' and to incorporate it in to the school curriculum. This incorporation, the argument goes, would ensure that pupils of 'ethnic minority' back grounds would have a positive self-image and would therefore be more in sympathy with the school as an institution and with the society at large. Let us examine each segment of thought.

This 'progressive' multicultural approach is one that has been prevalent in Scottish schools. There has been a focus in primary education in developing a multicultural focus in topic work.

For example, primary schools throughout Glasgow can be seen studying "The Tenement" whose inhabitants are families from different ethnic backgrounds, while totally avoiding or ignoring the racism that could be part of those families' lives. As Brandt states: "The problem with this approach is that it fails to acknowledge the stratification of British society along class, race and gender lines and the oppressive structures that maintain that status quo...." If we were in any doubt about this analysis, the Green Paper on education [on which, as I argued earlier, Strathclyde Region based its policy] states that "The education appropriate to our imperial past cannot meet the requirement of modern Britain. Even if one assumes 'good intentions' what is blatant is that the ideological framework for the problem does not allow for the consideration of racism - especially institutional racism- and starts from the assumption that the racist education of imperialist Britain would be perfect if only there were no black people here."

Robert Jeffcoate, an influential figure in the Schools Council, a British Government appointed group that had been commissioned to produce the report on *Education for a Multicultural Society* (1981), based himself categorically in the multicultural education camp. Jeffcoate (1982) identified with the liberal view of education that he says is "primarily concerned with the aims of schooling, specifically with meeting individual and social needs.... Schooling can and should serve as an arena for self-realization .... The stress lies on the enhancement of individual life-chances not on the diminution of group inequalities."

Jeffcoate (1979) had rejected any argument based on the assumption that "British society suffers from an endemic malaise, racism, which has acquired the status of a cultural norm and moulds children's attitudes." He argued that racism was a matter of individual prejudice and ignorance and argued for a multicultural education model that aimed at the celebration of "international friendship and under standing."

Troyna and Williams(1986) criticize such programmes: "The aims and objectives of multicultural education programmes are premised along precisely the same lines as their ideological forerunners. They are geared to a perspective which sees education as the main distributor of life chances; they are also committed to the belief that black students must be persuaded to accept the meritocratic function and credibility of schooling." They argue that The 3 S's (saris, samosas, and steel bands) interpretation of cultural pluralism was advanced as the operational mode through which the 3 R 's (resistance, rejection and rebellion) would be contained and defused. Such a formulation could only be explicable in terms of assimilationist imperatives.

This is what Salman Rushdie criticized in 1982:

"And now there's a new catchword: 'multiculturalism'. In our schools this means little more than teaching the kids a few bongo rhythms and how to tie a sari - Multiculturalism is the latest token gesture towards Britain's blacks. It ought to be exposed - like 'integration' and 'racial harmony'- for the sham it is. Unfortunately, sixteen years later, there is little evidence in Scottish schools or in the National Curriculum of England and Wales of this sham having been exposed."

To return to Brandt's continuum, the next position he discusses is one where multiculturalism includes anti-racism. Andy Green, a London secondary school teacher, argues that " genuine multicultural education must by definition be anti-racist." [3]

This is perhaps the position which many Scottish authorities (the inheritors of the former SRC's policies) now espouse. Following the publication *Education in a Multicultural Society*, a Policy Development Committee was established to put the policy into practice. This committee referred to Multicultural Anti-racist Education (MCARE), and its priorities included the development of guidelines on tackling racist incidents, ethnic monitoring and curriculum initiatives. The Director's report (SRC, 1989) which established the Committee seemed to refer to multiculturalism and anti-racism as one and the same thing: "...all curriculum initiatives should wherever possible take into account the multi-racial and pluralist nature of British society.... Further, a multicultural and anti-racist curriculum should fully recognize the role and place of

- 273 -

the African and Asian continents and their contribution to our economic, social and cultural heritage."

Chris Mullard, Director of the Race Relations Programme at the University of London's Institute of Education, disagrees with Andy Green's position, and therefore with that espoused by many education authorities: "There can not be anti-racist styles of multicultural education. Anti-racist multicultural education is a theoretical contradiction. Anti - racist education stems from structure; multicultural comes from culture. Multicultural education emphasizes the cultural criteria and practices of ethnic groups. Anti-racist education comes from structure; - it begins by identifying the problem as seen and viewed by black people who occupy lowly structural positions in society---it concentrates on the issue of racism.[4]

Brandt goes on to identify two further positions which Mullard would see as theoretical contradictions. The first of these (position 3 on the diagram; x:y) suggests that a multicultural curriculum can get taught in an anti-racist way but Mullard sees multicultural education as a white form of education. Brandt himself points out: "What tends to get missed out in this approach is the specificity of the construction of the curriculum, both in terms of content and context and both in terms of omissions and inclusions."

The second position that I believe Mullard would see as contradictory, again on the grounds of the origins of the two positions (structure versus culture) is that anti-racism is by definition multicultural.

There are clearly a wide variety of positions in this debate and it is one with which neither the policy makers nor the practitioners in Britain have come to grips. A primary head teacher was seconded in the early 1990s to the post of regional MCARE staff tutor. Her function was to multiculturalise the primary curriculum. This has typified the response of many education authorities to the debate: anti-racist is included for the terminology, not the practice.

Educational policy documents in Britain make very little reference to the perceptions of ethnic minority parents and pupils.

The only mention in the 1989 SRC Director's Report is to state that an incident will be treated as racist if a pupil or parent alleges that it is. There has been no consultation with ethnic minority parents over how they perceive the multiculturalisation of the curriculum.

In the ACER video, "*Anti-racism - 3 Perspectives*", Cheryl Adesanya, a black parent, expresses her concerns about mainstream education. She believes that multicultural schools are not doing enough; they are "all talk and no action". As a result of this concern, she believes it is necessary to establish mainstream black schools staffed by conscious black teachers and involving black parents.[5] This is not the view held by all black educationalists but the view has led for example to the opening of state-funded Muslim schools in some areas of Britain in recent years.

Adesanya suggests that the bureaucracy of schools militates against parental involvement and that the schools do not welcome parental support. These concerns have been echoed by Mukami McCrum, a Scottish black parent and community worker[6], although her conclusions were not the same. McCrum suggested that major barriers to parental involvement were the fact that the school is a white institution and that parents are aware of the assumptions that are made about black children's home background. Ms McCrum expressed ethnic minority parents' concern that their children may be victimized if the parent becomes involved in the child's education. She believes that an open-door policy, whereby parents are welcome in the school at any time, as opposed to the formal appointments system that operates in most schools, would break down a lot of barriers and that parents should be involved in the policy making.

These parental views are all given theoretical credence in the work of Maureen Stone (1981) whose research tackled a specific aspect of institutional racism in operation, namely how multicultural education can be detrimental to the achievement of black children, in its analysis of black children's culture needing to be compensated for in the curriculum. Multicultural education thus gives already powerful white professionals yet another tool with which to define the reality and situation of black children for them.

The implications of this for Stone are that "Teacher training should emphasize that teachers' professional interest lies in the inducting of children into knowledge, skills and abilities rather than in the provision of social work or therapy to children. ...Disproportionate stress has been placed on knowledge of the cultural and home background of 'immigrants' 'in teacher training...it may reinforce stereotypes and not enable the teacher to regard black children as potential intellectuals, worthy of their best teaching efforts instead of potential clients for therapy."

The position at the right end of Brandt's continuum is anti-racist education; that is an education which addresses the power inequalities in schools and society and helps children to understand and deal with racism, prejudice and stereotyping. In order to facilitate a definition of anti-racist education, I have adapted another of Brandt's diagrams that juxtaposes some examples of the language of multiculturalism and anti-racism. (see next page)

The Swann Report, *Education for All*, (Department of Education and Science, 1985) stressed the need for all educational institutions to prepare all pupils for life in a multiracial society by examining resources for ethnocentric bias, combating racism and developing school policies. However the report did not offer guidance to teachers or schools as to how to proceed with these recommendations.

Schools and teachers have been required to develop school anti-racist policies without a theoretical framework in which to work, and with no distinction being made between multiculturalism and anti-racism. Strathclyde Region's policy document, for example, understands Britain as a pluralist state, whereas Brandt states that "Anti-racist education starts from the premise of a racist state and therefore acknowledges that the essential aims of education are not necessarily in the interest of the racially defined dominated groups in the same way in which state education is not seen to be constructed for the ultimate benefit of working class pupils."

COMPARING THE LANGUAGE OF MULTICULTURALISM AND ANTI-RACISM

Phenomenon	Multicultural approach and language	Anti-racist approach and language
Perception of societal base	Failure of consensus within cultural pluralism of majority and of minority groups	Conflict between racist state and individuals and racially defined oppressed groups
The problem	Institutional and interactional monoculturalism/ethnicism and ethnocentricity Non-recognition, marginalization negative image, intercultural misunderstanding	Institutional and interactional racism, Racial exploitation, oppression, containment, cooptation, fragmentation (divide and rule) power maintenance, marginalization
The key concept	CULTURE awareness, equality, parity of esteem, racialism	RACISM Equal human rights, power ,justice
The objective	EQUALITY Prejudice, misunderstanding	JUSTICE Structure, power, context
The process	INTERCULTURALISM	ANTI-RACISM
The solution	Provide information, cultural exchange, cultural/ ethnic awareness, permeation, special interest	Dismantle, Deconstruct,Reconstruct The 3 O's (Mullard): Observation, Orientation, Operation, Struggle

(After Brandt, 1986)

Brandt goes on to say: "It seems to me that regardless of whether or not an authority has a policy, any school wanting to actively engage with an anti-racist practice should be considering the formulation of an anti-racist policy statement, implementation strategy and monitoring/evaluation procedure. This is so because whether or not there is a policy statement, the school is operating a policy. Therefore it seems imperative that a school that is serious about realizing the aims of anti-racist education would want to formulate a policy".

Mullard makes it clear that tacking 'anti-racist' onto a policy title is meaningless without a corresponding change in understanding: "Without a radical reappraisal of multiracial education theory and practice, our society's materialist and racist culture will continue to be transmitted by all schools: without a radical reconstruction of our society and of the meaning and practice of multiracial education in particular, we shall for some time to come continue to talk about black kids in white schools rather than merely children in schools."

Troyna and Williams made a study of the policies of seven local authorities in England purporting to be anti-racist. They found that Mullard's formulation was "evident in theoretical terms but absent from concrete policy observations --- simply not confirmed by what is contained in anti-racist education policy documents." Lax (1984) has pointed out that the extent to which anti-racism can become an effective accepted educational practice within mainstream schools operating within a fundamentally racist society is clearly limited and serves to remind all anti-racists of the need to be involved in the wider struggle.

The polarization of the debate in the British education system has resulted in internal dilemmas and contradictions. In the myriad of definitions what is clear is that there do need to be educational responses to the changing populations of democracies. In Britain, the debate continues but has been diffused somewhat in the eighteen years of Conservative government. Educationalists have been fighting to retain child-centred education in the face of the Education Reform Act and attacks by the government and the media on anything that could be termed progressive education.

Gilroy (1992), lecturer in sociology at Goldsmith's College, University of London, and author of *There Ain't No Black in the*

Union Jack, insists that there is more to the emancipation of black people than an educational opposition to racism. He poses the creation of a radical, democratic civil society which will link immediate local concerns to globalizing economic and political developments, forging links for example between the black communities in Brixton who experienced nail bombings in 1999 and black South Africans as they develop their economic and political power in the aftermath of apartheid.

De Vreede (1998) suggests that there are four types of educational response to the fact of plurality in societies and these are based on two variables. The target group may be either the ethnic minority or the whole society and the purpose may be either remedial, i.e. undoing deficiencies, or facilitating, i.e. making desirable processes possible. He claims that the combination of these two variables leads to four types of plural education: induction programmes, ethnic programmes, societal problem-solving programmes and educational change. De Vreede defines these types of education as follows: "Induction programmes help ethnic minority pupils to overcome their problems and to make a smooth insertion into the educational system possible. Ethnic programmes address themselves to the ethnic minority with the purpose to facilitate processes that are desirable for this group. Societal problem-solving programmes aim at tackling specific societal problems such as discrimination and racism. Educational change is the strongest reaction to society's plurality ... and will change or even transform society. " (De Vreede, 1998, p. 4) The method by which these educational programmes are transmitted will be dependent on the values of the society within which it is operating.

The interdependence of societal values and educational responses proposed by De Vreede is what has to be considered in the devising of educational reactions to increasing plurality in societies.

There have been and continue to be a wide range of educational responses to ethnic diversity in Britain. The terminology of multicultural anti-racist education carries many layers of meaning, some of which have been explored in this paper. It is of importance that the educational responses to diversity in the coming century do not perpetuate the stereotypes and prejudices which have been shown to be a contributory factor in the continuing underachievement of black pupils in British schools.

Bibliography

Brandt, G. (1986) *The Realization of Anti-racist Teaching*. London: Falmer Press. Department Of Education And Science (1971) *The Education of Immigrants*. London: DES.

Department Of Education And Science (1977) *Education in Schools: a Consultative Document (The Green Paper)*. London: DES.

Department Of Education And Science (1981) *West Indian Children in our Schools (The Rampton Report)*. London: DES.

Department Of Education And Science (1985) *Education for All (The Swann Report)*. London: DES.

de Vreede, E. (1998) *Underlying Assumptions in Plural Education*. Paper presented to the conference of the Association for Teacher Education in Europe, Limerick.

Dhondy, F. (1981) "Teaching Young Blacks" in James, A. and Jeffcoate, R. *The School in the Multicultural Society*. London: Harper and Row.

Gilroy, P. (1992) "The End of Anti-racism" in Donald, J. and Rattansi, A. (eds.) *'Race', Culture and Difference*. London: Sage Publications.

Jeffcoate, R. (1979) *Positive Image: Towards a Multiracial Curriculum*. London: Writers and Readers.

Jeffcoate, R. (1982) *Ethnic Minorities and Education*. Milton Keynes: Open University Press.

LAX, L. (1984) "Anti-racist Policies" in *Challenging Racism*. London: ALTARF.

Minority Ethnic Teachers' Association (1986) *Comments on Education in a Multicultural Society*. Glasgow: META.

Mullard, C., (1982) "Multiracial Education in Britain" in Tierney, ed., *Race, Migration and Schooling*. London: Holt, Rinehart and Winston.

Nieto, S. (1992) *Affirming Diversity: the socio-political context of multicultural education.* New York: Longman.

Rex, J. and Tomlinson, S. (1979) *Colonial Immigrants in a British City.* London: Routledge and Kegan Paul.

Rose, S., Lewontin, R.C. and Kamin, L.J. (1984) *Not in our Genes.* Harmondsworth: Penguin.

Schools Council (1981) *Education Of A Multicultural Society.* London: CRE

Scottish Office Education Department (1991) *Curriculum And Assessment In Scotland: National Guidelines English Language 5-14.* Edinburgh: Soed.

Scottish Office Education Department (1992) *Curriculum And Assessment In Scotland: National Guidelines Expressive Arts 5-14.* Edinburgh: Soed.

Scottish Office Education Department (1993) *Curriculum And Assessment In Scotland: National Guidelines Environmental Studies 5-14.* Edinburgh: Soed.

Scottish Office Education Department (1993) *Curriculum And Assessment In Scotland: National Guidelines Religious And Moral Education 5-14.* Edinburgh: Soed.

Scottish Office Education And Industry Department (1993) *Guidelines On Teacher Training.* Edinburgh: Soed.

Strathclyde Regional Council (1986) *Education In A Multicultural Society,* Glasgow, SRC.

Strathclyde Regional Council (1989) *Director's Report on Multicultural and Anti-racist Initiatives.* Glasgow: SRC.

Stone, M. (1981) *The Education of the Black Child in Britain: The Myth of Multiracial Education.* London: Fontana

Troyna, B. and Williams, J. (1986) *Racism, Education and the State.* London: Croom Helm

Endnotes

---

[1] CIAC 2nd Report, quoted in Troyna and Williams, *Racism, Education and the State*. London:
Croom Helm. 1986. p. 12

[2] Institute of Race Relations Satement to the Rampton Committee, quoted in Troyna and   Williams, *opus cit.*, p.43

[3] Green, A. speaking on 'Race and Education': Radio Cassette 3 for Open University course E354: Ethnic Minorities and Community Relations

[4] Mullard, C, speaking on 'Race and Education': Radio Cassette 3 for Open University course E354: Ethnic Minorities and Community Relations

[5] Cheryl Adesanya speaking on "Anti-racism; 3 Perspectives": video produced by Afro- Caribbean Education Resource Centre (ACER)

[6] Mukami McCrum, speaking at Inservice for teachers of English as a Second Language

- Chapter 15 -

Civic Education And Education For Citizenship: Continuous Education for Democracy in Multicultural Societies

Mitja Žagar

Introduction: Entering The Twenty-First Century

The information revolution has followed the industrial revolution. The industrial world we have known is changing and in some ways rapidly disappearing. The information society is replacing the traditional industrial society. The speed or unheard of rapidity of the transformation has astonished scholars and analysts; people are often not aware of the rapidity, global nature, depth, and the range or scope of the changes. Nobody knows their consequences. How will our world look tomorrow? How do we design and develop education for the "new world?"

The development of a new strategy for education in the twenty-first century is an enormous and challenging task. We know that education in the new information age has to become a continuous process that starts at an early age and does not end until death. The education of adults must be an important part of the process. Our societies must transform into learning societies. Therefore, we must focus upon how to design the "new education."

We know that the "product-oriented" education of the twentieth century is no longer adequate. The education and content studied by graduates from formal educational programs, at all levels, has only had a very limited life-span. Everybody, including these graduates, will have to be included in permanent educational and training processes, be they formal or informal, so they can cope with the rapid transformation and change in their respective field and in society. Their formal education, knowledge, and even skills, may become obsolete several times in their lives. The need to adjust to the changing world underlines the importance of the need for continuous education. The concepts and strategies of education in general, and of the education of adults in particular, that have prevailed are inadequate. The education of the adults of yesterday is no longer adequate.

This paper presents, and critically reviews, some of the characteristics and the nature of education as the world enters the new century and millennium. Special attention is given to the importance of the education of adults, civic education, and education for citizenship in democratic societies. This review is followed by suggested guidelines for the education of adults for the new century. The paper concludes with a proposal for a "Global Concept and Strategy for the Education of Adults in the Twenty First Century."

Education and its Nature in a Changing World

When we speak of education today, we usually think as we did before, of formal educational programs of the past offered by authorized or licensed educational institutions. Children enter such programs at a very early age and spend an important part of their young life in schools. Primary, secondary and higher education are traditionally the main stages or levels of the educational process. Authorized schools issue their certificates or diplomas to the students who successfully complete these programs. A certain level of formal education is usually an important precondition for almost every job. There is a general presumption that the students who graduated from the formal educational programs actually acquired the requisite knowledge and skills in their specific fields. Will this do for tomorrow?

The world has always been changing, but the speed and intensity of the changes have increased in the past few decades. The production of information and knowledge is enormous and is still constantly increasing; few can easily cope. Teachers and their educational programs are no exception. Consequently, a large portion of the knowledge and skills taught at schools and in different educational programs -- especially in fields conditioned substantially by the progress of technology -- is outdated, inadequate or obsolete. Companies and institutions are complaining that they have to train new employees who have just graduated from educational programs before they can successfully include these employees in the workforce or process of production. Nevertheless, employers usually still insist on the formal education of applicants for different positions and jobs. They know from experience that they can more easily and rapidly train or retrain persons who have completed a 'formal' educational program. Furthermore, companies often recognize that the education and training programs for different professions and jobs can be effective preparation or background.

Most do not want to abolish the existing concept and systems of education despite all their flaws. The systems are a good basis for transformation; they are an existing infrastructure upon which people can build. For example, primary schools give their pupils/students basic literacy and knowledge in different fields. The schools are an important provider of basic socialization in modern societies and a preparatory stage for the future education in secondary and higher education programs, different training and job education programs, and programs of continuous education including the education of adults. These post elementary programs give students specialized knowledge and skills necessary to begin their professional lives. All of these programs together represent existing educational systems that are basically product-oriented. The student graduates and leaves school with a set of skills, a bundle of knowledge, and the right attitudes.

However, we need to constantly update and develop these educational programs and systems. New knowledge, and now especially new ways, technologies, methods, approaches and some new educational concepts[1] should be introduced into the programs and systems so as to increase the interaction of education with life. Most especially, education should become a permanent and lifelong process in which all participants or actors -- teachers, educators, students and everybody else connected in the process -- play different, interchangeable and active roles. Employed or participating teachers, lecturers, trainers and experts in different fields would make their knowledge and experiences available to their students and provide them with opportunities to learn different skills. Students should not only be active learners in this process, but should also participate as teachers and trainers in the process of education. Students might present their specific or specialized knowledge, skills and experiences (for example, computer skills, creative abilities, research and study projects) to other students and teachers in their particular program and to other interested individuals. Information technology can be utilized to spread the information about these activities and offerings; at least sometimes, the existing technology and equipment could be used to transmit or broadcast the activities directly to the interested public. The roles of teachers, educators, and students should become interchangeable; everyone would play, simultaneously, several roles in the continuous process of education. The process would include a variety of several formal and informal programs and activities. The education would be enriched. Students could choose educational programs consistent with their needs and specific interests. In this context, education as a permanent and process oriented activity would require a developed counseling mechanism for all participants. Personal and specialized counselors and advisors would help the adult students design and develop their own educational process; counselors would assist with the necessary communication and help people to select the relevant information. The core formal educational programs would still issue official diplomas and certificates to students who complete the programs successfully; all other programs and educational training activities successfully completed by participating students could be listed in their biographies.

The context of education differs substantially from country to country. Education in every society is conditioned by its specific cultural, religious, linguistic, social, economic and political conditions and characteristics. These factors will continue to play important roles. Designers and coordinators of continuous educational processes and programs operate in different environments. When developing an educational process, the designers will have to consider several factors; for example, the languages spoken by the people in a region or country, the traditions and cultures, the existing literacy and general knowledge of the population, and the traditional and new ways of socialization. Political socialization, existing and potential material and human resources, the existing infrastructure and its future development, available technology, technological progress and the skills of the population to utilize the available and future technologies, for example, will need to be considered. Different educational systems and different continuous educational processes and programs will continue to exist. Nevertheless, intense international cooperation, connections and exchanges, and interchangeable and joint international educational programs have already been established. Experts predict further globalization of education. The international connections, cooperation, and exchanges will enrich existing educational systems and processes; however, they must respect the different cultures.[2] Globalization should not commit violence against the existing cultures, but should enable coexistence and equal cooperation of different cultures by creating an adequate framework of knowledge, information, and mutual respect. Globalization should also take into account the existing levels of social, economic and technological development in each society and contribute to the development of continuous educational processes suitable to the societies.

Education of Adults

The importance of the education of adults and the social role of this education have increased rapidly with globalization. Adult education has accelerated the production, adoption and dissemination of knowledge and increased the social impact of the changes.[3] The education of adults, or adult education, is an important segment in the process of continuous education. Our knowledge and skills age rapidly and we have to update, develop and broaden them constantly to participate successfully in the job market. Jobs are no longer permanent. Often people have to not only change jobs but professions or professional fields in their lives. Simultaneously, new knowledge and technologies are constantly changing and transforming almost all jobs and professions. Even if people do not change their job or profession, they have to adapt to new conditions and circumstances. Consequently, each person will need to participate in the process of continuous education throughout their life.

Several adult education programs were developed primarily to educate or reeducate and train or retrain students for specific jobs or professions. Formal programs were organized and offered usually by existing educational institutions (especially vocational schools) and sometimes by factories and companies. Factories and companies also often organized informal educational and training programs that trained and qualified workers for specific jobs or roles. This vocational education was usually recognized only by the factory or the company that organized it. The education of adults was, and often still is, seen in this context as vocational training and education for the work place.

The education of adults is becoming much more elaborate today.[4] It ranges from basic education, (literacy and civic literacy programs, for those who did not complete primary education programs or for those who want to refresh and update or upgrade their knowledge), to vocational training or educational programs for new jobs or skills. It includes, for example, secondary and higher education programs, specific training programs, and educational programs for the elderly. It is no longer necessarily job, profession or work-specific or oriented and it tries to serve different needs and interests. Some enroll in adult education programs to complete the education that they have failed to complete earlier. Others enroll in programs to qualify for different jobs and to be more competitive in the job market. Many never had the chance to secure their desired education or qualifications before because of their financial and social situations. Others may want to improve their social and professional status. Everybody needs to refresh, update, develop and broaden their existing skills and knowledge. Some want to enroll in programs for pleasure; they may be able to finally afford to enroll in programs to satisfy their personal interests. Others may wish to devote time to their favorite arts or to fields of knowledge or interest.

The education of adults is today a number of formal and informal educational, training and information programs, courses, and activities offered by diverse institutions, companies, and individuals. The programs and course are intended to serve the needs and interests of the employees or workers, companies, and institutions that provide public services and public administration to states and societies. The adult education field is growing rapidly, and enormous sums of money are spent. The education of adult for the today's and tomorrow's world is 'big business.'

When we search for global concepts and strategies regarding the education of adults, its growth and development -- as surprised as we might be -- we discover that they do not exist. Important sectors of the education of adults are often linked with the existing official public and private educational institutions at all levels, but these institutions are obviously unable to serve all needs and interests. To capitalize on these deficits, new public and private suppliers of adult education programs and activities appear in the growing "knowledge market" daily. The suppliers offer diverse educational services to the interested public -- often paying little or no attention to the social functions of education. These social functions of education include social and political socialization and mobilization, promotion of civic literacy and rule of law (der Rechtstaat), including tolerance, democracy, justice and other social values. The neglect of the social roles and functions of education could lead to a social crisis, instability, and unrest that might endanger future democratic development. Democratic systems need people who are interested in political participation and who are capable of participating in the democratic political processes. The rapidity of social change and the complexity of modern societies stress the importance of life-long learning and the need that everyone participate in permanent formal and informal education. In this context, societies at all levels, including nation states and all countries in the international community need to develop adequate

- 289 -

global, national, regional and sub-regional strategies and concepts of education including the education of adults in the twenty-first century.

Civic Education and Education for Citizenship in Democratic Societies

Civic education programs are an important part of continuous life-long education in every community. They should include every individual who should participate in different permanent (re)educational and (re)training activities or in programs aimed at promoting democratic political participation. All educational activities must take into account the social situation, circumstances and needs of the learners. The programs should be learner (user) and goal-oriented and adapted to specific target populations. The programs should be open and inclusive by their nature and they should reflect the political, economic, linguistic, religious and cultural diversity in the society. Educational activities and programs have to be adapted to specific target populations, be they individuals or specific groups such as trade unions or clerks in a bureaucracy.

Goal- and learner-centered learning processes of civic education and education for citizenship should use different concepts, approaches, and methods to address the specific needs of different target populations. Permanent educational activities and programs should always be adapted to the specific situation, abilities, and needs of a target population. Target populations can be defined in several ways. A target population could be children in a kindergarten; pupils in primary schools; students in junior, secondary, and high schools; university students; professionals in a field; people in community education or media; or elderly people in a seniors' residence. I would especially like to stress the role the education of adults can play in continuous civic education and education for democratic citizenship.

Different approaches to activities are possible. Nevertheless, experiences from different environments – from schools and local communities to professional associations and to seniors– show that simulation activities, especially the simulations of political processes and decision-making exercises are successful methods for learning about citizenship and civic society.[5] Through simulations of political processes, learners learn not only skills but the knowledge and attitudes necessary for a successful political process. In this context, civic education and education for democratic citizenship will focus on, for example:

- human rights, both individual and collective rights in all spheres,
- interpersonal and inter-community relations, including the possibility of conflicts, and on the ways, procedures, measures and mechanisms for the (democratic) management of relations and conflicts, communities – their specific situation, organization, characteristics, needs and interests, social values and generally accepted goals, including the individual feeling of responsibility for the well-being of a specific community and a society as a whole, recognition of diversity and knowledge about different distinct communities and their specific features, tolerance, acceptance of differences and equal cooperation.

When we speak of civic education and education for citizenship in the context of life-long learning, we often mean voters' education. This education should start in kindergartens and schools before an individual gets the right to vote, and should continue throughout every person's life. This education also includes learning successful democratic political participation. Successful civic education and education for democratic citizenship are crucial for the very existence and stability of democracy in a society, but they are often underrated as are the roles that numerous institutions should play. Media, public administration and public and private organizations are key institutions in successful life-long learning for democratic citizenship and for civic education.

At the same time, people working in public administration and state bureaucratic institutions also need to be educated. They are a specific target population because of their dual role.

Simultaneously they are voters or citizens who are entitled to political participation in democratic society. They are also state employees and persons who should assist democratic processes and recognize the rights of individuals and communities. The same is also true for those employed in other public or private institutions that have the responsibility to assist democratic processes or to participate in decisions-making. Civic education and education for democratic citizenship are important for all public servants who participate in administrative procedures dealing with the rights and duties of individuals.[6] Public servants and bureaucrats need to know administrative procedures and in their activities should always respect the human rights and integrity of members of the public.

We should stress the importance of continuous civic education and education for democratic citizenship regarding the autonomy and self-rule of local communities. In plural, ethnically and culturally diverse societies, special attention should be paid to ethnic and cultural diversity. To be successful, civic education and education for democracy shall be based on the concept of multiculturalism and interculturalism, which is to ensure that every member of each ethnic, linguistic, religious or other distinct community has equal rights and access to equality.

Guidelines For the Education of Adults for the Twenty-First Century

Learning is a right. Education, as a continuous process, should enable everybody to develop all their existing talents and realize all their creative potential. Our world should become a "learning society" and knowledge should be valued. Formal educational programs with traditional teacher-pupil relationships are and will remain an important and irreplaceable part of the continuous educational process(es), but several new ways and forms of education or different formal and informal educational and training activities and programs are emerging based on the new relations of all the participants. These are enriching and transforming the educational processes.[7]

The importance of education for each child and for the society was recognized long ago, but access to education often has been limited. The right to education was introduced as the result of the century-long social struggle for equal opportunities and for accessibility of education. The recognition of the social importance of education -- especially general and basic primary education -- resulted in compulsory primary education for every child.[8] The education of adults was not given equal attention; formal education was usually completed by the end of childhood. Such a position and concept of education became inadequate with the enormous acceleration in the production, development, and dissemination of knowledge and new technology in the last decades of the twentieth century. Demand for the education of adults and for the recognition of its social importance and impact have grown massively.

The International Institute for Policy, Practice and Research in the Education of Adults detected policy contradictions and the lack of adequate -- national and international -- global strategies and concepts of education of adults.[9] They decided to initiate work on the development of an adequate global strategy for the education of adults in the twenty-first century and invited scholars connected with the International institute to present their proposals.[10] My proposal, based on practical experiences with the Students' Research and Training Project *"Democratization and Resolution of Ethnic Conflict: Management and Resolution of Ethnic Conflict in Democratic Societies,"*[11] was developed in this context. I outline it in the concluding section.

Conclusion: "Global Concept and Strategy for Education of Adults in the Twenty-First Century"

1. Education, including the education of adults should be a learner-oriented, open, and continuous social process in which everybody can participate. Societies, especially nation-states, a specific forms of social organization, have to assure accessibility to education for all based on the principles of equality, equal access, and equal opportunities. Adequate and generally accessible

information systems on the education of adults need to be developed.

2. Societies have to develop adequate social conditions and infrastructure for education and pay special attention to the specific nature and needs of the education of adults. States have to develop an appropriate legal and social framework as the basis for the functioning of public and private educational and training programs and activities for the education of adults. Criteria, standards and conditions have to be established for access to public funding for organizers and suppliers of programs and activities for the education of adults. Although fees generated by the education of adults and support from the private sector could finance some programs and activities for the education of adults, the state and public finances will remain the key financial sources. Adequate public control and accountability regarding the quality of the education and public spending must be introduced.

3. Specific strategies for the education of adults have to be developed at different levels taking into account the specific conditions, needs, interests and the environment. These strategies will lead to the formulation of educational policies and regulations regarding the education of adults by government. The realization of these policies and strategies in continuing education will require channels of communication and the development of procedures, mechanisms and institutions for the coordination of the continuous education activities and the programs at all levels.

4. Strategies, concepts and policies regarding the education of adults have to recognize and respect the existence of ethnic, linguistic, cultural, religious and social pluralism. Based on the concepts and principles inherent in multiculturalism they have to:

• improve the knowledge (and information) about diversity in modern societies,

• present the existing diversity an competitive advantage and richness,

• develop skills for successful and equal communication in diverse societies, and

• promote mutual understanding, tolerance and peace, equality and cooperation.

5. Knowledge and information about existing cultural diversity and the promotion of the concept of equal cooperation should be an integral part of every program and activity in continuing education, but they are especially important for civic education and education for citizenship in democratic plural societies. Constant, rapid and dramatic social changes in this era of global transformation require the redefinition of the traditional concept of education for citizenship. All adults are now permanently included in the educational activities and programs to enable them to successfully participate in democratic political life.

6. The education of adults should be organized in ways to address and serve their specific needs and interests. This applies to the organizational structure as well as to the nature and content of the educational and training programs and activities. Formal and informal educational and training programs and activities should be offered at existing educational institutions, in the workplace, and where people live. They should be easily accessible, both physically and financially. The programs should vary from official educational programs at all levels, to different formal and informal educational and training vocation programs, to specific formal and informal programs and activities for specific communities and public groups (e.g., programs for the elderly).

7. Although several, especially official and formal educational and training programs and activities will remain product-oriented, other types of programs and activities should be introduced in the continuous educational process as an important segment of the education of adults. The education of adults should become more process- oriented and able to adapt instantly to the changing situation, new needs and interests. Broad basic knowledge and learning skills should be included in adult education programs and activities to improve the adaptability of individuals to changing situations, new technologies and a variety of skills that can be used in various jobs or positions. However, educational and training programs for specific jobs and professions, in response to the

existing and expected needs of individual companies and of the specific economy, will remain important segments of adult education.

8. The fact that everybody will participate in different roles in the continuous process of education during of their lives also conditions the nature of continuous education. Almost everybody possesses a specific knowledge or skill that could be interesting to others. The roles of teachers and learners could be interchangeable and reversed in different programs and activities. Nevertheless, we could expect that the traditional teacher-pupils relationship will prevail in many formal educational and training programs and activities. Most educational and training programs and activities in the education of adults are likely to depend on the interest of the participants. These programs and activities are likely to include participants of different ages, genders, backgrounds, education, and experiences that could interact in different roles (as students, lecturers, facilitators) and contribute to the better quality of the education of adults. The concept of a learning society should be explored, developed and promoted.

9. All available and potentially useful technology should be used in the education of adults to make the programs and activities more effective, interesting, and accessible. Designers and organizers of the education of adults in every society have to consider the level of social and technological development in the society and adapt the educational process to the specific conditions of the society.

10. Cooperation, exchange, and the transfer of earned credits and the mutual recognition of certificates, providing that adequate standards of education are met, should become important characteristics of the education of adults within the continuous educational process. Educational programs should be open and accessible to all interested individuals taking into account all the dimensions of social diversity. Whenever possible, international cooperation and exchanges in education should be encouraged.

To sum up, life-long learning is a basic need of every individual in the era of global transformation. Successful continuous education should be inclusive, accessible and flexible It requires active participation of every individual and every public and private institution in a society and should reflect its pluralism and diversity. Successful continuous education includes formal and informal permanent (re)educational and (re)training activities and programs that are adapted to the specific needs of participants. In addition to skills and elaborate knowledge for specific professions and jobs (job and/or vocational (re)training and (re)education) and general knowledge, continuous education needs to focus also on civic education and education for democratic citizenship, thereby enabling every individual to participate successfully in a political process. Central themes of successful civic education and education for citizenship are human rights, basic constitutional principles, perceptions of social values and the public good, agreed-upon strategic social goals, knowledge about democratic institutions, and life processes including the skills for social and political organization and activity. In the context of continuous education, the education of adults is especially important.

Bibliography:

Adult Education in These Times: An International Perspective, a special issue of Questions de Formation/ Issues in Adult Education, Vol. VII, No. 13/14 (1996) published by the International Institute for Policy, Practice and Research in the Education of Adults.

Blondel, Jean (1995): *Comparative Government: And Introduction,* Second edition; Prentice Hall, Harvester Wheatsheaf, London, New York, Toronto, Sydney, Singapore, Madrid, Mexico City, Munich, 1995.

Bockstael, Eric & Feinstein, Otto (1996): "Policy Contradictions and Policy Obligations" -- in *Adult Education in These Times: An International Perspective*, a special issue of *Questions de Formation/ Issues in Adult Education*, Vol. VII, No. 13/14 (1996), pp. 1-7.

Colomer, Joseph M., Ed. (1996): *Political Institutions in Europe;* Routledge; London, New York 1996

Delors, Jacques, *et al.* (1996): *Learning: The Treasure Within, Report to UNESCO of the International Commission on Education for the Twenty-first Century*; UNESCO Publishing; France 1996.
Feinstein, Otto (1996): "Toward a Field of Research in the Politics, Policy and Practice of the Education of Adults" -- in *Adult Education in These Times: An International Perspective*, a special issue of *Questions de Formation/ Issues in Adult Education*, Vol. VII, No. 13/14 (1996), pp. 199-224.
Leirman, Walter (1994): *Four Cultures of Education: Expert, Engineer, Prophet, Communicator*; Peter Lang, Europäischer Verlag der Wissenschaften; Frankfurt am Main, Berlin, Bern, New York, Paris, Wien 1996.
Žagar, Mitja (1997 - forthcoming): "Exploring Ethnicity: Constitutional Regulation of (Inter) Ethnic Relations" -- in the *Question de formation / Issues* .

Endnotes

---

[1] This includes also the development, transformation and overlapping of different cultures of education. See e.g., Leirman, Walter (1994), *Four Cultures of Education: Expert, Engineer, Prophet, Communicator*; Peter Lang, Frankfurt am Main, Berlin, Bern, New York, Paris, Wien: Europäischer Verlag der Wissenschaften; 1996, especially pp. 123-137.

[2] See e.g., Stavenhagen, Rodolfo,"Education for a Multicultural World" -- in Delors, Jacques, *et al.* (1996): *Learning: The Treasure Within, Report to UNESCO of the International Commission on Education for the Twenty-first Century*; France: UNESCO Publishing., pp. 229-233.

[3] See, e.g., Feinstein, Otto (1996)."Toward a Field of Research in the Politics, Policy and Practice of the Education of Adults" -- in *Adult Education in These Times: An International Perspective*, a special issue of *Questions de Formation/ Issues in Adult Education*, Vol. VII, No. 13/14 (1996), especially pp. 199, 205-207.

[4] See, e.g., contributions in *Adult Education in These Times: An International Perspective*, the special issue of *Questions de Formation/ Issues in Adult Education*, Vol. VII, No. 13/14 (1996).

[5] See.e.g. Chesney, James D., Feinstein, Otto (1997); *Building Civic Literacy and Citizen Power*. Upper Saddle River. N.J: Prentice Hall.

[6] States and public administration differ substantially; nevertheless there are also several common characteristics – including basic organizational and working principles. There are many similarities also in legally determined

administrative procedures (See. e.g. Blondel, Jean (1995),*Comparative Government An Introduction.* Second edition. London, New York, Toronto, Sydney, Tokyo, Singapore, Madrid, Mexico City, Munich:Prentice Hall, Harvester Wheatsheaf. pp. 307-338; Colomber, Joseph M., Ed. (1996); *Political Institutions in Europe.* London, New York: Routledge.; Hague, Rod, Harrop, Martin Breslin, Shaun (1992). *Comparative Government and Politics; An Introduction,* Third Edition, Comparative Government and Politics Series Editor: Vincent Wright. London: MacMillan. pp. 342-366).

[7] See, e.g., Delors, Jacques, "Education: the Necessary Utopia" in Delors, Jacques, *et al.* (1996): *Learning: The Treasure Within, Report to UNESCO of the International Commission on Education for the Twenty-first Century.* France: UNESCO Publishing. pp. 13-35; especially, pp. 19-22, 35.

[8] See, e.g., Article 26 of the *Universal Declaration of Human Rights* (GA Resolution No. 217 A [III] of 10 December 1948) and Article 13 of the *International Covenant on Economic, Social and Cultural Rights* (GA Resolution No. 2200 A [XXI] of 16 December 1966; entered into force on 3 January 1976).

[9] See, e.g., Bockstael, Eric & Feinstein, Otto (1996): "Policy Contradictions and Policy Obligations" -- in *Adult Education in These Times: An International Perspective,* a special issue of *Questions de Formation/ Issues in Adult Education,* Vol. VII, No. 13/14 (1996), pp. 1-7.

[10] Activities of the International Institute for Policy, Practice and Research in the Education of Adults and these proposals were presented at the Fifth UNESCO International Conference on Adult Education "Adult Learning: A Key for the Twenty-first Century" in Hamburg in July 1997.

[11] The Students' Research and Training Project *"Democratization and Resolution of Ethnic Conflict: Management and Resolution of Ethnic Conflict in Democratic Societies"* was established at the University of Ljubljana five years ago. Despite doubts, it has attracted the attention of students. So far more than sixty (60) undergraduate and graduate students and several former students (who are already employed, some of them for several years, or entering the job market) participated in the project. Participants in this project play several roles simultaneously: they are involved as researchers in different research teams, students and/or lecturers and/or trainers in different educational and training programs and activities (e.g., on research methodology, public relations, conflict management, etc.), managers and coordinators organizing and managing different activities within the project, etc. (More on this Students' Research and Training Project see in: Žagar, Mitja (1997): "Exploring Ethnicity: Constitutional Regulation of (Inter)Ethnic Relations: New Approaches to a Multicultural Education," *Questions de formation / Issues in the Education of Adults,* No. 16/1997, Vol. VIII, pp. 141-155.)

AGMV Marquis

MEMBER OF SCABRINI MEDIA

Quebec, Canada
2001